The Place of Stunted
Ironwood Trees

DAVID P. CRANDALL

The Place of Stunted Ironwood Trees

*A Year in the Lives
of the Cattle-herding
Himba of Namibia*

CONTINUUM

NEW YORK · LONDON

2000

The Continuum International Publishing Group Inc
370 Lexington Avenue, New York, NY 10017

The Continuum International Publishing Group Ltd
Wellington House, 125 Strand, London WC2R 0BB

Printed in the United States of America

Library of Congress Cataloging-in-Publication Data

Crandall, David P., 1960–
    The place of stunted ironwood trees : a year in the lives of
the cattle-herding Himba of Namibia / by David P. Crandall.
        p.   cm.
    ISBN 0-8264-1270-X
    1. Himba (African people)—Domestic animals. 2. Himba
(African people)—Social life and customs. 3. Cattle herders—
Namibia—Otutati. 4. Otutati (Namibia)—Social life and
customs. I. Title.

    DT1558.H56 C73 2000
    305.8963906881—dc21

                                            00-034065

For Elspeth, Margot, Nicholas, and Andrew

and in memory of Dr. D. J. Hanekom

Contents

A Reader's Introduction

The Himba are a cattle-herding people living in a remote corner of southwestern Africa, half a world away from the place I call home. And, true to course, our meeting was one of purest happenstance. On a rainy afternoon, I stood in an Oxford bookshop thumbing through a photographic essay on Namibia. Perhaps half a dozen pages contained pictures of the Himba, but they were enough to begin a journey that would land my wife, our daughter, and me at a settlement in central Kaokoland called Otutati. Much of this book is rooted in that lengthy field study, but several of its roots go deeper still, back to my childhood fascination for peoples and cultures whose ways and means seemed utterly different from my own.

Two years of graduate studies prepared me somewhat for the field expedition and the research to be pursued among the Himba, but did little to ready me for the experience of living with them day to day. I found, however, this latter side of the field study to be at least as interesting as the former, and in certain ways, more enlightening. Thinking back now, I have no idea what I expected from the Himba. I admit with some embarrassment that the discovery of a vast reservoir of common experience linking our two worlds, despite the many differences in setting, struck me with a great deal of force. The fact that my wife and I could sit and chat with Himba about child rearing, in-law relations, economic uncertainties, jealousy, hurt feelings, the difficulty of belief in a world of countervailing experience, and a host of other topics, and genuinely understand one another, was nothing less than remarkable. Among them we recognized all the personality types familiar to us from our own social world; and over course of time, the process of discovery continued for both them and us.

It is this then, the richness of a shared humanity and the commonality of so much human experience and so many human tribulations, that lies at the heart of this work. For it unfurls not an immaculate story but an extended narrative of Himba experience in a world that at one level appears so different, while at another so strikingly familiar. In many ways this book is less about the Himba as a people and more about the lives of individual Himba, though the two must go hand in hand. Writing such a book has not been easy, for standard genres and typical conventions seem to convey an impression of neatness and obvious continuity in human events that simply is not so—except, perhaps, when viewed from afar. Thus, I have taken the events of a year in the life of Otutati, from season to season, and grafted them into the events of a lifetime, from birth to maturation, and from marriage to death, taking meticulous care to portray them as they occurred. The events are real, as are the people and their words (which I have translated from Herero into English); yet it is I who singled out these few from the many that could have been chronicled. Their varied details are not only the result of my wife or I having been present, but also derive from discussions with the participants afterward—both singly and collectively—to reconstruct the event, a bit of stock-in-trade for ethnographers. I have also chosen not to place myself or my personal reflections at the center of things but rather to allow the Himba to speak for themselves, as much as this is possible. The narrative builds one vignette upon the other, none of them isolated but all forming chains of events that lead to a deeper and ever more complex portrayal of the Himba of Otutati. And in so doing, the narrative corresponds closely with my own discovery of these people, their biographies and experience, and the events of the unfolding year.

If I am able to draw the reader into this world, along a path at once strange and familiar, and to lead the reader to an acquaintance with the Himba portrayed in the narrative, to understand them as people in their own right, and to see the common threads of experience that run through all human lives, I will consider my effort of some value.

Swakopmund, 1999

Southern Africa

Angola

Malawi

Zambia

Mozambique

Namibia

Zimbabwe

Botswana

Swaziland

Lesotho

South Africa

Namibia

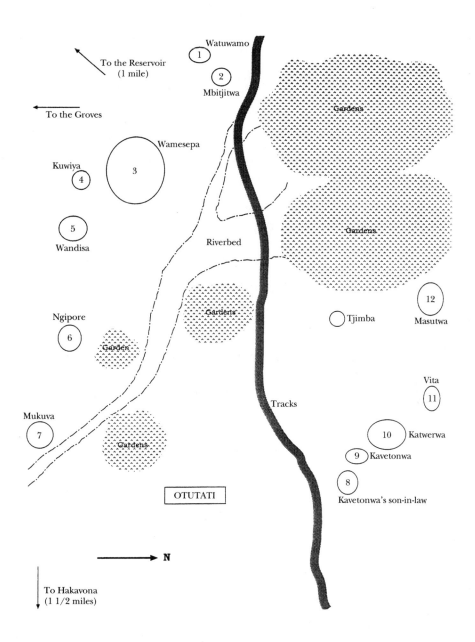

Living Arrangements

1. This is the homestead where Watuwamo ♀, her husband, and five sons live.

2. This modest homestead is occupied by Mbitjitwa ♂, his current wife, and children.

3. The very large homestead of Wamesepa Ngombe ♂, headman of the area, who lives there with his wife Ekuta ♀, son, Zorondu ♂, and other relatives including, Katere ♂ and his main wife, Wakamburwa ♀, and Katanga ♀ with her daughter, Rikuta ♀, and her youngest son.

4. This is a smaller homestead belonging to Kuwiya ♂, who lives there with his two wives and children.

5. In this homestead live Wandisa ♂, the elder son of Wamesepa ♂, his second wife, Wazurowe ♀, daughters Yapura ♀ and Kakara ♀, and their other children.

6. This is the homestead of Ngipore ♂, his wife, Mukahu ♀, their daughter, Wandjoze ♀, their youngest son, and the son of Ngipore's sister.

7. Mukuva ♂, his wife, and children live in this homestead.

8. Kavetonwa's daughter, son-in-law, and grandchildren occupy this homestead recently inherited by the son-in-law.

9. Kavetonwa ♂ and his wife have lived in this homestead for many, many years.

10. Katwerwa ♂, his three wives, and children, including Dakata ♂ and his two wives (though the first wife, Yapura ♀, often stays with her mother), live in this large homestead and adjoining homestead.

11. Vita ♂ and his wife, along with their son, Zondoka ♂, and their other children live here. Watumba ♀, a distant cousin of Vita's wife, her husband, Daniel ♂, and their children, share the homestead with Vita.

12. Masutwa ♂, with his wife and their children, occupy this rather isolated homestead near their gardens.

Relations to Wamesepa

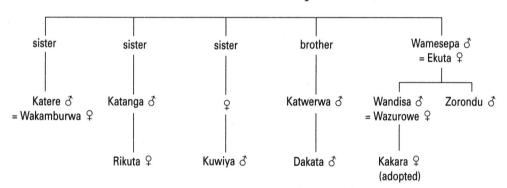

= represents marriage

The People of Otutati

Dakata—a young man, son of Katwerwa, and husband of Yapura and Penguka

Daniel—a man approaching middle-age and married to Watumba

Ekuta—an old woman, one of Wamesepa's wives, and mother of Wandisa

Francisco—a Hakavona man who came to Otutati as a youth, married to Wombinda

Kakara—a maiden, daughter of Wandisa

Katanga—a middle-aged widow, daughter of one of Wamesepa's sisters, and local midwife

Katere—a man approaching his elder years, son of one of Wamesepa's sisters, husband of Wakamburwa, and Wamesepa's heir

Katwerwa—son of Wamesepa's brother, cousin of Wandisa, father of Dakata, known for his lion attack, and husband of three wives

Kavetonwa—an ancient man, known for his wisdom and knowledge, friend of Wamesepa

Kuwiya—a man approaching his middle years and nephew of Katere

Masutwa—a man of middle-age with a large family, prominent in the community

Ngipore—a man in his late middle years from Kaoko Otavi, father of Wondjoze

Solomon—an old man whose mother was Himba and father Caprivian, an elder

Vita—a highly respected, hard working, middle-aged man, father of Zondoka

Wakamburwa—the beautiful, sharp-tongued wife of Katere

Wamesepa—the ancient headman of Otutati, husband to Ekuta, father of Wandisa, uncle of Katwerwa, Katanga, and Katere, friend and patron of many

Wandisa—a middle-aged man, son of Wandisa, father of Kakara

Watumba—a lively woman, wife of Daniel, and cousin to Vita's wife

Watuwamo—a woman entering her middle years, mother of five boys, wife of Ondjara

Wombinda—a middle-aged Hakavona woman, wife of Francisco, and spirit medium

Wondjoze—the proud, attractive, and playful maiden daughter of Ngipore

Solomon

Kuwiya

Kakara

Kuwiya's family

Watumba

Ngipore

Katanga

One of Vita's daughters

Katere

Katwerwa

Dakata

Watuwamo

One of the young thieves

Wandisa

The Valley Is Full of Life

. . . even before the seasons begin to change. The life of Otutati centers around the movement of cattle, the predilections of individuals and families, and the fortunes of the aged headman, Wamesepa Ngombe. Yet all these human activities are set against the backdrop of an earth created by Mukuru (God), and Himba know there is no sense in believing life to be anything other than what it is.

The gentle incline of the dusty tracks guiding our ascent contrasted with the stark, vertical facings of the surrounding hillsides. Heat-drenched hues of browns, golds, and blacks mingled and bestowed an impression of emptiness, of lifelessness, of timelessness upon the steeper, rockier slopes. As one's eyes fell on low rising hillocks, lofty grasses overshadowed glittering stones. The grasses had completed their cycle and the whiskers rising above the shafted seed pods were vaguely silver in color. Breezes fed upon the sun swept down these slopes like giant, lethargic snakes, slithering this way and that, forcing the grasses to bend in their courses, covering and uncovering the hardened earth.

Well behind us now was the provincial capital, Opuwo—the only urban stretch in the entire communal homeland called Kaokoland. Situated on a hill in the northwestern corner of a large and beautiful valley, Opuwo became a town in the 1930s when the former seat of central administration, a tiny police station near the banks of the Kunene River, was abandoned. The station lay in a malaria zone and the parasitic disease claimed the lives of several young officers who monitored the movement of livestock across the river. Chosen for its lack of permanent water courses—though springs and wells were plentiful—the Opuwo valley was also sufficiently long to accommodate the landing of military airplanes. Nestled here and there among the valley's foothills were scores of circular homesteads belonging to Himba and Herero cattle herders; and within their shadows the town slowly emerged, its name deriving from a local demand that outsiders encroach no further upon the territory.

For years, Opuwo was home to a handful of civil administrators, evangelists, and the sort of petty opportunists drawn to the exotic and the remote—people whose lives and works had comparatively little impact upon the greater population. In the several decades prior to national independence, the South African government embarked upon a number of public works projects: two small "native" schools were constructed (though not too well received) and a small but recognizably important hospital was built, offering medical services to the whole of Kaokoland. More recently, Opuwo and the surrounding region have passed through a severe drought, international relief efforts, a sometime border war, a United Nations supervised election and peaceful transition to independence, and the erection of an official cattle auction hall and barn. Each of these natural and manmade agitations has had a consequential impact upon Opuwo, especially in the growth of its population and the recasting of its activities and offerings.

Opuwo is a shabby town. Broken, dirty, and ill-rationed, it is the vanguard of change for the entire region, a place of movement and gathering, a crossroads of several worlds, with shanty villages springing up on its periphery. Yet for all its stirrings, for all its awkward pretensions, Opuwo is still small, and the whole of it can be traversed by motor car in less than a minute on the only tarred road in Kaokoland. Opuwos are scattered all over the world and they are all alike: filled with flies, quick striking reptiles, and litter that has no rightful place. To some, Opuwo is a pathetic and unseemly caricature of foreign-bred civil propriety. But for many of the locals and even country dwellers, particularly those of a younger generation, the fascination and attraction of city lights, even the dimmed and often fractured ones of Opuwo, proffer an allure and mystique, a cosmopolitan novelty to be found nowhere else in their world. Opuwo is a place of want and consumption, of old lives blending with new ways and new lives blending with old ways, a place of miscalculation, misjudgment, and uncharacteristic haste. And like all other Opuwos, the life it breeds is both confusing and addictive.

Beyond its glare, the Kaokoland Province in northwestern Namibia holds a munificence of stark and rugged beauty. Bordering on the high Vomboland plateau in the east, the landscape gently declines six thousand feet in elevation, reaching the towering sand dunes of the northern Namib desert as the Atlantic Ocean laps at their ever shifting foundation. The climate is hot and dry, and many regions receive fewer than three inches of rainfall in a good year. Central Kaokoland is hilly and broken, a vast conglomeration of hills and valleys carpeted in a variety of thorny grasses, bushes, and trees. From the air, the texture of central Kaokoland resembles a lattice work, as mountain tentacles stretch from east to west creating valleys of about twelve miles in length and perhaps four or five in width. These valleys are home to a sparsely distributed group of peoples, mostly cattle herders and rainy season horticulturalists, who have, for generations, grazed their animals, planted their maize, and endured the tempests of human life. The most numerous of them are the Herero, the Tjimba, the Hakavona, and the Himba. And it was the latter people, the Himba—by far the most populous group in Kaokoland—whose lives and whose world we had come to study. After an exploratory stay several months previous, my wife, daughter, and I were now returning to spend a year with them.

We paused at the summit of the easterly hills guarding the small valley that stretched before us under a cloudless sky. Otutati, the place of stunted ironwood trees, lay only half an hour's drive beyond the foothills. It was there our Himba acquaintances had invited us to take up residence, to pitch our tent, and make of it a home. The valley shimmered under the noonday sun, and in the distance, heat swelled upward from the irregular patchwork of red and creamy soils, gently swaying the branches of trees and bushes. Carefully, we eased our way down the summit as the width of the tracks and the width of Old Rover were nearly identical, and followed a course along the middle of the valley floor. Heavy sand, dry riverbeds, angular boulders, and wide, deep pockets of fine dust occasionally broke our way. The air was hot and filmy, but it was nearing the end of *okuni* (time of dryness), and though not a drop of rain had fallen in six or seven months and much of the vegetation had receded, everywhere tender new deciduous shoots were visible amid the jumble of shriveled leaves and vines.

Otutati was a collection of homesteads where we had been granted residence and familial ties by the old headman of the region, Wamesepa Ngombe. It lay nearly at the center of the valley, and as we drove along, only the hum of the motor and the cadence of the wheels produced accompaniment for our ears. The trees, the bushes, the contours of the eastern side of the valley seemed quiet and lonely, and time passed before we could identify one of the threescore interruptions in the valley's natural landscape: a homestead. A homestead is a small, circular hamlet of huts and work shelters that house the members of an extended family—persons who dwell together round an *okuruwo* (ancestral fire) and a central livestock enclosure. Both the ancestral fire and the livestock are believed to influence the success and well-being of each member of the family. For without the presence and blessing of the ancestors in their lives, and the ancestral protection afforded by the fire, provident living from day to day and season to season would be impossible. In the absense of livestock, especially cattle, proper manhood, proper womanhood, proper relations between human and ancestor, and the only respectable means of livelihood would be virtually unobtainable.

The small homestead appeared empty but not abandoned. Sturdy boughs and unwieldy stones secured the doors of the round huts, discouraging meddlesome animals and free-roaming youths from disturbing their peace. Last season's thatching reeds lay weighted down atop the flat-roofed work shelters along with other sticks and poles. The people of the homestead had not yet returned from dry season pasture—a three or four day trek along narrow paths in the northerly hills and mountains carved generations ago by migrating herds of elephant. But as the signs of a new season were clearly present, the women and younger children would likely journey homeward before too long.

The tracks led across a great central flood plane. On either side of us stood tall garden fences made from narrow timbers set deep in the ground, held together by interwoven brush and long strips of bark. Some were hundreds of paces in length as they circumscribed single gardens, always in contorted yet loosely circular patterns. In the distance, near a wide, sandy riverbed, stood three enormous thorn trees in almost equally paced succession. The largest of the trees, the most westerly of the three, stood well over a hundred feet high with many heavy limbs pushing farther and farther into the sky. Its lower trunk was mighty, and four men joining hands would barely master its circumference. For hundreds of years, these resolute sages had stood near the deep watercourse as sentinels marking the settlement called Otutati.

Soon we slowed and left the tracks, veering southward over a flood plane toward the large homestead belonging to Wamesepa Ngombe. As we approached the dry riverbed that separated the flood plane from a number of homesteads, we saw Kuwiya looking toward the approaching noise, using both of his hands to shield his eyes from the sun. Kaokoland is full of sounds. And though a stranger might at first hear only silence, the beat of a distant drum, the bicker of chatting voices, the grinding of stones, the bleating and lowing of livestock, the rushing of wind, the chirping of birds, the clicking of insects, the stamping of feet, and the clapping of hands form a constant and familiar stream of sounds. The intrusion of a foreign noise, such as the din of a motor car, is heard above all other sounds, not only because of its intensity, but because of its rarity. Kuwiya raised his arm in greeting. On the other side of the riverbed, people emerged from their houses and work shelters, interrupting their gossiping and light toilings to learn the source of the noise. Old Rover labored across the gravelly river bottom and up the embankment, and momentarily we pulled alongside a weakly thatched shelter where Wamesepa often passed his afternoons.

Rather quickly, a dozen or so adults, mostly women, and a greater number of children surrounded us. The women were dressed in mahogany colored leather skirts, front and back, with small, folded goatskin bonnets on their heads, iron beaded belts about their waists, and jewelry of differing manufacture around their arms, legs, and necks. Their lean, graceful shoulders were draped with long, tightly plaited locks of hair drenched with mahogany coloring, their skin beautifully adorned with a rich mahogany cream. As we took leave of Old Rover and touched hands and arms with the people, salutations and enquiries were exchanged. Some of the people were only acquaintances, but most were related to us through Wamesepa Ngombe.

The central government in Windhoek had long acknowledged Wamesepa as an important leader in Kaokoland. But more significantly, he was recognized as headman and revered as one of the greatest of all *ovahona* (superior men) by the people of his region, indeed by the whole of Kaokoland. Wamesepa was a man of vast cattle wealth—some of it inherited, much of it husbanded. It was a wealth he shared with hundreds of people, clients whose fortunes in life had improved because of his generosity. At the time of our meeting, he had served as headman for at least forty-five years, though now, because of age and natural deterioration, his elder son, Wandisa, fulfilled many of his political and social obligations. Wamesepa was an ancient man, humped over and reliant on his walking stick. His physique was frail, his breathing somewhat labored, but his eyes, which age and sunlight had turned an azure blue, were mostly clear and sharp and focused.

Katanga, Ngipore, Watuwamo, Katere, Watumba, and others who had come to greet us, retired somewhat to allow our reception from Wamesepa. It was important that we formally present ourselves before the headman and greet him before any of his fellows or subordinates. We walked several dusty paces over dung strewn ground to the rustic, open-air pavilion. The old man was seated in a folding metal-framed chair upholstered with a piece of stained, degenerating canvas. Although the timbers supporting the pavilion's roof stood an arm's stretch apart, the northwest corner of the structure was the designated threshold. We stooped low and entered, Michelle and Elspeth first, though this was contrary to Himba custom, and greeted Wamesepa not by name, but by his familial position in relation to us, *Tate* (father). The use of given names is highly regulated according to distinct gradations of age and sex, and the accompanying levels of respect. A child never speaks the names of his parents, not in life, and more especially, not in death. And one must never refer to persons of an older generation, relative or stranger, by given names, for such an utterance implies one considers oneself the equal of that person— something that simply cannot be.

Wamesepa leaned forward and his chair groaned. He took his walking stick and held it under his chest for support and watched as we approached him. His eyesight had dimmed with age and prolonged exposure to sunlight, and he strained to recognize the people drawing near to him.

"Ah, my children," he began after a period of silence, his eyes widening, "you've come to reclaim your father!"

"Yes, *Tate* (father)," I replied with some deliberation, "we have returned to your homestead and wish to stay with you. This time though we hope to stay longer, if you are willing."

The words tapered off into silence as a gust of wind blew against the roof, further exhausting the already weakened thatch.

"We've brought you a few simple gifts, *Tate*," added Michelle, "sugar, meal, and medicine for your aches and your cough. But we must unpack our belongings before we can bring them to you."

The old man sat back in his chair, his eyes following the line of shadows beneath the roof. At last, he pulled his walking stick to his side and let it drop to the ground. "Ah, thank you, my children, thank you," he said, almost whispering. "This is your home, you are always welcome here. But we are simple people and I can't imagine you'd need more than a few days to learn everything there is to know about us." And then, as if to say something more, he opened his mouth widely enough to stretch his wrinkled lips, but nothing followed.

We thanked him and inquired after his health, an obligation of sorts as Europeans were thought to possess powerful and effective medicines.

"Ah, nothing has changed," he lamented. "Some days I feel better than others. But I'm an old man and only Mukuru (God) knows what's to become of me."

We visited a moment longer before excusing ourselves to organize camp. There was no shortage of helping hands and by sunset our westerly facing tent had been pitched and furnished and shade cloth stretched above the whole encampment. Elspeth searched the ground for precious stones as we sank deeply into our chairs to watch the closing of the day. In the far sky, just above the furrowed hills bordering the western edge of the valley, stood the sun, its mature strength nearly drained. The crimson globe fell lower and lower, scattering long, irregular plumes of red and orange across the darkening sky. Milk cows were returning to the homestead for the evening, mostly guided by boys. Nearby, Katere reclined against a fence and called his daughters to hobble an unruly dam lowing for its calf, that it might more easily be milked. The sun disappeared. Soon, only the pale light of cooking fires, scattered throughout the homestead, broke the sullenness of evening shadows.

Evening shadows fell into darkness, but out of this early blanket of night rose a delicate glow as stars appeared one by one and then cluster by cluster on the eastern horizon. Slight, alternating flows of warmth and coolness drifted from the north until the last vestige of day had retreated. Now it was the time of the night. Wooden pails and gourds filled with milk hung from an enclosure fence as the cows were led away from their calves for the night. Masculine and feminine silhouettes lifted the containers from their perches and moved gracefully toward the light of cooking fires.

As the fires grew, their light moved in waves and captured spaces that moments before had lain in darkness. The fires' light had not overcome the dark but shone warmly in the faces gathered round the hearths.

Sometimes the world is strange, but mostly it is familiar; occasionally it seems inscrutable, but often explanation can be found. With floods, drought, lightning, sickness, and death, the world can be a frightening place. Such things are not for us to control, but remind us of our frailty and dependence upon Mukuru and the ancestors.

The earth on which we live is flat. What other form could it possibly take? If it were shaped like an egg would we not find ourselves constantly walking either uphill or downhill? If the earth were egg-shaped then stones and cattle and other objects not securely fixed to the ground would topple over and roll down the sides of the earth! We know this is not so; simple experience tells us otherwise. It is absurd, against all common sense to believe the earth is anything but flat. All of the earth's land sits together in one great mass. The mountains and valleys of Kaokoland, along with the mountains, valleys, and rivers of all other lands, lie together, con- nected, adjoined. The true size of this land mass is beyond guessing, such a thing can only be known by a man who has walked the width and breadth of it. And a man who attempts this can know he has come to the end of his journey when his feet touch the sea and he looks far into the distance and sees nothing but water standing between him and the edge of the earth. For the earth's land is completely surrounded by water. And though the earth is flat, it is not square or rectangular but as Himba houses—circular. Earth is a disk with the land at the heart and water at the extremities.

The creation of the world was deliberate and progressive, and followed the same course as the sun's journey from east to west. The waters and lands lying to the east of Kaokoland were created before Otutati and its surrounding valley; the land on which we now move was created before the lands and waters of the sunset. What lies beyond the waters or underneath the earth is not known. No man has ever seen it. The sun goes down there, on the underside of the earth, to slumber for the night. Some people say one-armed and one-legged creatures live there—creatures that re- semble humans, but are only half human. This is just a fable though; no one really believes it. In truth, only Mukuru knows what lies beyond the waters and why everything is thus shaped. It is not for us to comprehend these things, and a person who claims to know and understand it all is most certainly a fool. Can a man or a woman cause the winds to blow, or clouds to form in the sky and drift over the valleys and drop their charges of rain on the earth below? No, a human being cannot cause such things; neither can we fully understand such things. Only Mukuru knows, comprehends, understands, and guides these processes. High above our heads roam the sun, the moon, and the stars. We observe their minglings and movements in the vault of heaven, but how they move and what causes their motion cannot be known. And what, if anything, stretches beyond the vault of heaven is understood by Mukuru alone. Yes, we have heard stories that explain such things, but they are truthful only to those who already believe them.

As the cooking fires burned low, quiet settled over the homesteads of Otutati. The disturbing hours of darkest night were approaching and people retired to their houses. Carefully, glowing coals from the cooking fires were set upon darkened inner hearths and blown into flames. Feeble wooden doors were secured from the inside and only the moon and stars shared their light.

No community of human beings knows precisely how the world came to be. And though Himba are at a loss to describe this process, they see a distinct order and sense of beauty in both nature and human life. The cool shade of a tree, the well kept appearance of a man or woman, the gracefulness of the kudu against the plodding clumsiness of the rhinoceros are things of beauty in their world. Their aesthetic sense is not rooted in the fanciful image of a child of nature living free and unencumbered by the burdens of civilized life. There is no such thing. But neither is that sense grounded in sheer practicality and elemental function. Human beings have never been singularly guided by the stomach and the loins.

The mystery of human origins and destiny, the inequity of human bounty and human distress, and the privations of choice and consequence are troublesome questions attractive to many Himba. And though Himba are interested in explanations of how things came to be, of technical processes, more important are explanations of why things occur in the precise manner they do. A satisfying and comfortable life is found with a bow and arrow, a digging stick, or a herdsman's staff, if these simple technologies are joined to a portrayal of the world as comprehensible and meaningful. Nowhere is human life conducted in the dark and answers to the basic questions of experience are offered in all human societies. The uniformity of these basic questions stems from a uniformity of human beings and human life. Making a living, coping with spouses and mothers-in-law, the trials of child rearing, the upheavals of love and hate, the attraction and revulsion of wealth and poverty, the difficulty of expectation and failure, and the wavering nature of belief in something absolute frame the common pool of human experience. It is a pool from which human beings can never drift too far, and it is a commonality that allows us to understand one another.

Though the questions are perennial, their answers are far less so. Approaches seem to reign in absolute certainty for a span of time, only to be, at some inevitable point, defrocked, cast aside, and eventually ridiculed by subsequent generations. So much of human thought is mere window decoration, little more than fancy dress. For it is not the answers we find but the questions we ask that shatter the grim illusion of primordial uniqueness.

The seen and unseen forces of the world penetrate our activities and thoughts; they prickle, irritate, and upset our well-being and self-satisfaction. But they also offer explanation and understanding. We know that Mukuru created this world and the beautiful valley in which Otutati lies. The world was created for people to inhabit and all peoples of the earth are descended from the same original parents. But one day, so long ago it is beyond memory, the rope that hung from heaven to earth and allowed the original man and woman to visit Mukuru at will, was severed. The woman was milling grain in a mortar with a long handled pestle. Carelessly, she struck Mukuru in the groin as he was descending the rope to visit his children. The woman's attention was so fixed on delighting her stomach that her appointment with Mukuru was forgotten. "If human beings are so busy with trifling matters," thought Mukuru, "they have no use for me. Let them find me with great effort." He ascended into the heavens and cut the rope, and the separation of heaven from earth has brought us unremitting toil, hunger, sickness, and death. We live because Mukuru gives us life, and when we die we are not lost. We become ancestors to a new generation of kinsmen who depend on our blessing every day of their lives. Yes, the world is what it is and must be accepted as such; to do otherwise is foolishness.

· 2 ·

Faces in the Crowd

. . . become recognizable only after we come to know something about the people behind the faces—their lives, their preferences, and their habits. Strangely, not only do their faces vary according to physical appearance, but once their characters and personalities are known, their very countenances seem to change.

As days passed into weeks, the sun's warmth increased and clouds began to drift across the deep blue skies. Kaokoland is a land of warmth and even afternoons in darkest winter are warm, though winter evenings and nights are cool, and early mornings occasionally frosty. When the summer sun stands at full strength, large clouds, like huge tufts of cotton wool, form above the Indian Ocean and float westward across the continent progressively spilling their moisture until, enfeebled, they reach the eastern edges of Kaokoland. Being dependent on an ocean thousands of miles away for rain is unfortunate, but the cold Benguela Current that flows from the Antarctic to the southwestern shores of Africa is frigid and rain clouds do not form along Namibia's coast. The sun helps create blankets of fog that creep inland over the western Namib desert, but these do little more than help provision some of the desert's fragile inhabitants.

The valley's powdery soil was giving way to new life as small, tender shoots grew into stems and blades and tendrils. Ironwood trees teemed with smooth, glossy butterfly-shaped leaves of dusky-red hue, and here and there wildflowers appeared in the dust. The full blossoming of the new season, though, awaited the rains. But these first tangible signs were enough to spark an initial return of people from their dry season pastures, and two or three milk cows, together with their calves, accompanied each family as mostly women and children began journeying back to their homesteads. Most of the livestock would remain in dry season pasture until the grasses around Otutati had grown sufficiently dense to support them. Many of those returning would have preferred to stay with the cattle, but gardens had to be readied for planting by the time the rains began to fall.

The initial commotion generated by our arrival had waned, allowing us to settle into a comfortable routine. We were still somewhat of a curiosity and people continued to gather at our camp, though increasingly less to visit with us and more to meet and chat with friends and passersby drawn to our strange looking homestead. We were the first Europeans to live at Otutati, though most had encountered Europeans before—often in connection with medical treatment. During the Border War of the 1970s and 1980s, a contingent of South African soldiers was stationed in northern Kaokoland. Part of their strategy was to foster good relations by operating mobile bush clinics. This experience left many Himba with the impression that every European adult, if not a genuine physician, at least possessed an array of tablets capable of curing the widest variety of physical maladies. Consequently, anyone living in or around Otutati who suffered any kind of bodily affliction—from headaches to social diseases to infertility—felt confident we could treat the problem satisfactorily. All we could actually offer was proper disinfection and a clean bandage, and most mornings and late afternoons people in varying states of physical distress waited under the shade cloth for attention.

The afternoon was warm and cloudless. A woman we had met during our previous stay named Watumba, and her daughter, who was nearing the age of physical maturity, appeared in the distance. Each carried a large bundle on her head, yet walked gracefully across the land. Though her bundle was heavy, Watumba easily moved her head from side to side to greet people as she neared Vita's homestead. She was not as tall as some women, but her figure was stately and her face evenly proportioned and beautiful. As she spoke, her teeth glistened, and when she smiled, the missing lower incisors, removed ceremonially in youth, along with her two upper midline incisors, diagonally filed in half to enhance her beauty, came fully into view, for her smile was generous. Her daughter was tired, and while Watumba spoke with other women she searched the landscape for company her own age. But the greetings were momentary and the two continued along their course.

Their posture was stiff and smooth with their heads held firmly above taut shoulders and slender necks. Their upper bodies were resolute and straight but angled slightly forward. It was a distinctly feminine posture, a teasing posture, one that accentuated the size and shape of their buttocks. Large, well-proportioned buttocks are highly sensuous and desirable, all the more so when a woman's front and back skirts modestly separate to reveal full and supple thighs, and below the skirts, when her calves and ankles are beautifully curved and shaped. By watching the posture of her mother and other women, Watumba's daughter was learning to imitate the ways of standing, kneeling, and walking that she might enhance her comeliness until the movements became a natural, unconscious part of her bearing.

Again Watumba and her daughter paused, this time waiting for two weary milk cows to emerge from the woodland before entering Vita's homestead. As they passed through a break in the wooden fence encircling the collection of homes, Vita's wife and several other women and girls greeted them from the shade of a work shelter. It was the completion of a two-day journey that had taken Watumba and her daughter four days, but Watumba was carrying a child. It was the beginning of her eighth moon and she knew that when it became full again, her baby would soon be born. Both Watumba and her husband, Daniel, were pleased about the coming birth as the baby would be their second child. Daniel was somewhat older than Watumba. He was not considered handsome but pleasant, and his manner was jovial though lacking somewhat in the maturity expected from a man of his age. And while he possessed sufficient livestock to fill the needs of his immediate family, Daniel was not known among his fellows as a diligent herdsman. His most noteworthy feature was a soft, spongy growth nearly the size of a man's thumb lodged within his left earlobe. Watumba had left him at dry season post, and he planned to return before too long with his sheep and goats.

Daniel and Watumba were comparative newcomers to Otutati. Wayfarers normally offer a genealogy of their previous whereabouts before a headman grants them permission to stay in his region, and Watumba ex-

plained that they had moved because they felt central Kaokoland was more
hospitable than northern Kaokoland. It was an explanation many found
odd, but Watumba and Vita's wife were distant cousins, and since Vita
allowed them to settle in his homestead the matter was given no further
thought.

Vita was among a small number of people who had not left Otutati
that year, having instead entrusted the care of his cattle herd to his elder
son and nephew. There were, of course, those who rarely left the main
homesteads—mostly the elderly and infirm, sometimes mothers with very
young children, and the occasional poor family that had so few cattle,
sheep, or goats they could be comfortably grazed in the surrounding areas
year round. Vita was neither rich nor poor and had given his son undue
responsibility because he felt it was needed. A number of times Vita had
traveled to his cattle post to bring the herdsmen fresh grain, and finding
things in order, returned home to look after his wife, children, and grandchildren. Daniel and Watumba had caused him no grief and Vita's wife
was often happy for the companionship. Daniel spent almost as much time
away from his family as he did with them, knowing Vita would see to their
welfare in his absence.

My daughter, Elspeth, and I walked along the tracks hoping to visit a man
named Kavetonwa. His onetime bustling homestead was well east and
slightly north of our camp and he lived there with his second wife as sole
occupants of the compound. He was old, older than Wamesepa, but his
aging physique bore the difficulties of his years more easily than his good
friend's. Kavetonwa's father had been headman of the region prior to
Wamesepa, and though as a younger man he was not politically ambitious,
Kavetonwa had served as a careful, thoughtful, and trusted advisor to Wamesepa for many, many years. Now that age was an impediment to his
involvement in public life, Kavetonwa was admired for a knowledge and
understanding of Himba ways few others had attained. And though his
public esteem was considerable, he seemed largely unaware of it.

His youth was spent in a time when strangers, foreigners, and outsiders
were neighboring peoples—Hakavona, Ngambwe, Vambos and others—
not the agents of a central government, let alone Opuwo's world of budding consumption. In secure moments, Kavetonwa described the tensions,

motivations, influences, and enticements he felt pervaded modern Himba life. Not all of them were harmful, but he found the desire for money, alcohol, and motorcars, a general want of things that had nothing to do with real life, and the deception, thievery, and willful disregard of familial obligations that accompanied them, to be shameful death warrants. "I don't know why so many people are choosing death," he often said. It mattered little that few understood his words and that fewer still agreed with them. His standing as the wise old man of the community did not depend on whether or not his opinions were agreeable.

The cool of the morning was pleasant and on the northern horizon, high wispy clouds slowly drifted southward. Leaving the tracks, Elspeth and I walked a serpentine path through a patchwork of fenced gardens, and where fences dipped we greeted people working with short chopping hoes, removing the stiff, fibrous remains of the previous year's maize crop. Portions of some gardens had already been cleared and the heaped remnants of maize stalks burned lazily. The work of clearing a garden was difficult but always moderately paced, with plenty of time for a friendly chat. Soon the fences disappeared and Kavetonwa's homestead came into view, its rather shabby and forlorn condition obscured by its remove. Immediately south of his compound stood a large homestead, completely encircled by a high wooden fence. Kavetonwa's son-in-law had recently inherited the great homestead and his first and senior wife was Kavetonwa's younger daughter. She was still away at dry season post, yet throughout the season she had returned to Otutati every few weeks to see that her parents were well provisioned.

The old man's house was still. The outside timbers needed plastering and in places the thatch looked too thin to repel the rain. Draped over a large, gray stump was a blanket and we bent low to call through the partially closed doorway—but the house remained silent.

On days when he felt particularly agile, Kavetonwa made the rounds, normally winding his way to Wamesepa's homestead where the two of them discussed the comings and goings of their favorite and least favorite people, and reminisced about earlier times. Elspeth and I turned back, and when we arrived at our tent, Kavetonwa was sitting on a flat stone beneath the shade cloth talking with Michelle. His wife had left for the gardens early in the morning and he had come to greet us and collect a few tablets to soothe their innumerable aches and pains. It was particularly difficult to diagnose his ailments, for as soon as he began describing his lower back pains he would switch to his knees and then to his chest or his elbows. During his first self-diagnosis, we saw that his eyes had grown blue like Wamesepa's and wondered how he would account for the change. Pointing to my eyes, I began to question him when he broke through my sentence. "Oh yes," he said, "my eyes, my eyes—they are painful too!"

"Ah, my father, does the morning go well for you?"

Kavetonwa extended his long, slender arm toward me while inclining his head to one side. "Thank you," he replied, mimicking my voice, "it does indeed. And you, does the morning go well for you?"

I took his hand and crouched beside Michelle. "No, the morning has brought me trouble. I went to visit someone, but he wasn't home, in fact the whole homestead was empty."

Withdrawing his arm, Kavetonwa adjusted his turban, sensing the weight of his hair had loosened it. Meticulously, he pulled forward two worn strands of soiled fabric and tied the ends together, the knot resting well above his forehead. With both his hands, he moved the hair beneath the cloth toward the crown of his head and shaped it until he was satisfied.

"I say," he replied, "this man probably knew you were coming and warned the others to leave. There are those whose visit is unwelcome, you know."

Shifting his weight, Kavetonwa bent one of his legs and drew the knee to his chest, comfortably stretching the other one before him. He was a tall man and very lean. His legs and arms had muscular definition, but his muscles no longer performed the tasks of a younger man and the skin about his upper arms was loose. His eyes were filmy and he suffered from cataracts, and his long, twisting eyebrows, as well as the stray hairs peeking from beneath his turban, were white. The skin of his face was smooth, even around the eyes; indeed, his chest and stomach were far more wrinkled than his face. Behind his right ear, Kavetonwa kept a long metal snuff spoon. From time to time he took the spoon and forced it into a tube of coarsely ground wild tobacco, milling the leaves into a delicate, powdery inhalant. Using the flat end of the spoon, he carefully extracted a measure of snuff and divided it, then breathed a pinch into each nostril, allowing the residual powder to form a grayish-green mustache.

"Have you noticed," asked Michelle, "the Angolans are no longer working on Katere's fence?" She pointed across the riverbed to an ongoing enlargement of Katere's garden. The fence was only partially completed and a stack of timbers lay idle on the ground. "You don't think he'll finish it by himself, do you?"

"Oh no," answered Kavetonwa. "No. Something must be up, there must be trouble. Perhaps Katere is playing one of his tricks."

He reached for his walking stick and eased himself to his feet. "I must be going now, I told my wife I'd meet her in the garden." Stretching his legs, he took a forward step, then turned slightly and held up an envelope containing aspirin tablets. "Thank you for these." He walked a few paces and spoke a farewell. Kavetonwa's slow gait was sure and steady for his age. A hollow gust of wind blew at him, lifting his back skirt slightly before he could place a hand to preserve his modesty. He passed a few small trees and large shrubs, and then disappeared into the riverbed.

Watuwamo had sent one of her young sons with an invitation to visit that afternoon as she would be making *ongoniha*. Himba cuisine is quite limited and the basic diet is one of maize porridge and soured milk. Meat is had on festive occasions, wild fruits and nuts are collected in their seasons, but milk and porridge are daily fare. The quality of a good porridge depends on the delicacy of its grind, the hand that guides its cooking, and the seasonings prepared as side dishes. Among the sauces considered most delicious are two deeply cooked butters, especially the one called *ongoniha*.

Watuwamo lived in a large, well maintained homestead a short walk from Wamesepa's. Her husband, Ondjara, was a hard working man who preserved a tireless degree of order in everything he did. Though his expression was often dour, he was an amiable husband and father, and affectionate with his children. He was tall and slender and set within his middle years. His rugged face was engaging but overshadowed by a prominent nose. Its flesh was perfectly shaped, just unusually large among a people of more subtle features.

Sitting beside the cooking fire at the edge of her work shelter, Watuwamo's legs were outstretched and her leather skirt was tucked between her thighs. She was quite a large woman, with her corpulence pleasantly distributed throughout her body. Her generous proportions only enhanced her appearance, as a fuller figure was thought more beautiful than a willowy frame. Watuwamo was fortunate in this respect, for though

women generally aspired to such a voluptuous figure, relatively few obtained one. It was truly a gift since the size and shape of one's physique
had nothing to do with nourishment.

*How could this be otherwise? Do not all women eat more or less the same amount
of food? When we gather for a meal, no one has opportunity to eat more than
anyone else; no one is more generous with herself than with others. If we see two
women sitting together and the first one is beautiful and fat but the second one is
thin, it is not eating that has made them that way. It is Mukuru. Mukuru has
made the one woman to be fat and the other woman to be thin.*

"Good day, good day, good day to you!" Watuwamo greeted us, bidding
us to sit. "Tell me now, what's the news from over there? Tell me everything that's going on!"

We unfolded our chairs and Michelle began to visit. Elspeth noticed
several children staring at her from a small hut across the homestead and
ran to them. Two of them were Watuwamo's; her other three children
were nowhere to be seen. Over the cooking fire stood a large, three-legged
cauldron whose contents steamed and hissed. Taking a wooden paddle,
Watuwamo stirred the cooking butter. "This is very important," she said,
"not only should the butter be moved around, but the bottom and sides
of the pot must be scraped. The richest flavoring comes from the butter
that sticks to the sides and bottom." The thick simmering liquid had had
its first cooking several days before, and after coming to a boil it was ladled
into a goatskin bucket to cool and congeal. As Watuwamo talked, she
emptied the last of the butter from the goatskin into the cauldron. "The
first time it cooks it has no flavor—we only use it to make *otjize.* This time
it must cook and cook and cook." A pungent aroma rose from the cauldron and hung about the work shelter in the still afternoon air, engaging
the attention of scores of black flies. Most of them risked their lives edging
ever closer to the golden liquid, finally succumbing to its allure. The lifeless specks, suspended in the rolling butter, bobbled along the edges of
the pot. Noticing my expression, Watuwamo said, "They are troublesome
things, but we'll be rid of them in the end."

"I'm not his first wife," she replied, loosening her bonnet, "but I'm really
his only wife. My husband married when he was a young man and his first
wife is a good woman. They were together for a long time, but she wasn't
able to bear children. She went to the ancestral fire where my husband's
father prayed to Mukuru and his ancestors, but nothing changed. They

thought perhaps someone was using *omiti* (bad medicine) against her and consulted a diviner, yet nothing they did opened her womb. Eventually, my husband spoke with her about taking a second wife, and though she knew that a man without children is nothing, she resisted the idea." Watuwamo paused for a moment and stirred the butter, carefully lifting several flies with her paddle and shaking them to the ground.

"I understand her, though," she continued, "because a woman without children is also nothing. It would be hard for me if I had no children, just as it would be hard for you. She must have been saddened by her barrenness and jealous at the thought of another woman bearing her husband a child. Perhaps she thought she would lose her position with him, maybe even his love. I'm sure my husband didn't think in those terms, but how could he—he's a man. My husband had an uncle who lived by our homestead on the Kunene River and we'd known each other for a long time. One day he came and asked my father about marriage. We were surprised because his wife wasn't with him, but he said she was ill and couldn't make the long journey. My father was a bit suspicious, because if the first wife doesn't make the inquiries it can mean she doesn't know of her husband's intentions.

"But I loved that man, and I wanted to marry him. My father knew he had a good heart, so he consented. We were married and came here to Otutati. But the moment we arrived at this homestead, I knew something was wrong. There was no one looking for us, no new house for me or anything. And when my husband's wife saw us coming—I in my bridal clothes and he wearing a groom's bonnet—she immediately called him to their hut. I knew exactly what this meant, and I was right. The next morning she left with several cows, a donkey, and all her belongings to settle with her brothers. That was never my husband's intention, and certainly not mine. I think she couldn't accept me as her husband's wife because she didn't know how serious he was about me. That was a very hard time, but now things are better for all of us. Though she and my husband are still married, they're more like brother and sister than husband and wife. He's provided for her all these years and I know he still feels love for her, but not as strongly as before. I think she no longer resents me. She speaks to me with respect and even asks about the children."

Watuwamo stirred the pot and found it had boiled long enough. The texture was smooth and thick, and the color was a deep amber. The single vessel now contained two different butters: the upper portion was *ongon-*

divi, and the lower, *ongoniha*. Pulling the cauldron from the fire, she set it to cool; and when it had, we helped her separate and store the butters. On the cauldron's lid was a wooden funnel, carved by Hakavona and shaped like a clumsy, long-stemmed goblet with a shiny bullet casing for a spout. Handing it to me, Watuwamo set a bird's nest inside the funnel to filter the butter and began ladling the warm liquid while Michelle held a bucket underneath. After every five or six ladlefuls, she removed the nest and shook away the flies. Soon, the leather buckets were full.

Dark clouds framed the edges of the valley and the sun stood nearly at the top of the sky. The air was heavy and low rumblings echoed in the far distance. The three of us accompanied a woman called Katanga, the local midwife, on her way to visit Watumba. We walked across the tracks and headed north toward Vita's homestead. There was some concern, for Daniel had not yet returned and Katanga felt Watumba was nearing the time of her confinement. Katanga was one of the few who addressed Daniel by his real name, Kurunga, meaning hindered, as he himself preferred the sophistication of Daniel. It was a name he received from a man wandering through Kaokoland when Daniel was a child. As the story was told, the man was a German from Swakopmund evading arrest on a murder charge. He passed several months with Daniel's family before trekking north and crossing the Kunene into Angola. His few words of Himba, combined with a rather slow tongue, put the boy's name beyond his ability to pronounce, so he christened him Daniel.

Vita's younger children greeted us as we approached the small homestead. Four houses stood in an arc along the eastern side of the ancestral fire. Vita's sturdy timber house lay directly east of the fire as he was the fire-keeper and this was his rightful position. The entrance to his house faced the hearth, and when he left his home his eyes viewed the valley's westerly hills. From this position the circular homestead was divided into right and left portions. To the left of Vita's home were two smaller but equally sturdy houses used as bedrooms by his older children. To the right of his house, though at some distance from it, stood Daniel's hut, a desert igloo constructed entirely of wattle and daub. The small dome-shaped structure would not accommodate a standing man and was no more than three paces in diameter. It was the kind of shelter used at dry season cattle camps; but within a permanent homestead it was a sign of poverty. Looking about the place, it was clear Watumba had gone somewhere, and when Katanga inquired, the children reported she was working in her garden.

Finding her would have been difficult except that Katanga's garden adjoined Watumba's. As we walked along a winding path, we saw both men and women toiling in the fields. Men were generally responsible for maintaining the fences, though most helped their wives turn and clear the soil. We passed Masutwa and his wife returning to their homestead and they confirmed that Watumba was in her garden. Winged insects and large black beetles collected in the shade wherever the ground was moist. At last, Katanga stopped and pointed her chin at a high fence. "That's her garden," she said, her gaze moving about quickly. "But I don't know where the entrance is." Michelle and Elspeth looked along the southern stretch and happened upon a slight depression in the fence. Resting against it was a crudely notched timber, and balancing her weight carefully, Katanga scaled the ladder and jumped to the ground.

Watumba lay resting in the shade of a blanket stretched over a few saplings. Under the leafy branches of a tree in a far corner of the garden, her daughter played with a doll made from an ear of dried maize, dressed as a baby. The girl spoke in a quiet voice, her eyes low to the ground—Yes, her mother had been sleeping for a while. As we looked around the garden, Watumba awoke and sat against the fence with her blanket gathered round her, just below her breasts.

"Come here," she called to us, eating a handful of roasted maize kernels.

Her daughter came too and showed her doll to Elspeth.

"Are you feeling well?" Michelle asked, taking a place beside her.

"Yes, thank you, Mikila, I do feel well—though my back hurts me. Would you have any tablets for an aching back?"

Katanga knelt close to Watumba and gently grasped her stomach. Quietly, her hands moved across the belly seeking a range of signs to determine the baby's condition. And though she said nothing, Katanga appeared satisfied with her findings.

"Is there any news about your husband's return?" I asked.

Watumba lowered her head. Her bonnet fell forward and one of its leather straps rapped against her forehead. She was silent for a moment. The garden too was still except for the heckle of a blackbird puffing its shiny blue breast. Watumba lifted her face slightly. "My husband will be here today before the sun leaves the sky," she said with deliberation. And pointing to a tree, she hissed, "That bird has just spoken it!" She eased her body forward again, deeply amused, and laughed. Katanga also laughed, but finally shared the secret with us. Earlier that morning, two men on donkeys had come to Watumba's house and given her the message that Daniel should arrive before nightfall.

Watumba was tired and wished to sleep a bit longer, and we prepared to return to camp.

"Mikila," she called, "remember that my back is still aching."

"Yes," replied Michelle, "it's good you reminded me." And taking a few steps toward the fence, she turned back. "Perhaps you might send your bird to remind me when I'm home—I wouldn't want to forget again."

Of Wamesepa's five wives, only one lived with him. He had endured two divorces and one death. A fourth wife had separated from him many years ago to care for her aging parents, yet never returned after their death. Ekuta was the mother of Wandisa, Wamesepa's eldest son. Occasionally, she cooked for Wamesepa and helped him in other ways, but Ekuta's soul was free and independent, and her temperament highly changeable. She was short and old. Her back was bent and it was said she walked like a chameleon. Though the strength and vitality of her body were clearly waning, it was not, according to local impressions, due to a life of exertion. For Ekuta was never fond of physical labor, and beyond Wamesepa's sight and hearing, her reputation was one of privileged indolence. Every morning, she bathed and refreshed herself with *otjize*, and while her toilet and coiffure lacked thoroughness, Ekuta never considered herself too old to maintain a favorable appearance.

Her position as Wamesepa's wife allowed her to make requests of her neighbors that they found difficult to oppose. In earlier times, she asked women of the area for help in her garden, but now that her gardening days were finished she requested milk, yogurt, butter, and maize meal, knowing her petitions would not go unanswered. Requests for assistance in one form or another were hardly unusual, but Ekuta stepped beyond the bounds of propriety and never returned a favor. Whether Wamesepa knew of his wife's dealings and simply turned a blind eye to them, or whether he was truly unaware of her reputation, no one could say for certain. But in view of his position, no one dared approach him about his wife's excesses. Wandisa knew all the details of his mother's scavenging, but he was also her son, and it was not his place to reprove her. Only his father could fittingly do that.

Ekuta hobbled along the dusty footpath to visit us again. Walking to the edge of the shade cloth, she lowered herself to the ground as if famished, spoke a whispered greeting with low cast eyes, and sat aloof, occasionally turning her head to watch our movements. Greetings and inquiries were rebuffed and we went about our business, having learned from her first visit that she would make her request known in her own due time.

"Look!" she called, rising to her feet. Straightening her frame, she began to shake with hunger, the convulsions growing ever more serious as her body fell toward the ground. Clutching her stick tightly, her knees wobbled and her breathing became rapid as her legs touched the soil and dust began coating her freshly bathed limbs. Ekuta grasped her right knee and drew it toward her chest, then leaned forward, her upper body supported by her other arm. Shifting her knee downward, she rubbed her empty stomach and softly moaned. Slowly, her aged head wandered one way and then another, and creeping toward us, her large, round eyes scoured the ground and her fingers sifted through its debris, looking for something to eat. A moment later, Ekuta had found a few blades of dried grass, a shred or two of tree bark, and several leaves. Gathering them in her right hand, she lifted the bundle to her lips, then slipped it in her mouth and chewed with vigor, her head moving back and forth. Finally, her lips trembled and the bundle of food fell to the ground. Looking directly at us, Ekuta lowered her head and then collapsed.

Men were assembling in the commodious shade of a great camel thorn tree to settle a dispute. Several hundred paces east of Wamesepa's homestead, a tattered collection of folding chairs, weathered logs, and flat topped stones were being arranged in a circle. Masutwa stood apart from the others and visited with the two plaintiffs. As Wandisa was in the far north attending the funeral of a relative on behalf of his father, Masutwa would preside over the court and render final judgment. The troubles brewing between Katere and his Ngambwe laborers were to be investigated by the gathering men. Katere had engaged two young Ngambwe to build a fence around his enlarged garden. The Angolan laborers, like so many others, had fled their country to avoid conscription into either of two factional armies involved in civil war. In Kaokoland, they worked at the sorts of tasks Himba were loath to perform. And for their trouble, they accepted livestock as payment with the intent of building up herds and flocks of their own.

Katere emerged from his house and walked slowly in the direction of the tree. He was more than sixty years of age, and though awkward physically, sustained a youthful appearance. His eyes were watery, his lips rather thin, and the bits of hair not gathered beneath his turban were deeply gray. Along his forehead and cheeks the skin was smooth and soft, but so too were his shoulders. Out of his hearing it was said he possessed the soft body of a woman. Katere was an odd combination of misfit passions—much of the time he was selfish, even mendacious, but other times his kindliness and hospitality were almost excessive. At root, he was a mild and gentle person. He was also the eldest son of Wamesepa's eldest sister, and as he would one day inherit much of his uncle's vast estate, he wished to be treated with the kind of deference and respect shown the old headman.

Katere's youngest years were spent in the southeastern corner of the valley. The tranquility of his childhood ended with the untimely passing of his mother, followed shortly by the sudden death of his father. On a peaceful morning before any rains had fallen, Katere's mother and several other women journeyed from dry season pastures to their valley homesteads. As they walked along the familiar course leading through the hills and mountains, a lone bull elephant stood upon the path. Hearing their footsteps, the huge creature turned its head and, spooked by their appearance, raised its long, gray trunk. The women scattered and ran, but it was said the elephant singled out Katere's mother and pursued her, eventually crushing her left hip. Still breathing, she was carried on a makeshift litter to her home where she passed several days of agony before succumbing to her wounds. Her husband was told by messenger and immediately took his bow and arrows and found the very elephant responsible for his wife's death and killed it.

But death and revenge are never so easy. No one dies solely from natural causes—they are but illusion. Beyond them lurk the true cause of death: the use of malicious omiti *(medicine) employed by someone consumed with enmity toward the victim.*

A diviner was consulted by Katere's maternal aunts and uncles, and the highly respected oracle revealed that Katere's mother had died at the hands of her husband: Katere's father had used *omiti* to kill his own wife by seizing upon the elephant's heart and mind. It was a frightful revelation and those privy to it knew of no appropriate course of action. A number of weeks later, however, Katere's father, a strapping and virile man, inexplicably fell into dire illness and expired within days. His baffling death was taken to the oracle, and when the diviner was apprised of all the details, he put Katere's family at peace. For it was the dead woman's spirit, angered by the circumstances of her death, that caused her assassin to lose his life, and now, without distress, she could pass into the ancestral realm. On that day, Katere was received into the care of his mother's brother, Wamesepa.

Katere had five wives. Most of his time was spent with his favorite wife Wakamburwa at Otutati—an arrangement seemingly agreeable to everyone involved. Wakamburwa was a handsome woman not yet beyond her childbearing years. She accepted public displays of her husband's character flaws without discomfort and was, according to those who knew her well, generally unaware of the gossip generated by his deeds. She knew Katere better than anyone else and maintained he provided for her in a considerate and loving way, that he never upbraided her physically, and even his verbal reproaches were soft and gentle. Wakamburwa herself possessed an unusually sharp tongue which she occasionally turned on her husband. She was highly fashion conscious and spent a good deal of time grooming and assuring herself of the uniformity of her body's mahogany covering. She cleaned her iron beaded anklets and the copper bracelets that ran from her wrists to her elbows on both arms, and took care that her children were properly and cleanly attired. These were not entirely selfish acts, for Wakamburwa knew her husband appreciated such things; and in her own way, for her own reasons, she was devoted to him.

Masutwa sat atop a short wooden stool, his back supported by the rough trunk of a young ironwood tree. Flanking him on either side were nearly a score of men willing to hear the case and influence the court's decision. At the end of the human ellipse sat Katere, and opposite him, the two Ngambwe men. Entirely absent from the gathering were women, whose presence was only necessary if the disputants were female. The proceedings began when Masutwa called on the Ngambwe men to declare their reasons for convening the court. As the taller one stood to address the gallery, the visiting and gossiping quieted.

"Honored sir and honored gentlemen," he began, leaning slightly forward to acknowledge Masutwa. "We bring the matter of a broken agreement before you. The man, Katere, asked us to build a fence around his new garden, and we were willing to do it. After discussing payment for our labor, we agreed the man would pay each of us two full-grown but still reproducing nanny goats, and three young kids, at least one of them a female. In addition to the goats, we agreed the man would provide us a sleeping house and two meals a day, one of which would include meat. I say, this was our agreement."

Masutwa signalled him to suspend. And looking at Katere, he asked, "Do you agree, Katere, were these the terms?" Without raising his eyes, the man nodded his agreement.

The Ngambwe quietly glanced over the gallery of faces. As he was not their peer he had to be cautious in gauging their reactions. "We felt the terms were a bit low, too much in the man's favor, considering how far we had to go to find trees suitable for posts. But it was fair enough. The next morning we began scouting and chopping in the ironwood groves near the small hill over there." His chin pointed south, and though everyone present knew the location of the groves, and knew they were too distant to be seen, every man turned his eyes and searched for them. "From those groves we had to carry the timbers on our shoulders to the garden site because the man said his donkey was not strong enough to pull such loads. If we had had use of a donkey, we could have saved many days of work. As it was, we cut and hauled wood for six or seven days, and piled the wood near the old garden fence.

"The man came to us then and said because so many lads were returning from post he was worried they might vandalize the wood. He told us we should carry the wood to his homestead and set it beside his house. We protested as this would greatly increase the amount of work, but the man insisted, so we did his bidding. Then five days ago the man told us we were working too slowly and eating too much food, and he would withhold one nanny goat from each of us to compensate himself for these extra expenses." The young man's voice lifted and strengthened. "He announced too that he would no longer provide meat at our meals. Again, we protested and said his actions violated our agreement, but the man said his mind was made up."

The Ngambwe lifted his gaze from the ground ever so slightly to read the gallery, then lowered it and spoke softly. "Now honored sir and honored gentlemen, we ask you: Is it right that this man violate the terms of our agreement? We've worked very hard, and every delay has been a result of the man's orders and his unwillingness to provide us with a donkey. I say, this is the matter we bring before the court."

The Angolan took his seat and onlookers began talking back and forth until Masutwa turned and requested that Katere stand and make his statement before the court.

"You've heard the words of this man?" asked Masutwa.

"Yes," answered Katere.

"Do you agree with his words? Are they correct?"

Katere stood quietly, leaning on his walking stick. Masutwa allowed him a moment to reflect, and then repeated his question.

"Yes," Katere said finally, "much of what he told you is correct. We did agree upon the goats and food and lodging as he said, but there was a time element. I asked them to have the fence completed early enough to turn the soil and plant the maize before the rains came—and I remember them saying they would. But now many gardens are half prepared while this one has yet to be enclosed." Straightening his back, Katere looked at his fellows. "So what am I to do about this?" he asked. "Perhaps I spoke too hastily about reducing their payment, but I did so hoping to prompt them to finish their work." He raised his chin and closed his eyes. "Yes," he said, "that's all I have to say."

The gallery was silent.

"Do you wish to add anything to your statement, Katere?"

"No. I've said all I need to say."

"Now," began Masutwa, looking toward the Ngambwe men, "as we've heard these two statements, they differ only in that Katere claims you agreed to complete the fence early enough for the garden to be planted before the rains. What's your response to this?"

The second Ngambwe man stood. He was considerably shorter than his companion, but his voice was deep and rich. "Honored sir and honored gentlemen, I've heard the man speak to you. And I say, part of what he's told you is true, but his other words were cleverly spoken to mislead you. Yes, it's true that time was a consideration, but we only said we'd try to complete the work by the time the ground in his current garden was ready for planting. And honored gentlemen, even as the man has spoken, his wife has not finished half of her garden preparations. And furthermore, the man himself has been the cause of our delay. He hasn't allowed us use of his donkeys, and what has taken us nearly seven days to carry, could have been done in a single day with a donkey and a sledge. Also, because the man won't permit us to leave the wood at his garden, everyday we have to carry it to and from the site. And even from here you can see how great a distance that is."

The Ngambwe paused as the men looked, their eyes following the path leading from the house to the garden.

"And there's one last thing I wish to say. Carrying the wood between the man's house and his garden is a new task—it wasn't part of our original agreement. If anything, the man owes us another goat or two."

The Ngambwe took his seat. And as the mellow sound of his words disappeared into the air beyond the shade, everyone shifted toward Katere, awaiting his response.

"This is strange," said Masutwa. "An agreement shouldn't have two meanings. You may remain seated, Katere, but we'd like you to respond to this man's words. Tell us whether the agreement was as he's said. And is it correct that you refused the use of your donkey and required them to move the wood from your garden to your house?"

Katere's eyes widened and his lips flared. He glanced at his peers, but would not acknowledge his opponents. "I say," he began haltingly. "I think there's been a misunderstanding. You know how it is when a man hires laborers to do a job, how a man must push and prod them forward—just as a man must prod and push a beast. My words were only meant to help them finish the task. I never intended to withhold payment. I always honor my word."

Several men clicked their tongues.

"I say, if you wanted them to complete the fence as quickly as possible, why did you refuse them the use of your donkey?" asked Makuva. "And why did you have them carry the wood back and forth?"

Katere ignored the questions.

"Come now," said Vita, wheedling him, "answer the question. You're keeping a lot of men from their work."

Breathing deeply, Katere retained his subordinate posture. "I couldn't let them use my donkey because I was thinking of making a journey to see my cattle. Besides, my children enjoy riding the animal. As for lodging the wood near my house, I thought if the wood were known to be mine, it might be carried away. Things aren't as secure as they used to be."

Ngipore lifted his chin. "If you were worried about theft, did you make securing the wood part of the agreement?"

"If you're asking whether I specifically said the timbers must be kept at my house, the answer is no. But isn't it common sense that building materials should be kept safe? Must I be explicit about something that's so obvious?"

Masutwa leaned to his right and conferred with Makuva and Vita, then asked the two Ngambwe to rise. "Katere's words must be answered," he said. "When a man hires you to build a fence or a house or anything else, where do you bring the wood that you've cut from the groves?"

"Honored sir and honored gentlemen," answered the taller one, "we've always stored the wood at the building site. Never have we kept the wood so distant from our project."

"Have you ever worried about wood being stolen?"

"Since coming to Kaokoland, we've never worried about the theft of building material. Together, we've built fences, houses, and work shelters these past two years, and nothing's ever been stolen from us."

"Thank you," said Masutwa. And shifting his eyes from the taller to the shorter one, he said, "Katere's stated that common sense should have told you to store the wood close to his home so it wouldn't be stolen. Does this seem reasonable to you?"

"Honored sir and honored gentlemen, common sense tells me the opposite. My experience, our experience, as my brother has said, is that building materials are safe when stored at the building site. Wood has never been stolen from us, and if I may speak frankly, I haven't heard of it being stolen from anyone."

"Yes," said Masutwa, "I see. How long have you known Katere?"

"Known the man?"

"Yes, how long have you known him?"

"We met the man a few days before we started his fence."

"Had you ever heard of Katere prior to this meeting?"

"We were told he was looking for someone to build a fence—that was all we knew of him. Nothing more."

Masutwa turned to the gallery. "Does anyone else have a question?"

After several further queries, the parties were excused and the deliberations began. Every corner of the gallery was searched until a consensus was reached, and as the morning sun moved to the top of the sky Masutwa's boy was dispatched to call Katere and the Ngambwe back to the tree.

Masutwa rose and spoke to the three. "The court has reached a decision," he said. "We find that Katere has acted wrongly. We find that you, Katere, have violated several terms of the agreement and added others that were unreasonable and beyond expectation. The court has decided that you must abide by the original terms of the agreement, and that you must pay each of the laborers an additional female kid for the trouble you've caused.

"Do you question the decision of the court?" he asked.

"No," answered Katere. "I do not."

Presently, the men of the gallery rose and mingled freely with Katere and the Ngambwe, taking care to speak nothing of the trial or its outcome.

Open and Close

. . . describes the Himba's relations with their ancestors; for the latter are always ready to hear their living kinsmen and wish to remain close to them. The configuration of a homestead reflects this relationship, an often difficult one—for human beings desire to be close to their ancestors yet remain apprehensive at what it might bring. Wandjoze also wishes to be close to someone, though not an ancestor, but then decides to keep her distance.

A bit of rain had fallen in our part of the valley. The scattered drops briefly settled the dust and inclined a few to hasten to their gardens, but its effects hardly lingered beyond midafternoon. Empty homesteads around Otutati gradually filled as people returned in greater numbers to open their homes and sweep their hearths.

Not far to the east of Wamesepa's house lay a homestead of two well maintained houses and a small work shelter set on the eastern side of the central livestock enclosure. As the homestead had recently been constructed, the timbers and thatching appeared clean and fresh, not yet fully discolored by sun and dust. The owner was a man named Ngipore who lived there with his wife and two of his children. Ngipore reckoned he had two families. His older sons were grown and married and had children of their own, but a younger maiden daughter and a son on the verge of maturity lived with him still. They had come from a place called Kaoko Otavi, a settlement with large perpetual springs several days' trek south of

Otutati. The countryside around Kaoko Otavi had seen little rain for several years and Ngipore decided, for the sake of his cattle, to divide the herd and leave a portion with his sons. The remaining animals he led to the more generous pasturelands of Otutati.

Ngipore was a patient and good-humored man. He was tall and wiry and had dark, thick whiskers. And since his wife was visiting her elderly parents, he had taken on the responsibility of preparing the garden. Soot and ashes lay all over the ground from its recent burning, and standing barefoot in the middle of the field, Ngipore raised his hoe slightly above his knees and struck the earth. The foregoing days had seen the return of his daughter and nephew from dry season pasture, driving the animals left in their care with them. His nephew was a handsome, seasoned youth, though fully absorbed in his own appearance and the difficulties of romantic life. From the brightly colored cloth he used for his skirts he had fashioned a swatch to cover his circumcision plait—the only tuft of hair on his otherwise cleanly shaven head. The long plait had been growing since his circumcision in late boyhood and should continue to grow for a number of years before the single plait would be ceremoniously divided and woven into two as a sign of his marriageability.

"So Wondjoze and your nephew have found their way home," I remarked after greeting him.

Ngipore turned and laid aside his hoe. I knew the mention of his nephew could be unsettling, for the lad had come to live with him less than a year ago when Ngipore's sister returned to Angola to look after their mother. Since the lad would one day inherit most of Ngipore's cattle, his mother decided it was best he learned herding and husbanding from his uncle. The youth had come to Otutati with expectations of license and idleness, but Ngipore had thought of him as another pair of hands.

"Yes, they're both home," he said walking to the fence. "But do you see them here helping me? No, they're off riding donkeys with their friends." And lowering his head, he lamented, "I just don't know what to make of children anymore—they're almost as naughty as we were!"

The sandy path wound through groves of ironwood trees growing at the foot of a steep hill. The slopes were littered with stones and hardened branches, and the way to the top was difficult. Near the summit, resting in a large, rocky depression, was a young baobab tree with new leaves growing from its uppermost limbs. The hilltop itself was nothing more than a small patch of even ground, but below, all the homesteads of Otu-tati stood in their peculiar forms. The meandering tracks stretched the length of the valley, dividing it into halves; yet never was the location of anything described in relation to them. The countryside was filled with locales, bunches, clusters, circles, arcs, and ellipses, of places securely built here or there, and not as if scattered by gusts of wind. There was order, pattern, and familiarity.

On the eastern side of the homestead lies the ancestral fire and hearth, where every significant event in human life is brought to the attention of Mukuru and the ancestors. The presence of the fire also separates the homestead from the wilderness that surrounds it. Every seven or eight days the fire-keeper approaches his fire to speak with Mukuru and the ancestors on behalf of his paternal relatives. Standing before the hearth with his eyes looking west, he petitions for a listening ear; and as sole proprietor of the fire, he must find it.

Do not all peoples have ancestral fires that they may speak to their fathers? Is it not the same god who looks over all the peoples of the world? Yes, it must be the same God and he is the most powerful being in the heavens. He understands every mystery and there is no other creature like him. But Mukuru dwells in distant regions and has much to do. Because of this, he has given us ancestors who watch over us, know our hearts, and bless us when it is right. These spirits dwell above the earth—though they visit us as often as they like. Their lives are orderly and the events of their days are similar to ours. They keep cattle, but their cattle are always fat, their pastures are ever green, and milk and meat are never scarce. They do work, but it is easier for them and their lives are very pleasant. No longer do they age, illness has no place in their realm, and death can never touch them. Their lives, though, are not so simple, for there are always things that weigh upon their hearts. They worry about their living kinsmen and will chasten us when we need it. And for blessings, all they ask is that we remember them.

The hilltop's southern view was of sharp and rounded peaks, and beyond that, nothing but sky. To the west, the valley continued till it met a line of mountains. Homesteads, a small reservoir, stands of trees, open savannah, and dusty red soil rolled into the foothills. The eastern view was little different, only the mountains seemed more distant. Drifting clouds cast shadows across the valley floor and the map was nearly done.

Near our tent stood a tawny gray donkey. The stoic beast, tethered to a stone, held itself in absolute rigidity—even its black encircled eyes gazed forward without straying from its focus. A group of loitering youths, maidens, and older children huddled behind the tent, laughing and chattering. Among them was Ngipore's nephew, who seemed to be a leader among his peers. But moments before, another lad had arrived, and as he joined the gathering, attention shifted toward him. He was a handsome, tall, solid, muscular youth with black skirts and an iron beaded necklace. His circumcision plait was stiff and shiny, and he had spent two full days traveling from Etanga to stay with relatives near Otutati. It was rumored that Wondjoze fancied him, and when she learned of his coming, she and her friend, Wahona, returned home to refresh their skin with *otjize*, a cosmetic made from cooked butterfat and finely milled ochre. But now that he had arrived and was visiting with the other youths and maidens, Wondjoze was nowhere to be seen.

Two older girls stood near the entrance of our tent holding a large blanket that rippled in the soft breeze. The sun shone along the opposite side of the screen and one of the shadows cast upon the blanket was Michelle's. As I approached the tent, the two girls warned me away, saying that matters behind the screen were private and no concern of mine. Wondjoze, it seemed, was injured. She and Wahona had planned to ride a donkey and attract the youthful visitor's attention. Straddling the beast at its shoulders, Wahona waited until Wondjoze had climbed atop the rump, spread her skirts, and slipped her hands around her midriff, before taking the reins. The two maidens rode up and down the footpath linking Wamesepa's homestead to Ngipore's, shouting, laughing, and calling to others.

As the carefree trotting continued, beneath their leather skirts the donkey's bristly hide began to irritate the maidens' unprotected skin. Wondjoze was the first to notice and asked Wahona to slow the donkey's pace that she might rearrange her skirts. But the continued friction proved unbearable, and she dismounted the animal and walked toward the tent, preserving as best she could the appearance of a normal gait.

"I've been riding the donkey," she said quietly, "and now there's pain between my legs. Do you have any medicine to help me, Mikila?"

"Perhaps," answered Michelle, "but I must see the wound."

Wondjoze stiffened at the thought, but finally agreed to be seen on condition of absolute privacy. Behind the screen she leaned forward and pulled her rear skirt aloft. Her injury was a series of weeping abrasions, and with great care the wounds were cleaned and dressed. Afterward, Wondjoze wrapped herself in the blanket and cautiously looked about before heading toward her father's homestead. Deliberately, her footsteps led her away from the gathering, but not before the youth from Etanga noticed her. And after chatting with Ngipore's nephew, he quickly stepped forward to greet her.

"Wondjoze," he called after her, "I've come to see you."

Without upsetting the succession of footsteps, she acknowledged and dismissed his words by lifting her hand.

· 4 ·

A Cry at Dawn

. . . is finally heard when Katanga draws Watumba's child from the womb. At this meeting place of all humanity, Katanga's knowledge of midwifery is taxed to its limits as she seeks to bring forth a living baby from a woman who has not given life in many years.

Cool night air had settled along the valley floor and the moon was dropping peacefully toward the far horizon. Animals were still and people slumbered; only the mischievous spirits of the night roamed the landscape. A small fire on the hearth at the center of Kantanga's house burned and smouldered, dispersing just enough light to cast a dull, hazy glow within the house. Rising smoke, held captive by the heavy grasses tied to the roof's conical framework, idled slowly in the closed air, inciting creatures of the thatch to rub their legs and twitch their wings. The fire turned its quaking light upon skin that shimmered with the perspiration of effort. Shadowy breasts, silhouetted against the wall, hung low, noticeably rising and falling as the chests beneath expanded and contracted with breath. The three women had removed their *erembe* bonnets, and their long, thick plaits appeared as darkened tentacles.

Katanga and Yoroka had been with Watumba since late afternoon when her travail had begun in earnest. All three were weary, yet the outward signs revealed the baby was still no closer to relinquishing the womb. From the very outset, Katanga felt this birth would not be without complication, for though Watumba had borne a child within a year or two of her marriage—a birth unmarked by difficulty—her baby was now a budding young woman, and all those years had passed with a silent, empty womb. When seed had taken root, Katanga was among the first informed of Watumba's circumstance. As soon as a woman knows her womb is full, when her menses have failed to come according to females' time reckoned in the waxing and waning of the moon, her mother and husband are told the glad tidings. It is a time of happiness as well as a time of anxiety, a time when moral restrictions are more fully obeyed and marital fidelity becomes absolute, a time when the assurance of a safe delivery becomes primary. As a trusted friend and neighbor, Kantanga was asked to prepare the unborn child for its journey into the world. And within her practice, the most essential preparation was the fortnightly fetal massage —a technique Kantanga had learned from her mother and mother's mother.

This fundamental provision was offered to Michelle when she spoke of her condition to Katanga and Miranda one afternoon in the shade of a tree near the well. Miranda, a middle-aged man visiting from Okangwati, confessed prior knowledge of the condition. He had observed the unusually forceful pulsation at the base of Michelle's throat—an obvious sign that a baby has joined its breath to the breath of its mother. Katanga had also suspected pregnancy, but on rather different grounds. One morning, not long after breakfast, Michelle rushed from the tent and quickly lost her porridge. As our comings and goings were subject to the scrutiny of scores of eyes, ears, and nostrils, Michelle had been observed by at least one set of eyes that alerted every willing set of ears. But such circumstances are private and only introduced into general conversation by the experiencing party. And with Michelle's casual announcement, Katanga felt secure in tendering her prenatal services.

At the foundation of her practice lay a belief that a fetus must be active. An expectant mother senses mild flutterings and tickings within her womb, but these stirrings are more than a sign of the baby's health. Such movements ensure a safe and timely delivery, for the mother alone does not draw her child from the womb. The baby must pull itself along the canal of birth, a journey made possible by developing its strength of movement. Katanga's massages were simply a means of urging the fetus to enlarge its capacities.

Katanga entered our tent with an air of gravity and seriousness. We had not known Katanga as a midwife but as a spirited and rather playful widow who had lost her husband many years prior to our acquaintance. During his life, she had borne him three sons, and within several years of his death, she bore another son and a daughter. Katanga's firstborn was now a man more than half her age; her next two boys were twins, a circumstance that altered the course of her life. The mother of twins is endowed with unusually rich generative powers. Round her neck hangs a peculiar necklace that sets her apart from all others, as such a woman is perilous and may unwittingly challenge the fertility of Nature.

Human beings, Nature, and the Powers upholding the world mingle together and influence one another. Our conduct honors or offends these Powers, but the actions of a mother of twins are even weightier. When dark, heavy clouds begin to drift across the sky at the beginning of the rainy season, ordinary people discuss the possibility of a storm. But the mother of twins must take charcoal and draw circles and crosses on her forehead and breasts so that the rain will fall. For though she has given birth to twins, she is still human, and her capacity to give life is nothing compared with the rain's capacity. Arrogance, though, is blinding, and the Powers require that we acknowledge our feebleness before them, otherwise they cannot bestow their gifts.

Katanga placed her bundles on the floor near a sheet of plastic set out to contain her personal effects. Discreetly, she surveyed the contents and arrangement of our tent. It was our one vestige of privacy and its canvas walls held within them a fragment of our world, a world as curious and perplexing to Katanga as hers was to us. Michelle was bidden to recline on the floor and uncover her abdomen. Reaching for a small wooden container, Katanga dipped her forefingers inside, replaced the lid, and rubbed her hands with *otjize*. Michelle raised her upper body slightly as Katanga took her place on the ground. She doubled her legs and slid beneath Michelle's back so that the patient's head and shoulders might rest comfortably on her thighs. Then, leaning forward, Katanga stretched her torso and arms to make certain she could reach beyond Michelle's waist. From this position, Katanga's right side lined up with Michelle's.

Determining the sex of the baby was important to Katanga for it would guide the course of her prenatal massages. Although an idiosyncratic test, Katanga felt she could establish the sex of a child during the beginning stages of pregnancy when fetal movement was far less expansive. In her experience, males and females spent more time on one side of the womb than the other: Girls nestled on the mother's left; boys lodged on their mother's right. But determining the sex of a child growing in the womb was different from understanding why a child should partake of one set of physical dispositions rather than another. And on this point Katanga could offer no explanation.

No one is certain how the sex of a child is decided; it is simply an act of Mukuru. However, if a child's appearance or temperament favors one parent or the other, the cause is easily understood. A child is formed from the liquid substances each parent contributes at conception. But the strength of one's substance is variable— one time it is strong, another time it is weak, and different people may have weaker or stronger substances altogether. When a child's appearance or disposition favors one parent, it is because the favored parent's substance was stronger at the moment of conception.

Katanga rubbed more *otjize* onto the palms of her hands and carefully smoothed it onto Michelle's belly. The movement of her articulate fingers and the appearance of her smooth, steady stroking hardly corresponded to her hands' activity. For in the midst of gentle, circular movements, Katanga's fingers bore down assertively upon the child. Grasping one way and then another, she probed the womb searching for the baby's underside, a view Katanga felt necessary in determining the sex. It was an uncomfortable examination, but for one properly trained in the arts of medical divining, the signs revealed through touch and sight were unmistakable. The baby was lodged on Michelle's left side; she was carrying a girl.

The heavy movements were taxing and Katanga broke for a moment's rest. When she recovered her breath, she placed her hands on Michelle's lower abdomen. Her fingers moved pliantly across the skin until they detected the baby's figure nestled on the lower end. With less firmness and rigidity, Katanga applied pressure at various points on the womb while continuing to massage the whole of it. Her long arms rounded and her fingers met below Michelle's waist. Slowly, she pulled them toward her, wedging her fingers deeply into the skin to cup the child. Gradually, and with great care, Katanga relaxed the pressure and drew her hands over the belly. From time to time she redirected the movement of her massage—inclining the baby from top to bottom—but counteracting the normal propensity was her greater intent. For more than a quarter of an hour she kept at her task, and as she neared the end of the massage, droplets of sweat fell from her brow to the object of her toil. One last thrust from bottom to top and the massage was finished. Wearied, both women fell back without exchanging a word.

Watumba's baby had been encouraged by Katanga throughout her pregnancy. Though now, in the midst of a protracted labor, it was difficult to know whether the massages were proving helpful. The house quieted as each woman collected herself apart from the others. Then, moaning so softly it was almost beyond hearing, Watumba inadvertently signalled the rise of another contraction. Katanga's eyes met Yoroka's, and pointing with her chin, she directed Yoroka to take her position at Watumba's back. Watumba had been resting on her knees, but feeling the support of Yoroka's body she pivoted backward, pulled her ankles under her buttocks, and leaned her full weight against Yoroka. Watumba's body quivered involuntarily as weary muscles were urged to readiness. Feeling a stab of pressure at her knees as Watumba stiffened against her for support, Yoroka secured her footing by leaning against the wall of the house. She laid a hand on Watumba's glistening forehead and drew what moisture she could from the tense brow, wiping it on her own thigh. Watumba's expression remained stoic, her turbulent breathing the only recognition of her suffering.

As the contraction's pull diminished, Watumba's limbs softened and she slid from Yoroka's grasp. Katanga blinked wearily as she handed her a gourd of tea brewed from *otati* bark, an antidote for pain. Noticing the fire had died to a smolder, Yoroka set another piece of wood at its smoking core and watched to see whether it would catch. Watumba's ailing body stiffened instinctively as the pains of birth returned. All three women assumed their birthing positions, though Watumba's strength had so waned she could no longer squat unassisted. Gradually, the scene unfolded, but as before, its conclusion was not encouraging. Yoroka, whose stamina and patience had fallen to low ebb, whispered firmly, "Who is it, Watumba? Tell us his name!"

It was a challenge to uncover hidden knowledge. For birth is not merely a physical process, but a moral process as well—both physical and moral forces work upon a birthing mother. However isolated labor and birth may seem, every human act and every human intention is eventually returned. A baby ought to be born after a reasonable period of labor, and if it hesitates too long, its restraint can no longer be considered natural.

Something beyond the physical has intervened, and the process of birth will not continue to its close until the offending circumstance has been resolved. If, during her pregnancy, a woman receives other than her husband's embrace, the seed of the stranger is repulsive to the growing baby, and within her womb, struggles ensue between the personalities of the two seeds. Such wayward actions cannot be hidden, for the Powers will retaliate by sealing a mother's womb until she confesses. Her paramour too will suffer until he openly acknowledges his deeds and makes appropriate compensation.

"There is no one," murmured Watumba, "there is no one."

No longer could Katanga ignore the dull bleating and lowing of livestock or the clamor of hooves knocking against an array of hardened surfaces. Through the crevices of her doorway fell the first light of morning. And as she noticed this her anxiety deepened, for she knew the length of Watumba's travail was inordinate and she worried the baby might be stillborn. Katanga came from a family of midwives, but her knowledge, like that of her mother's and grandmother's, was gained in different ways—techniques learned through assisting other midwives, advice gathered in consultation with others, and a few peculiarities developed in the course of her own practice.

Katanga gently laid Watumba on the floor. Quickly and incisively her hands and fingers examined Watumba's belly to determine whether the baby was moving, but her probings went unanswered. Watumba still lay on the cool, shiny floor as the fervency of a new contraction overtook her body. Yoroka rushed forward and slipped her arms beneath Watumba's, and with great effort began raising her to a squatting position. "No!" whispered Katanga sharply. Yoroka turned, puzzled at Katanga's words. But as her eyes met Katanga's, she understood and relaxed her arms, allowing Watumba to pass downward. Cautiously, Katanga straddled Watumba's rigid figure, crouching just below her breasts. She raised her head and stretched her hands in the same direction the baby must travel. Breathing heavily, Katanga spread her fingers widely and set them on Watumba's belly precisely where she determined the baby to lay. Down rushed the strength of her arms, harder and harder, bearing against the womb, nudging, pushing, straining, driving the baby forward. But it was a burgeoning of affliction Watumba could not endure and her mouth widened to its fullest. She turned her head slightly and exhaled with such vehemence that Yoroka laid an ironwood shoot in her mouth and stepped back, watching as her teeth bore into the water-soaked twig.

The contraction seemed endless and glistening liquids issued ever so slightly from the birth canal. As Katanga's fingers sensed Watumba's abdomen softening, she eased the pressure of her hands and finally rose to her feet. Droplets of reddish perspiration trickled down her forehead and brow and fell to the ground. Watumba cast the twig from her mouth and lay silent. Motioning to Yoroka, Katanga spoke with her back to Watumba, "Soon the baby will come."

Twice more Watumba tensed and relaxed. A third tension brought the crown of the head to passing view before receding, which was a sign of encouragement and cheered the three women as they waited. The fire had dimmed again, discharging a brackish haze that mingled with the fatigue of their minds and bodies and created a dreamy sensation. The spell had not yet lifted when the muscles of Watumba's abdomen began to pull. Yoroka rose and took her position behind Watumba. Katanga bent toward Watumba's ear. "This must be the last one," she admonished.

"Lift her! Lift her higher—the baby must drop down!" ordered Katanga, as Yoroka struggled to support Watumba's resistant body. "Push," she said, turning to Watumba, "press your eyes together." After a long moment, the baby's crown became visible and Katanga angled forward on her knees, resting her shoulders and head on the floor. The position was awkward, but Watumba's groin was low to the ground and Katanga had to see the baby. In an instant, the crowning gave way to a rush, and a delicate little head with moist, shiny locks dangled from Watumba. The tiny head turned ever so slightly from one side to the other, but advanced no further. Katanga got to her feet and firmly laid her hand on Watumba's belly—the contraction was dying. "Push!" she called again, "you must push one last time!" Watumba obeyed. She set her chin against her breast and curled her upper torso over her abdomen as tightly as she could. With her remaining strength, Watumba pushed as forcefully as her body would allow.

Katanga withdrew from her position. The baby was coming—of this there was no doubt. Its shoulders, though, refused to pass through the narrowness of its mother's circular exit. Again, Katanga bent low. As Watumba bore down, the baby edged forward, pressing the skin around the exit to the limit of tautness, the limit of thinness. Tenderly, Katanga grasped the head and neck, and firmly but with exquisite care attempted to augment Watumba's efforts. But the head was too delicate and the skin too resilient to yield to Katanga's pull. Pressed now by the tapering effects of Watumba's final thrust, Katanga made her right hand into a fist, extended her thumb, and directing her thumbnail, gouged the skin surrounding the exit until it broke, and incised a crude path. Watumba seemed oblivious to the episiotomy, but her child finally broke free of the womb. Hurriedly, Katanga pressed her wrists together and spread her fingers to receive the descending head. Her left arm shifted forward to support the child's underside, and when its feet had cleared the birth canal, Katanga cradled the tiny living body and laid it on a soft goatskin. The infant's ruddy eyelids fluttered clumsily and his shining lips parted, but he uttered no sound. Katanga cautiously drew a circle round the inner circumference of the baby's mouth with her forefinger. His little chest expanded and he gave birth to his first cry.

His cries grew louder and Watumba moved her head in the direction of the sounds. Her eyes searched for her child and found the tiny body trembling from the force of his own lungs, his skin covered with the salve of birth. Watumba's white teeth shone. Her body, so fatigued from the ordeal of birth, lost its muscular composure and Yoroka, equally unable to continue her support, allowed Watumba to sink to the ground. Katanga worked on, awaiting the contractions that would expel the placenta. Already inside the hut, on the westerly edge, lay a shallow hole ready to receive it. For placenta is not merely the debris of the womb, but a part of the child, an element so connected with the child's life that its resting place must be safeguarded. Any danger or ill experienced by the placenta is no less injurious to its companion child. As Watumba's belly strained to discharge the afterbirth, Katanga and Yoroka waited, and then severed the umbilicus and carefully interred the placenta.

"I'm cold," whispered Watumba, who now lay on a stiff cattle hide beside a few glowing coals. Yoroka pulled a blanket hanging from the rafters and spread it over her shivering body. From a bucket she drew a cup of water and set it beside her. Watumba lifted her head slightly and drank, her eyes following Katanga all the while.

The baby had passed several moments outside his mother's womb, without affection. Finally, Katanga lifted the child and curled her left arm round his tiny body and held him fast. Her other hand reached for a knife. Deftly, she reshaped the umbilical cord and knotted it. The same hand took a remnant of fabric and immersed it in a water-filled tortoise shell. While drawing the cloth from the water and wringing its excess, Katanga looked deeply into the baby's eyes. The dampened cloth was cool and briefly stilled the child's cry. Carefully, Katanga cleaned round his eyes, clearing the residue of birth secretions. Satisfied, she dampened the cloth again and bathed the rest of his face before turning to his neck, shoulders, and back. While Katanga swabbed his breast and around his nipples, the baby relaxed and urine trickled onto Katanga's knee. Meticulously, she labored to remove the stains from his skin and then laid him aside. From a leather bucket near the wall, Katanga scooped a palmful of cooked butterfat. It was cool and stiff to the touch, and she kneaded the amber ball in her hands till it warmed. Again, she reached for the baby and glazed his tiny body, except for his scalp, in the sparkling cream and then nestled him in Watumba's arms.

Watumba held her baby close to the warmth of her bosom. Katanga knelt at her side and lifted the blanket, concerned about the flow of blood. From one of her bundles, Katanga gathered shreds of leather and set them on a rag; adding other bits of absorbent material and aromatic leaves, she fashioned a pad and managed, with some effort, to lodge it between Watumba's legs. She then rose and replaced the blanket.

Prompted by the nearness of his mother's breasts, the baby cried loudly and insistently. A low rapping at the door was answered by Yoroka—a request for news of the birth, to be conveyed to Daniel. When her whispered interview finished, she joined Katanga who had pulled the baby from his mother. He seemed hungry, and following this assumption, Yoroka searched for a spoon while Katanga filled her cup with water. Kneeling beside him, Yoroka patiently spooned drops of water into his mouth, but he cried all the louder. By now the sun's glow was visible around the door and through weak patches in the roof. Katanga opened the door slightly and Yoroka laid the baby at Watumba's breast, softly directing his mouth toward a nipple. He latched on and suckled for a moment before Katanga pulled him away to check the flow of Watumba's milk. Her suspicions were correct: there was no milk in her breast, just droplets of a transparent secretion known to upset a baby's stomach. Katanga spooned more water into the begging mouth, but he refused to drink. Yoroka's breasts were large and full. She had not nursed her own child the whole night through, and the newborn's cries released her milk, causing it to trickle down her stomach. She reached for the boy and laid him at her own bosom, and when he finished drinking, she nestled him in his mother's arms.

5

The Forces of the Unseen

... are powerful and clever. Vita's daughter is ill, but even after the physical symptoms have cleared, the problem is not resolved. Unseen forces often work unwanted in human lives—whether on Kuwiya's hunt, in Zondoka's heart, on a newborn's umbilical cord, or in a presumed connection between a person and his name.

Vita's young daughter was not well. His eldest son, a short, muscular lad, had come to ask if we might visit her. And after finding our portable medicine chest, we walked across the riverbed and headed toward Vita's homestead.

A good rain had fallen the previous day—the first of the season—and even now, the morning after, large pools and smaller puddles were slowly turning the soil to mud. The morning sky was clear and tranquil, with just a few high clouds hovering near the northerly and southerly mountains. Vita's son led the way, his eyes darting from side to side as he looked for snakes forced from their holes by the rain. These, he reasoned, would be lying in wait after passing a miserable night. The rain had brought an absence of dust and the sun shone all the more brilliantly. Trees and bushes reverberated with life as a myriad of birds congregated in dense foliage after a long season of want. Grasses and flowering ground covers were spreading across the more fertile soil, yet even in the barren sands new sprigs of green had emerged overnight. The rain had washed dust and dirt from houses, fences, and work shelters, leaving the wood fresh and youthful; and though the morning was still cool, the sun rapidly drew moisture from the ground and the air was thick and heavy.

Zondoka was an older youth approaching the time of manhood. In appearance and stature, he favored his father, though his personality was strictly his own. Vita sometimes commented in private that he was a confused and unsteady boy, looking for something Vita could not supply. Zondoka was drawn to Opuwo, and whenever his father could spare him he would find his way there. The skirts and belts of Himba tradition no longer suited him, and while he occasionally dressed to please his father, most of the time he wore blue trousers cut above the knee and a shirt stitched from the cloth of maize meal bags. Yet, it was more than his appearance that disquieted Vita. It was the lad's indifference toward their way of life, the authority of their tradition, and the obligations that bound them together as a people that caused him the most distress. "Yes," he said, "who doesn't go through this? But then we all come out of it too." Zondoka had yet to do so, and it was his lack of progress in moving beyond youthful immaturity that so troubled Vita.

Many, many seasons ago, a lone young man named Nondo had come to Otutati and was taken in by a family without sons. Though that family had since moved north, the Ngambwe lad remained in their homestead, living beyond the company of others. He was handsome, sporting, and considered a good companion by the older youth of the area. Over time, he acquired a circle of friends, yet despite his congeniality he continued living apart—a state of affairs everyone considered peculiar. As his life and activities were largely free from interference and familial obligations, he enjoyed a degree of liberty his youthful companions simply could not. Young Nondo slowly acquired the habits and tastes of Opuwo life and indulged himself though he worked little and was thought to be virtually propertyless. Zondoka deeply admired Nondo and the two had become inseparable friends, a friendship that worried Vita.

We entered the busy homestead as Watumba's daughter arrived with a container of water. Her mother was still convalescing, but the baby's umbilical cord had fallen away and soon he would be taken to his father's ancestral fire and formally presented to Mukuru, his ancestors, and the local community. Daniel had gone to Opuwo the previous day on some urgent matter, asking Vita's wife to attend Watumba until he returned.

Zondoka looked about the place and then directed his gaze toward his approaching father.

"I've been out looking for a cow that wasn't driven home last night," said Vita, after greeting us. "I haven't found a trace of her, but there are other places to search."

He turned and brought us to the corner of an oblong work shelter where his wife sat on a blanket comforting the baby—holding her close and offering her a breast. Quietly, we greeted the woman while Vita took the ailing child from her arms and kissed the baby's head.

"You see, Odavido, this side of her face is fine, there is no sickness. But this side," he said, turning the child slightly, "isn't well. It seems very painful, especially in her ear." It was the left ear, and its distress was internal and hidden. But the child's left cheek and jaw were heavily inflamed and an infection extended from her ear to the tip of her chin, even her lips appeared puffy and sore.

"Is she able to drink?" asked Michelle, looking at Vita's wife.

"No," she answered. "And every time I set a nipple in her mouth she refuses it and cries all the more."

Secretions from the child's eyes had gathered on her lashes, crusting them together, and her nose ran ceaselessly.

"The illness is very strong and she needs to be seen by a doctor in Opuwo."

"Yes," said Vita, "I knew it was serious. All my children have gone through this before, though in their cases the sickness came and went within a matter of days. But this little girl has been suffering for a long time—for some reason the sickness is unwilling to leave her." And handing her back to his wife, he asked, "Is there something you can do for her?"

"We can give her a medicine that will help her feel better, but it won't cure her. Only the doctor in Opuwo has medicine to do that."

Vita spoke with his wife and then turned toward us. "If you'll give her some medicine, we'll prepare ourselves to leave."

We opened the bag and found the suspension, and drawing the medicine into a dropper Michelle pressed the rubber nipple and forced the sweet liquid onto the girl's tongue. Vita's wife quickly packed a few belongings while he went looking for his donkey, and well before midday the little girl was on her way to Opuwo.

Kuwiya had driven his small herd of cattle from dry season pasture to a place well east of Otutati. Here, the grass was quite plentiful and no homesteads lay in the immediate area. Kuwiya and a nephew built an enclosure of thorn branches that stood waist high. And although the barrier was makeshift, they assured themselves it was sturdy, for Kuwiya's only two cows had recently calved, and the young animals were precious to him.

Sometime during the night a predator had breached the thorny fence and killed one of the calves. The attack seemed all the more distressing as the carcass, now teeming with flies, was only partially devoured and lay but a few dozen paces from the enclosure. Kuwiya's story quickly circulated and another man reported the loss of several goats, plundered in a similar manner. The soft earth was carefully scoured for spoors. And though a few suggested it was malicious theft, the spoors implied a young leopard. It was not uncommon for leopards to prey upon livestock, but Kuwiya would not stand by and see his livelihood threatened.

He approached a young man named Dakata and several others to help him devise a plan to capture the leopard. Hunting the creature was never considered due to the animal's cleverness; and since a deep hole lay in the ground not far from the enclosure, the men thought it best to construct a pit trap. Looking over the hole, they decided it was deep enough, but needed some widening around its mouth. The heavy clay soil was loosened with walking sticks and heavy staves, and then removed by hand and pail. The men took turns digging, extracting, and shifting the ground, and by midafternoon Kuwiya felt it was time for the pit to be overlaid. The plan was to spread branches and leaves across the opening to conceal the hole, and then to secure a piece of fresh goat meat at its center to lure the animal. Once the leopard had fallen through, its life would be taken by spear. The men separated and chopped branches from nearby trees and bushes and dragged them to the site, trampled them slightly to weaken the wood, and finally spread them over the opening. After haggling a bit over the direction of the leopard's approach, they returned to Kuwiya's homestead for a meal.

Kuwiya and Dakata returned to the pit as darkness began enfolding the valley, carrying with them a freshly butchered leg of goat. As the center of the overlay was beyond arm's length, setting the meat in place proved more difficult than expected. But once secured, the two men secluded themselves at what they felt to be a safe distance from the trap and gathered thorn branches around them. There they waited in silence, listening for the leopard's movement but hearing only tiny creatures of the night. Now and again, the cattle began a round of lowing—a sound that might draw the leopard from its hiding place. Both men knew tales of the leopard's ingenuity, for of all predators they were thought the most clever, most dangerous, and the most capable of outwitting their pursuers. The evening wore on and a large yellow moon rose overhead. Its light fell heavily over the landscape below, causing shadows cast by trees and bushes and contours in the land to stir ever so slightly as it moved along the heavens. A light breeze rose from the nearby hills and both men thought of cloaks forgotten in their haste. Their eyelids grew heavy and soon the whole world was dark and peaceful.

A light rustling of branches and leaves stirred Kuwiya from his easy slumber. He reached over and touched Dakata on the shoulder. The leopard's moist nose twitched as it found the meat's scent. Its luminous eyes searched back and forth until they spied the meat lying on the branches. But the leopard was cautious, wary of such a rare gift. It circled the pit, never taking its eyes from the succulent flesh, then curiously backed away. Kuwiya and Dakata silently grasped their spears and watched, fully captivated by the nearness and intelligence of the animal. The leopard stood aloof, gazing at the overlay. Finally, the creature swept its glance across the scene, then turned and left the clearing. Kuwiya and Dakata remained silent and motionless, for this was the time when a leopard proved most dangerous. But where had it gone? Was it roaming the darkened earth in search of surer prey, or was it quietly circling the area, looking to uncover a deception? Both men knew they were in danger. Perhaps their actions were rash, they thought; perhaps they should have considered things more carefully.

Their anxieties lifted when the leopard reappeared at the edges of their vision. Slowly, it circled the trap again, its eyes probing every hidden shadow. The animal stopped and looked over its shoulders. Cautiously venturing to the rim of the trap, the leopard extended a front paw to test the branches. Its head rose slightly and it sniffed the fresh meat. The men stood and watched the animal advance. Softly growling, it bore down on the branches; the wood crackled, but the leopard chose not to withdraw. Its other front leg came forward and rested on the trap's edge. Another step or two would bring the animal to the savory meat. Lowering its body, the leopard strode toward the leg of goat. Immediately, the branches gave way and the creature tumbled to the bottom of the pit.

Springing from their barricade, Kuwiya and Dakata ran to the trap, hoping it was deep enough to contain the leopard. Their arms tensed as each man raised a short jabbing spear and aimed it at the hole in the overlay. Breath rushed sharply from Dakata's mouth as he threw his spear; a moment later, Kuwiya released his. The leopard shrieked and the two men retreated to the thorn bushes, not at all certain their throws had inflicted mortal wounds. Gradually, though, the leopard's cries died away. But thinking it was a ploy, the men waited, and the moon slid behind a thin cloud. There was no movement and no sound. Finally, Kuwiya took a throwing stick and several stones and followed Dakata, who held their remaining spear, and edged toward the pit. Straightening his body, Kuwiya hurled the stones with all his might and then ran for cover. Dakata stood by and strained to hear the impact of the stones, but the sounds were empty and final, no cry had been raised. They believed the leopard was dead, yet remained cautious lest the beast be waiting to attack them. Moments passed and there was only quiet; then the two moved forward, Dakata holding the spear in readiness. Crouching beside the pit, they peered into the hole, but it was too dark to see, and pressing even closer, all was black and still. They began removing the overlay branch by branch and the moon pushed beyond the cloud. Again, they lowered their heads into the pit, but there was no leopard. There was no meat and there were no spears, only a small pool of blood.

Where was the leopard? And how could it have escaped without being seen? Neither man had any explanation and they walked home hardly exchanging a word. But when the morning finally broke, they called upon Wamesepa to tell him their strange tale. A few people gathered to listen and were enchanted by the mysterious report. Someone raised the possibility of witchcraft, others saw it as a powerful foreboding. Around midmorning, a boy marched into Wamesepa's homestead with a message from Kuwiya's nephew. A leopard had been found in the sparse undergrowth not far from their trap. A spear lay in its rib cage, another, in its rump. It was the largest leopard the youth had ever seen.

Vita and his wife and child returned from Opuwo on the same day as Daniel. Five long days the little girl had lain in a hospital bed before her strength and vitality returned. The swelling along her jaw was gone and her ear was no longer painful. Vita was grateful to the doctor who had treated his daughter, and though it was explained to him that a virus had caused the illness, this explanation was far from complete. Vita needed to know why his daughter had been singled out, why specifically the virus had struck her with such power, and not some other child—questions the doctor at the clinic could not answer. But these questions were not mere curiosity; instead, they entered the very heart of the illness.

All of us succumb to common sicknesses from time to time, but how rare that a common sickness becomes life-threatening. And when this happens, when the ordinary becomes extraordinary, a further explanation is needed. Extraordinary events do not simply happen; they are willed, they are caused, they are brought about by unseen forces. And when the result is sickness or tragedy, most often the unseen forces are acting on behalf of jealous, malicious, and envious human beings. Life is filled with misleading appearances and European doctors only treat the physical symptoms. Beneath their practice lies a truer order of things, and learning the underlying cause is vital to the cure. For unless this is done the physical symptoms will return.

While in Opuwo, Vita inquired after a practitioner who might reliably uncover the circumstances of his daughter's illness. Such inquiries were troublesome and required discretion, as those with the loudest voices were often the least effective. While it was common knowledge that a practitioner's reputation should be verified by a satisfied clientele, doing so was unusually difficult since even a practitioner of solid repute was bound to make faulty diagnoses on occasion.

Vita was directed to a Zimba man living slightly north of Opuwo. He was completely unknown to Vita, but recommendations from several of his clients convinced Vita he ought to visit the man and discuss the case. On the afternoon before they left Opuwo to return home, Vita walked to the unassuming homestead at the foot of a steep hill where the man lived with his two wives and children. Entering the homestead without prior notice, Vita was graciously received and bidden to relax in the shade of a tree. The Zimba man's demeanor was light and personable, and the skirts gathered at his waist were clean and brightly colored. On his belt hung a long metal snuff tube and his walking stick was stout and old. Sitting with Vita, the man listened carefully to his story before asking a number of important questions. When the answers had been given, he tipped his head backward and thought. Finding the true cause of the little girl's illness was possible, and Vita repaired with him to his chamber. The diviner drew upon all his talents and knowledge, and after much painstaking work, the oracle revealed the source of the illness.

A man dwelling in questionable circumstances near the Kunene River was consumed with bitter anger toward Vita. Its origin was obscure and the oracle only revealed that it was unfounded, misplaced, and had no true, moral connection with Vita. Yet, while the anger was directed at Vita, the man had targeted something Vita loved most—his young daughter— for her death would cause Vita a life of sorrow. His wife was the unwitting agent of this evil. The angry man was working strong medicines against her breasts, causing her milk to be poisoned. Vita's ancestors, though, were intervening by suppressing the little girl's desire for breast milk. The child would become whole again if Vita followed the oracle's prescriptions. Firstly, the girl had to be weaned from her mother's breast immediately as nursing would only weaken her again. Secondly, Vita's deceased fathers asked that a sheep be sacrificed. They stood ready to fully counteract the evil medicine and protect Vita's family, but desired his humble acknowledgment of their blessing hand.

The oracle was both disturbing and comforting. Vita now knew the cause of his daughter's ailment and knew further it could be treated quite easily. When he returned to Opuwo, his wife was relieved to learn of the oracle's revelation, and on the morning following their return to Otutati, once the livestock had been led to pasture, Vita approached his ancestral fire and slaughtered the sheep. By the time he took his knife to hand, he had searched his memory and was certain of his distant foe's identity.

Watumba was gladdened by Daniel's return. The baby's umbilical cord had indeed fallen away, and the infant was ready to be presented to his deceased fathers and receive his name at Daniel's ancestral fire. Watumba opened a small, folded piece of cloth holding the crumbling remains of her son's navel cord. Placing the dried, flaking skin in a small wooden container, together with a lock of the baby's hair, she left the sleeping child in her husband's care and walked across the peaceful land to a lonely spot in the banks of a deep riverbed. There, she carefully looked around, and seeing no one, buried the precious relics. It was important that this be done, for Watumba did not wish to leave her baby vulnerable to the attack of malicious people. Such people would secretly hunt for loosened hair, nail parings, bodily waste, even treasured possessions to serve as carriers of fatal medicines. For the things of the body remain connected with the body, even if separated by great distance, and whatever harm is done to them will surely find its way into the body and cause it to sicken, wither, and die. It was this Watumba sought to avoid.

Daniel and his family returned to Otutati after journeying northward to his father's brother's homestead. It was his uncle who kept their ancestral fire, and after several days of preparations Daniel's son was brought before the fire, presented to his living and deceased fathers, and given a name. While they were away, good rains had fallen on three successive days, soaking the pastures and watering the gardens of Otutati. Some fields of maize were fully planted, even sprouting, while others were still being sown. Watumba's garden was in a desperate condition. The weeds she had toiled so long to remove had been generously replaced by others. But now that her son had been laid before Mukuru, she felt secure in leaving the homestead with him, and as she walked along the field's mostly unbroken ground, she worried about the bounty of her harvest.

The garden adjoining Watumba's on the northeast had lain idle for several rainy seasons. Recently, Masutwa had taken a portion of it to enlarge his family's maize crop. Much of their seed had already germinated and soon the weeds would have to be cleared again. Walking in that direction, Watumba heard voices and moved toward the fence to see who was there. Masutwa's wife, two married daughters, and an older woman who lived in their homestead sat in the shade of a tree round a small cooking fire. Watumba called to them and they invited her to share their meal.

Gourds of soured goats' milk hung from the tree and a basket of freshly ground maize meal lay near the old woman's feet. The water in the kettle was warming, but had yet to reach a boil.

"Is your son well?"

"Yes," replied Watumba. "He drinks and drinks and drinks, and is very fat."

"When did you arrive home?"

"Yesterday, yesterday afternoon. It was a happy time for us, being with my husband's people, but it's good to be home again." Watumba lifted her head. "Though after seeing the state of my garden I feel overwhelmed. Everywhere I look there's nothing but weeds. I'm not sure what to do."

She looked across Masutwa's planted field.

"I see your maize is already growing, but our soil hasn't even been turned. I think my husband will have to hire Solomon to come and plow the field—we can't possibly do it by ourselves."

"I'd be happy if my garden were plowed," said Masutwa's wife, "but my husband says Solomon charges too much and his work isn't as careful as mine!" She looked downward as the others laughed. "I think he also finds it odd that maize should be planted in rows rather than clusters—though I don't see what difference it could make."

"I don't know either," replied Watumba. "But unless we get our maize planted we'll starve when the cold weather comes."

Steam rose vigorously from the three legged pot and the younger of the two sisters climbed to her feet. She took a paddle in her left hand and with her right began pouring meal from the worn, shallow basket into the boiling water.

"What name did your husband give the baby?" asked the older woman.

"Two names," replied Watumba, "he gave his son two names. The first name he spoke was Enyando [joy, happiness] because his birth has brought us great happiness. He also gave him the name Zumawa [quaking ground] because, my husband said, to have a son was as great an occasion as when the earth shakes. His uncle carried the baby to the fire and gave him the first name, then my husband named him, and finally his brothers."

"I say," interjected Masutwa's wife, "your husband's family is like my husband's. They give every child name after name after name. But even so, I always end up calling my children the names I had in mind—somehow they seem more fitting."

"I know your words too well. My husband's father wanted to name our first daughter after his grandmother Opore [calm]. I thought, 'How can we name this little girl Opore?' She has never been calm. As a baby, she never slept, never stopped moving, so I called her Hayanda [inexhaustible]. And even now, though she's almost a maiden, nothing she does is done slowly. Hayanda either runs or dances wherever she goes."

The porridge was bubbling and hissing, and everyone turned, worried it might burn. Lifting the pot to the edge of the fire, the younger daughter gave it a stir.

"Do you know how I came to have my name?" asked the older woman. "After I was born, my mother's auntie came to visit. Mother was still in pain and lying in, but the family didn't want to upset Auntie because we thought she was a witch. She had lived for years near Hakavona and learned their ways. Every time she came to visit us, at least as I remember things, she had gifts for us, always tobacco for my father and mother, but good tobacco—the kind that must be bought in a store. I remember she wore a very long snuff tube on her belt, and we children asked among ourselves, 'Who is this Auntie that she always has gifts for us and wears this long snuff tube when her husband has so few cattle? How can she be so wealthy?'

"She came to our homestead a day or two after I was born and, without warning, immediately crept into the house where my mother was resting and snatched me from my mother's side. She startled my mother with her clicking sounds and I began to cry. Auntie put me in my mother's arms and stared into my eyes. Finally, she told my mother, 'You must name her Ehandu [naughty].' But my mother said, 'How can I give her a name like that? Can a newborn baby be naughty?' 'I see in her eyes,' replied Auntie, 'a certain redness that tells me she is a naughty person.' 'Hah!' said my mother. But she was too scared of Auntie not to go along with her, and when Auntie told the family what I should be named, they went along with it too, even my father. And everytime I got into trouble, when I let the goats wander too far or refused to help my mother around the house, I was always told, 'Auntie was right about you.'"

"I say," remarked the elder daughter, "aren't these names of ours curious? Most of the time I never think about my name or what it means. But sometimes when I hear my name spoken [Ouzikame] I ask myself, 'Am I really so constant, so steadfast? Am I truly what my name implies?' Or if I meet someone else with my name, I look at her and think, 'Are we sisters? We share a name, but are we so alike?' I think some people are what their names imply, but I'm not so sure that I am."

"Yes," said Watumba. "Some people are their names, but others are exactly opposite their names. It's a strange business, isn't it?"

6

A Woman Must Be Strong

... since a man is already strong. He has two lungs and a large heart, but a woman's heart is smaller and she possesses only one lung. A woman's strength is her will, her resolve, her ability to see what is to be seen. A woman's strength can thwart a man, as Ngipore's wife has done. And now that Kakara is becoming a woman, she too must learn. But, as Kantanga knows from her daughter, Rikuta, it is not easy to teach a girl to be a woman, for budding womanhood is more than an interest in boys.

A good rain had fallen after Watumba's garden had been plowed and seeded. Solomon's furrows were curved and imprecise, but her maize had sprouted and the sprigs of green were reassuring. On her field's southerly edge lay Katanga's garden. It was a large garden, far larger than Katanga needed, and only half of it stood under cultivation. Most of the maize was now waist high and growing well despite the lack of drenching rain. The once tall fence that had separated the two gardens, nearly fifty paces in length, had vanished, and in its stead was a curving line of cinder and ash. Part of Katanga's crop had also been reduced to ashes. Her daughter, Rikuta, was responsible.

Rikuta was a young maiden, and though her body appeared fully mature, the time of her first menses had not yet come. Her appearance was her mother's, and she was a beautiful girl. Her face was symmetrical and smooth, her brow haughty, her lips full and precisely formed. Her arms and legs were long and slender yet held the promise of becoming rounded and shapely. Rikuta had been asked to prepare a final portion of the garden for planting in case a lack of rain should reduce the normal yield. Katanga had cleared and planted most of the field by herself, occasionally aided by her youngest son. And though she felt the garden appendage was not truly necessary, she recruited her daughter out of a sense of duty. Rikuta was approaching the age of marriageability. Soon enough she would take charge of her own garden and the responsibility to harvest sufficient maize to feed her own family, a skill that a daughter ought to have learned from her mother.

Teaching sons and daughters the essential skills of life required patience and forbearance, qualities Katanga felt she possessed in ever-waning supply. As her two younger children grew into their youth, she expected them to assume a greater role in household maintenance and other tasks appropriate to their age. But she also knew that encumbering them with the obligations of adulthood was wrong, that the two of them needed to enjoy themselves and their friends, and that resentment would surely build if she were overly strict.

News had reached Katanga that her eldest son's wife was ill and she decided to journey to their homestead to help tend the small children while her daughter-in-law convalesced. Rikuta was charged with completing the garden and looking after the household while her mother was away. Work on the field was casual and sporadic, and the girl spent far more time in the company of her friends than in working the soil. Several days passed with only slight changes to the ground's contours, but on the fourth day Rikuta arrived before sunrise and began turning the earth with unusual resolve. Wondjoze had told her of relatives traveling from Otjitanda to Opuwo who would likely stay over at her father's homestead. One of her cousins, a young man somewhat older than she, had already arrived, and the remaining group was a day or two behind, including several of the young man's peers. Rikuta wished to have the planting finished that she might greet the main body of visitors.

The softening effect of the previous week's rain was lost in the earth and the thick, deeply rooted weeds remained firmly anchored in the creamy soil. Rikuta tugged, hewed, pulled, and hacked at the weeds, but progress was tedious and slow. The morning cool was now gone, and as Rikuta paused from her work she walked along the space her mother had outlined as the new garden. Not all of it was thickly overgrown by weeds, but most of it was covered with the dried remains of maize stalks her mother had neglected to burn. Touching the fibrous material, Rikuta let her hoe fall to the ground and stepped to her small cooking fire where she bent low and blew on the smouldering coals. Moments later, three had turned from gray to red. She reached for a long, metal spoon, scooped a glowing ember, and carried it to a place where the dry stalk fragments were deep. She dropped the ember and blew it into small flames. Twice more, she returned to the fire and brought a glowing coal to another part of the field. And as the hardened stalks and leaves slowly caught fire, Rikuta walked back to her blanket and lay down. The low flames moved in hesitant, irregular steps and Rikuta turned aside to rest. She was fatigued from her labors and closed her eyes.

Daniel's shouts awakened her, and as she opened her eyes she saw that flames had spread across the field. Furiously, Daniel chopped away at the burning fence, hoping to contain the fire. Already he had freed one end, and with another few strokes the leaning fence fell into the burning garden. He bellowed at Rikuta and she took his directions without complaint, and before long they isolated the flames and watched the fire burn low.

"How could you do such a stupid thing?" asked Daniel. "Even a child knows that fire's dangerous!" As he continued chastising her, a bit of a crowd gathered, curious about the smoke, and his words became less harsh. He pointed to a part of his own garden ruined by the flames. It was his wife's private reserve—that portion of a garden whose produce a married woman sets aside to be used in any manner she wishes.

"And when you plant this ground, you must plant enough to compensate my wife for her losses," he said. And looking briefly at the crowd, he added, "Child, do you hear my words?"

Rikuta nodded; there was nothing more she could do. She knew her mother would be angry at having to build a new fence. But more troubling than her mother was Daniel's tongue. For the afternoon would not pass, she reasoned, before everyone in Otutati knew of the fire. Rikuta cut a branch from an ironwood tree and fitted it to the hoe blade, darkened by the flames, and worked until nightfall. She and her brother ate with another family, and when the sounds of clapping hands, singing voices, and stamping feet rose in the evening air, she walked to Wondjoze's homestead and joined her friends.

In most of the gardens, the maize had reached half its eventual height, and though many plants were green and lush, wilting leaves and ailing stalks were becoming more common. The need for rain and the deterioration of the maize crop were general topics of conversation, but conversation alone could not encourage a vigorous cloudburst.

The earth and its plants and animals do not yield to human desires. Sometimes we perform rain ceremonies learned from Angolans, but most often we supplicate our ancestors for rain that no one should be hungry in the coming dry season. Sometimes our petitions are successful, other times they are not, and it is difficult to know why they are granted on one occasion but not on another. Our lives are often precarious, but is it not so for all peoples? Do not all peoples suffer from reversals of the natural world, and this against all their earnest pleadings?

The passage of life brings a succession of years, of rainy seasons and dry seasons, of harvests of plenty and harvests of want. Unless Mukuru or the deceased fathers intervene, Nature is indifferent. It takes no account of our sufferings or joys, and though it belongs to Mukuru, it is neither cruel nor accommodating. The world cares nothing; it wills nothing; it thinks nothing. The world only is. Nature does not protect human beings, only Mukuru does this. There will be good seasons and bad seasons, but not because Nature is good or bad, but simply because this is the pattern of life. Nature works without heart, without intent. Only Mukuru and our fathers know our circumstances, and they provide for us—though not always as we might have chosen. One year may vary from the next, but over a person's span of years the good of life outweighs the evil, the generous seasons are more numerous than the grudging ones. Our families have increased and our cattle herds have enlarged. Our life is the present, concentrating on the problems at hand; soon enough the future will bring its problems. But we know both grass and thorn.

Ngipore was alone, sitting in his garden. The ground within the high fence was covered with green but for a small, dry patch, and it was there he sat in the cool morning air. Because his wife had not yet returned from visiting her parents, a circumstance thought most curious, Ngipore had planted the garden with little help from others.

A smooth, flat stone was his seat, and we took places beside him, allowing Elspeth to walk among the growing stalks. Ngipore's voice was mellow and resonated through his nose. He was known for his humor and amiability, but his observations about the world and human beings were thoughtful and occasionally solicited by other men. Unlike most Himba, Ngipore cared little for snuff. He preferred to smoke a pipe, and as we sat together he opened a leather pouch that lay on the ground beside him.

Removing his pipe, he filled it with wild tobacco and then closed the pouch. The pipe was a goat bone, as long as a man's middle finger, the wider end holding the tobacco. So smoothly had the vessel been rubbed and polished, it was easily mistaken for ivory. He lit the pipe with a small coal picked from a weak fire by his heavily calloused hand. The smoke rising from the pipe and his darkened mouth was pungent and its pleasure short lived. When Ngipore finished, he set his pipe in its usual place— between the first and second toes of his right foot. It was a peculiarity for which he was known, but with his pipe thus lodged, Ngipore could walk after his livestock or work in the garden without fear of losing it.

The conventions of Himba life had become convictions deeply seated within him. The threads and fibers of common thought, so easily accepted as explanation for the occurrences of everyday life, were more than passing sentiments. Ngipore was committed to Himba beliefs; his experiences in life assured their general correctness. In his youthful days, a contract labor concessionaire lured him into a two-year agreement to work on a dairy farm near Gobabis in eastern Namibia. Ngipore's days were filled with work from dawn to dusk, but the farm itself and its manner of operation, the variety of tools and machines, the strength and expanse of its buildings, the vigor and size of the cattle, the rich array of foods, and the appurtenances of European civilization (though he only shared in those from a distance) impressed him and caused him to reflect with mild contempt on the circumstances of his own life. "I was better than these Himba. I was an *omuhona* (superior man) because I knew of things my family and friends did not. And I wanted to stay in that place with those things."

When his contractual obligations were finished, Ngipore was transported back to Kaokoland with the several head of cattle his labors had purchased and his few remaining banknotes. When he was taken from Kaokoland, the concessionaire hid his naked primitivity under a pair of blue coveralls, and when he returned, those coveralls, now faded and somewhat tattered, were Ngipore's link to the world he had left behind. "As long as I wore them I was still in Gobabis." Life was good for him and his fortunes increased steadily.

During the season of cold, Ngipore fell ill with chills and fever. He lay in his bed waiting for the sickness to leave him, but as the days passed his condition only worsened. The progressive relief granted to others laboring under the identical illness was denied him. And as the fever lingered, he grew weaker and weaker, finally realizing the sickness could only end in death. Ngipore requested a medical diviner, and when the expressionless man finished laying out the instruments of his practice, he began to penetrate the malady's somber face. At the root of the illness was Ngipore himself—his arrogance and independence. The illness was a gift from his deceased mother. Who was this man among the Himba clothed in a ridiculous garment? And what was his pride in wearing such a thing? Speaking through the diviner, she told her son to cease his foolishness and remember he was Himba—that it was good to be Himba. He was to burn the coveralls, sacrifice a sheep to his parents, and retain the horns as a reminder of his folly. Ngipore did as his deceased mother directed him and almost immediately his strength returned.

"Ah," said Ngipore, "I think we're at an end. My wife's a good woman, and I have much love for her, but she's a naughty woman too. This time she's been too naughty—I think we're finished." He rested forward and looked into the center of his garden. "I'm very sad. My heart feels heavy, but what can I do?"

Ngipore and Mukahu had known each other since childhood. Over time, their young friendship grew and matured into youthful fancy despite Mukahu's early betrothal to an elderly man. When the fullness of womanhood had finished shaping her limbs and loins, Mukahu was married, becoming the youngest of three wives. Her parents knew her longstanding objections to the marriage and persuaded Mukahu's husband to allow her to remain with them until they finished training her in the skills of managing a household. Reluctantly, he agreed. And during his absence, Mukahu and Ngipore deepened their mutual affections. When the seasons turned, the man came for his wife and Mukahu left her world to enter his. She had never closely observed the lineaments of his form or demeanor. He was mild in temperament, but Mukahu revolted against his aging and deteriorating physique, and refused him marital embrace. In turn, he sought to restrict her movements, but with limited success. As the years passed, Mukahu bore him three children: all boys, and all fathered by Ngipore. Rightfully, the boys were taken by Mukahu's husband to his ancestral fire and initiated into his lineage and the care and protection of his ancestors.

Ngipore was a man of limited means. But he persevered and entered the labor contract with the intent of building up a herd sufficient to make the compensatory cattle gift to Mukahu's husband as a divorce settlement and take Mukahu to wife. It was years, though, before the old man agreed to a divorce—despite the fact that Mukahu spent most of those years in Ngipore's homestead. There is great distance between separation and divorce. A wife may live separated from her husband for many years and, no longer bound to marital fidelity, bear children fathered by another man. These children, however, belong to her estranged husband, not her paramour, and will be presented at his fire and live in his homestead. It is divorce and remarriage that finally sever these rights of paternity. A husband relinquishes his right to any future children his wife may bear and grants that right to her new husband through a decree of divorce and remarriage. And it is a loss demanding compensation.

Ngipore paid the divorce settlement, and his cattle pen stood nearly empty. The three boys born of their premarital union remained with Mukahu's former husband, as they deserved the nurturing and protection of their own fire and ancestors. But Ngipore's vision was blurred. He felt the three boys were his, not the old man's, and decided to contest their residency in a headman's court. A preliminary council was convened by the headman and elders of Kaoko Otavi to ascertain the merits of the case. Mukahu's former husband had been asked to join them; and knowing in advance he had nothing to lose, the old man told the council the three boys had not been fathered by him. Privately, the headman questioned each of them. It was their collective desire to live with their mother and Ngipore. But the case was not about wishes or desires, but parental rights. By lineage, by fire, by ancestors, and by properly obtained rights, the boys belonged to the old man, and there was nothing human or ancestor could do to reverse the flow of events. Ngipore accepted the decision of the court, but Mukuru was good to him and in time Mukahu bore him a daughter, Wondjoze, and a son, Kamanga. After the passing of their father, the three boys, now edging toward manhood, came to reside with Ngipore and their mother. It was a happy reunion. But the contentment of those years was coming to an end.

"I say," repeated Ngipore, "she's a naughty woman, but this isn't easy." He excused himself and rose to help his son water their goats.

Night had fallen. A few weary stars appeared on the eastern sky and the moon was rising in the west. Between Wamesepa's house and the ancestral fire stood a makeshift hut. It was no more than willowly saplings feebly secured to the ground and one another, supporting an array of blankets and skins. Deliberately set within the *omuvanda*, a place of absolute safety on the eastern side of the homestead, the shelter housed Kakara, a maiden the age of Wondjoze, and several of Kakara's friends. Her father, Wandisa, and mother, Wazorowe, had retired to their own homestead once the mighty ancestral fire had foundered into coals. Earlier that evening, when the skies had just begun to darken, Kakara reposed somewhat uneasily and listened to her friends' serenade. Some of their ballads were lively, even rambunctious, others were melancholy; but each recalled the circumstance bringing them together:

> *Here's our little girl,*
> *Give her a bone to chew,*
> *Give her the marrow,*
> *For she has found her menstrual blood,*
> *Our beloved one is crazy and dumb,*
> *crazy and dumb!*

Amid the singing, Kakara was finally led to the fire. With her grandfather, Wamesepa, present, she knelt at the hearth while her father successively placed three large gourds of milk in her hands. She lifted each gourd to her lips and swallowed once. The gourds were filled with milk drawn that evening from her grandfather's sacred herd—those beasts representing Wamesepa's deceased fathers. As such, the milk was both sacred and dangerous: only persons directly related to these fathers patrilineally might drink it, and even then, only after Wamesepa had tasted the milk at the fire. Tasting the milk of ancestrally owned cows is both a supplication and an acknowledgment of their blessing. It is a humble gesture offered by the fire-keeper for the benefit of his extended family; it is also a solitary performance, one rarely extended to others. Only three occasions in the life of a woman are significant enough to make this responsibility hers: her first menstruation, her wedding, and the days immediately following each of her births.

When the celebrations finally quieted, Kakara entered the hut followed by her girlfriends. All but one of them had raised a gourd of sacred milk to her mouth in the past year. Inside the hut it was dark, but as the moon and stars shone more brightly, distinctive figures emerged from the blackness. The rest of the homestead lay under a slumber as the maidens groped in the shadows for their sleeping skins and blankets, laughing and chatting good-heartedly. Their voices lifted and carried in the cool night air, but if they disturbed anyone, it was well, for this was a great occasion in Kakara's life: the evening was hers.

"Tell us Kakara, how did it happen?" asked the youngest maiden as they settled in, "How did you know when to go to the field?"

"To the field?" she replied, taking care as she drew back her hair and rested against a wooden pillow. "How did I know to go to the field? In truth, I didn't know at all." Wrapping the edge of her blanket about her neck, she added, "I didn't even suspect what was happening to me."

The night's coolness was rapidly turning inimical, and without concern for the faint, intermittent passages of laughter and hand clapping emanating from a distant homestead, the maidens nestled deep in their covers.

"Most days I wake early," continued Kakara, "before the sun comes over the hills. I wrap myself in a blanket and go out to start the fire and make coffee for my parents. When I awoke this morning, my stomach ached and I looked down at it and thought, 'What's this hurting me?' I had to go to the bush, and quickly, so I crept from the covers and left the house, hoping not to disturb anyone. It was dark outside, much darker than usual. But when I returned I felt better and took a branch off the hearth and lit the fire. It flamed and I crouched beside the warmth and closed my eyes. When they opened, the fire was hot, and I poured water in the pot and set it to cook. The ache started rising again in my stomach and I could no longer sit upright, so I slid closer to the tree and leaned against it. The sun was rising behind the mountains, but my eyes were heavy. I closed them and must have fallen asleep, for the sound of my mother's voice shook me from a dream. She called from the doorway, 'Kakara, Kakara, are you well this morning?' And without moving at all I replied, 'Yes.' A few moments later, when I felt able, I stirred a handful of coffee into the water.

"Holding three tins in her hands, my mother joined me at the fire. Soon the coffee was finished and she began filling them. By then my head was aching as much as my stomach and I asked her not to pour me any—I didn't think I could drink it. 'Why not?' she asked, 'you always take coffee in the morning.' As I made my reply she held the tin in her hands and looked at me. 'Is there blood between your legs?' she asked, 'have your menses come?' I hadn't even thought of that, so I told her, 'No, I don't think so.' But she was clever and came again, 'I think you have. We must see.' She helped me to my feet and we saw dark spots on my skirts and the ground beneath me. She squeezed my hands and told my father. And with a small bundle tucked under her arm, she led me to the groves."

"Did it hurt?" asked the same maiden again. "Was the bleeding painful?"

"No," replied Kakara softly, "the trickle of blood didn't hurt at all, only my head and stomach did."

Kakara's eyes closed as she spoke these words. A slight, patchy breeze had steadied; it blew through the hut causing blankets and skins to flap and the framework to quake. But the sounds and movements roused no outward attention.

"You were fortunate, Kakara, that your mother was so near," spoke another maiden. "I was away from everyone when it happened to me.

"One evening I had light pains in my stomach and back; they were strange but not troubling, and I figured by morning they'd be gone. When I rose the next day, my father asked me to take the goats to pasture and watch them. My brothers were off with the cattle and though I wasn't feeling well, I told him I would. Mother handed me a packet of maize, and after a long drink of water, I took my stick and drove the flock between the mountains. The walk was long, but I wanted a pasture where the animals could graze safely and I could rest.

"I was weak and hungry when the pasture came into view. I urged the animals forward before opening my maize packet and eating. Afterward, my body suddenly felt cold and I shivered. My eyes searched for a place to rest and settled on a large, flat stone where I lay in the warm sun and fell asleep. By the time I awoke, the sun had moved to mid-sky. Slowly, I sat up, not recollecting exactly where I was. When my mind became clear, I remembered the goats and listened for their bleating, but I could neither hear nor see them. At once I got to my feet and walked almost to the banks of a dry river before spotting them high on a slope. My mind was much calmed.

"Walking back to the stone I noticed a wetness between my legs. 'What's this?' I wondered. 'You're no longer a baby that you should wet yourself!'

I crouched beside a bush and lifted my front skirt: my thighs were bloody. I hadn't any idea why. For a long time I'd known my mother and older sisters bled during their menses, but I thought myself too young for such a thing. When I saw blood smeared on my legs, I panicked. I left the goats on the hillside and ran for home. From a distance, my father saw me rushing, saw I was alone, and feared the worst. He met me calling, 'What's happened? Are you hurt? Where are the goats?' My eyes filled with tears and I said, 'Daddy, I'm bleeding!' He looked down at my legs and, taking my arm, led me to the shelter where Mother was grinding maize. She received me and held me close, explaining I was becoming a woman, and that it was a time for happiness, not worry or sorrow. Mother spoke to a few women before walking me to the groves. By then I was no longer scared, but wanted her to stay with me."

"Is it good to be a woman?" asked the youngest maiden.

"I don't know," answered the eldest, "I haven't been one long enough. My mother told me it's good to be a woman, though a woman must be strong. After my night in the hut, Mother came and said, 'Walk with me as I lead these goats to the mountain.' I followed her, but we traveled in silence until we were far from our homestead. We stopped and rested. 'Varama,' my mother said, 'I want to tell you something. I want to tell you what I wish I had been told when I was a maiden. Now that you've menstruated, boys will look at you and see your *erembe*. They'll take you aside and whisper, "I love you, come and be my girl." There's a time for boys, Varama, and when that time comes you'll know it. But until then, be strong and let no one force you into something.' Then, without warning, she got to her feet and began walking back to the homestead, leaving me with the goats. Much of the afternoon I thought about her words. They weren't new to me, only unclear. But now—though I'm still uncertain whether or not it's good to be a woman—I understand why a woman must be strong."

Night deepened as the moon crept through the steady evening breeze into the eastern horizon. A solitary figure emerged from a house and wrapped herself in a blanket. She strode along a well-worn footpath, pulling the blanket more tightly around her bare head. At first her footsteps were unsure, but as her eyes saw more clearly through the night shadows her step became certain. Quietly, she walked toward the hut in the *omu-*

vanda. After looking over her shoulders, she parted a skin from the frame and gazed into the protected darkness. Her eyes fell upon her sleeping daughter where a delicate patch of light folded like drapery below her breast. For a time all movement ceased.

Abruptly her head turned, for she heard another's breath. Wazarowe stepped aside and allowed Wandisa to peer through the opening. He withdrew a moment later and slowly began retracing his steps home. Wazorowe lingered though, and when she was satisfied she let the cattle skin fall back into place and walked the pathway home.

Much of the morning billowy clouds gathered in the sky overhead. It was a welcome sign, a hopeful sign that rain might fall and restore the weakening plants. Around midday, the clouds darkened and settled on the mountaintops and the air became thick and still. In a far corner, lightening struck near a hilltop and almost at once, rich, deep claps of thunder rolled across the sky and shook the earth. A heavy wind arose as if from nowhere and the first droplets of rain touched the soil. Hardly a moment had passed when the rain started falling with such vehemence that the rising dust, generated by the first raindrops, was thrust to the ground where it vanished beneath a sheet of water.

People ran for cover. Those in the fields collected under makeshift canopies and shelters that only slowed the rain's penetration. Michelle, Elspeth, and I huddled with Katanga and listened to the sound of the rain as it pelted her house, a sound mollified by the densely thatched roof. As the force of the rainfall lessened, Katanga opened the door slightly, for though the rain had cooled the earth, inside it was smothering. Outside, the skies were still dark, and for a long time the rainfall continued in widely varying intervals of strength and weakness. Eventually, sunlight broke through the clouds as they shifted over the southerly mountains, and as the break increased in size, the dampened world below turned lustrously bright. Young girls and maidens, wrapped in blankets, gathered to walk through the homesteads, trilling songs that praised the rain. The soddened earth beneath our feet seemed to flow, yet off ran Elspeth to join other children splashing in the puddles.

The riverbed separating the homesteads from the gardens was moistened by the rain but held no flowing water. Afternoon grew into evening and the higher portions of land appeared dry and stable to the touch; by sunset the clouds had drifted beyond the mountains and were completely out of sight. Cooking fires burned as cows were milked and then turned into their enclosures for the night. Surrounded by the familiar evening sounds, Kuwiya lifted his head and looked eastward. Faintly, we also heard a distant, muffled roar; others also noticed it, yet continued in their tasks. But when the noise began dominating the evening air, people rose and gathered along the riverbank. We followed and stood with them before an empty channel. "Look," cried someone, "here it comes!" In an instant, the power of a flood burst down the rivercourse, pulling in trees, boulders, and other debris and sweeping them downstream. A moment ago the bed had been dry; now a rapidly moving river, deeper than a man's height and more than twenty of his paces in width, flowed past the body of spectators, disgorging its precious contents onto the flood plains north and south of the tracks. Posts and rails creaked and trembled as the rush of water washed through the fences and flooded the gardens.

The waters subsided shortly after sunrise, and by midmorning the riverbed was passable. Most gardens were saturated, still immersed in water that nearly touched the lowest leaves on the stalks.

Afternoon sun bore down upon the valley floor through a cloudless sky. In a shady thicket of trees near the riverbed, a judicial gathering had finished its work, and lingering in conversation, men began rising from their seats and smoothing their skirts. Three youths, who had been secluded from one another around the edges of the gathering, emerged from the thicket and walked side by side along a path leading to a group of homesteads beyond the ironwood groves. One of the youths lived there; the other two were strangers. Their heads were cleanly shaven except for their curved circumcision plaits, which rode motionless despite their hurried pace.

Katanga's daughter lay on a cattle skin in the shade of a work shelter, her head resting on a wooden pillow. Behind her, smoke lazily rose upward in the still air from the smouldering remains of the fire that had cooked their midday meal. Rikuta's body was stiff and tense and her eyes tightly closed as two pairs of hands skillfully unplaited her thick, dark hair. It had been one season, if not two, since its last dressing, and after a morning chat with her girlfriends, Rikuta felt the time for renovation was at hand.

"She wishes to enchant the newcomers," teased Katanga, referring to the two youths who had arrived before dawn to appear in court. "So we must make her very beautiful!"

The women moistened their fingers repeatedly in a tin of water as they unraveled the long strands and carefully removed the parched *otjize* that overlay the hair. As thumbnails delicately scraped the excess coating so as not to break or tear Rikuta's tresses, long, fine shreds of leather, bits of rope and string, the bristly filament of cattle tails, and other fibrous materials used to lengthen and beautify the plaits, were pulled from her head and laid on the goatskin beside them.

"Who are these boys?" asked the other woman in a sonorous tone. "What business can they have here?"

"I'm not certain who they are, only that they live near Otjitanda and are friends with Musete's son," answered Katanga, as she took the last plait in her hands.

The other woman nodded. Her fingers had stiffened and slowed, and when she finished cleaning the plait, she swept the residue from her skirt and eased her hands. Her shoulders drooped as she stretched her chin upward and turned her neck from side to side. A whispered sigh escaped her lips as she shifted her body forward and leaned her straightened back against a thick, smooth post and demurely allowed her eyes to follow the motion of Katanga's fingers.

"As for business, they are said to have stolen a goat and eaten it while at dry season post with Musete's son."

"Ah," said the other woman, her eyes closing. "I see."

Rikuta felt her mother's hands soften and release the loosened hair. She opened her eyes and hesitantly peered into the daylight. Her girlfriends had long since walked to the other side of the ironwood groves to await the strangers. But neither she nor they had known the circumstances that required the strangers' presence at court. Katanga rose and stood for a moment outside the shelter, looking across the homestead.

"Court must be over," she said quietly. "I see the boys walking toward the groves."

Slowly, Katanga ambled her way round the houses and work shelters on the northerly side of the homestead, her eyes only turning from the image of the boys once they disappeared from view. She moved her gaze eastward and for a time engaged a distant vision, then retraced her steps and bent low to enter the shelter. Katanga knelt at the remains of the fire and felt the ashes along the periphery for warmth before setting three generous handfuls on the goatskin. The other woman opened a container of *otjize* freshly made that morning and waited while Katanga settled beside her. Though the plaits had been undone and cleansed, the hairs so long cradled together refused to mingle with those of other plaits but remained in long, tufted strands. Katanga pulled the hair tightly and began weaving, knowing the greater the tension, the longer the plait would retain its shape.

"And what interest does Rikuta have in these goat thieves?" asked the woman as she reached for a bit of ash.

"I think," replied Katanga, "her interest in the boys is the same as any maiden's."

Rikuta moaned softly as her head began to throb from the tightness of the plaits—a tightness that would relax as the days passed.

"Yes, perhaps," said the woman. "But goat thieves? Should she be interested in goat thieves?"

Katanga made no reply and the two women dressed the maiden's hair in shaded afternoon heat—pulling, twisting, dusting, appending, and pulling again. The work was tedious and fatiguing. Katanga stilled her fingers for a moment and wiped her brow. The plait lying across the palm of her hand needed lengthening, so she coated strands of artificial hair with ash to strengthen the bond as she added them to Rikuta's natural hair, piece by piece. Several times she measured the plait, and when it stretched well beyond the maiden's shoulders, the end was secured with string.

The other woman noticed the finished plait and rubbed her forehead. "I say, Katanga, you haven't answered my question. Would you be interested in a man who's a thief?"

Katanga looked away for a moment and then answered. "No," she replied, "I would not. But then I'm a woman, not a maiden."

Shadows crept eastward as Rikuta's finished plaits were smeared with *otijize.* Carefully, patiently, the creamed ochre was applied to each plait, coat after coat, until her tenebrous hair disappeared beneath a smooth, glistening mahogany glaze. As their labors ended, Katanga handed her daughter a small, precious fragment of blackened glass. Rikuta held the jagged mirror in her palm and looked deeply into it, moving her hand from time to time to catch a different reflection of her beauty.

The sun had fallen behind the westerly mountains to begin its restful journey toward the east. Ngipore's nephew led a group of boys, including the two strangers, across the plain. As they walked, branches and twigs were sought and carried. The sky was clear and dark, and already the cooling draughts of night rippled along the valley floor. The boys descended a riverbank and gathered in the middle of the large, dry bed to light a fire. Musete's son balanced a live coal on a notched paddle, and though its reddish glow had faded, a surfeit of young breath and a handful of dried grass quickly brought it to life. The riverbed was a reluctant host. Its surface broke easily under the vigor of youthful feet, but the floodwaters had compressed the bed and the late summer sun had baked it into a hard, shiny surface that should endure an evening of dance.

Someone laid a twisted branch of greasewood on the growing flames. The dry, porous wood quickly warmed, drawing its liquid heart near the surface. The branch crackled and hissed for a time amid the talk and laughter of the boys, but suddenly it exploded into flames, catching all but the fire-maker by surprise. Branch after branch was set across the flames until the fire blazed high and illuminated a wide circle of ground. The alluring glow enticed creeping and flying insects to draw near; the creatures hovered about the light and then mysteriously disappeared. As the fire grew, three more boys walked down the riverbank and joined their friends.

Wondjoze said little as she strolled with Rikuta, Wahona, and a number of other maidens toward the riverbed. There was laughter and frivolity, but twice since leaving Wamesepa's homestead the group had stopped and quieted. The boys were at the fire, even the strangers—of this they were certain. But crossing the divide and engaging the boys' attention was an awkward, uneasy matter. Again their footsteps ceased, this time not far from the riverbank. The maidens exchanged heated whispers, straining through the darkness to recognize faces partially unmasked by quivering light. But they failed to recognize movement behind a nearby tree.

"They are here! They are here!" whispered the spy as he entered the circle of light. "They're waiting—standing over there and looking at us."

"Do they know we're here?" whispered one of the maidens.

"Perhaps, but I think not," answered Rikuta. "We've been quiet and have seen no one about."

A light gust of wind passed over them as they stood erect and gazed at the fire, straining to hear the boys' voices.

"Let's move over there," said one of them, pointing with her eyes, "and crouch in the bushes near the edge. We'll be much closer but still hidden from view."

The maidens walked a few paces then crouched low, lest they be spotted. Though the distance between them and the riverbed was but a score of footsteps, it was traversed slowly and carefully, for their early evening had been spent in grooming, and they wished the beauty of their appearance to remain unspoiled by the dust of the ground.

"There they are," whispered Rikuta, "the goat thieves. Can you see their faces?"

"Yes," answered another. "And they're as handsome as was said."

"Quiet!" warned Mbaba, "or they'll catch us."

The maidens' position lay safely beyond the fire's glow; and though kneeling in the bushes was uncomfortable, it was only a temporary stop. The boys played—laughing, mocking, and teasing—but not a word was said about the morning's events. From the shadows appeared another boy, and instantly the boisterous conversation died. Strangely, all the lads came to the southern edge of the fire and turned their backs on the veiled maidens. Softly, the grasses and shrubs bent forward toward the river as the darkened outlines of hesitant maidens leaned closer to the riverbed. Only rustling leaves disturbed the confusing silence. Overhead, the moon and stars shone brightly. From the darkness behind the maidens, the sound of a heavy walking stick breaking against the face of a large stone caused them to jump and scream. Soon, an overly deep voice called to them, "You've kept us long enough!" The riverbed stirred with laughter.

Near the edge of the firelight, four maidens timidly clapped their hands amid the roar of unrestrained voices. As their percussion grew in steadiness, the rhythmical movement of their long, supple arms and richly anointed heads became their expressive accompaniment. Though their movement did not escape notice, most of the youths chose to wait for others to heed the summons while they themselves remained chatting. But the message was not easily ignored and the steady clapping seemed to undermine the already weakening conversation. One by one, a few lads and several more girls joined the four maidens, separating by sex into two distinct corners. The clamor of laughter and visiting never entirely ceased, only fell as anticipation of the dance rose. The numbers in the separate corners slowly expanded until, almost imperceptibly, they loosened and stepped forward to form an ellipse of about twenty-five paces in length and perhaps four in width. But the maidens and youths remained apart.

Hands now clapped louder and faster, and joined with stamping feet, the night-born reverberations filled the riverbed and overflowed its banks. A group of maidens began singing in falsetto—a song praising the beauties of an ox. The lyrics turned on a recurring pattern of four tones, and as the singers repeated them again and again, they cast their eyes down and sobered their expressions. No sooner had the song concluded than another began. Its pattern of tones was similar but the lyrics were entirely different: "He is the one I love, the one I love, the one I love." As the voices faded, Ngipore's nephew broke ranks and stepped to the middle of the ellipse to dance. His feet moved in quick, short steps while his arms began winding in great circles. The pace of the clapping was rapid and the lad turned his head toward the maidens standing on the opposite side and imitated the movements of a bull, lowing to them his puerile affections. The maidens stepped back as he passed. His movements, though, gained in speed and power as he danced ever closer to the end of the line. Then, lost in a frenzy of clapping, he leaped high into the air and turned his body before his feet touched the ground. Driving steadily to the other end of the ellipse, he hesitated before the maidens, but was again rebuffed. The youths began clapping in crescendo as their friend raced to the end of the ellipse and hurled himself into the darkness. Lightly, he descended from his leap, and suddenly the clapping stopped. The lad looked over the human chain and then retreated to his place.

Slow, steady clapping began anew. All heads were bowed and fixed, and all eyes were low. Cautiously, each set probed the stance and tension of those in the ellipse, searching for an indication of likely movement. Round after round, hands and arms and eyes stirred, but nothing more. Someone began a peppered clap to rouse a dancer from the wings. The others followed his lead, yet no one emerged, and the clapping fell to its former calm, almost melodious pace. The moon had grown very bright, but the gesturing shadows of the riverbed were no less uncertain. A heavy *crack* sounded, followed by an immediate cry from Musete's son, and he was pushed into the ellipse by his friends. Straightaway, the clapping turned sharp and crisp, and the youth, his buttocks still smarting where the willowy branch had crossed them, awkwardly began a dance. His first steps were unsteady, but quickly the percussion led him away. He turned his shoulders and arms and head as Ngipore's nephew had, but in a lively, feminine mockery of it. He moved quickly, his footsteps gaining speed until he vaulted upward.

"We've heard your friends' confessions," said Masutwa, "and we believe you took part in the theft. Is this true?"

"Yes, honored sir, I did."

"We now wish to hear your story. So stand here and face us—your friends can't hear your words, so you may tell us the truth."

"Yes, honored sir, I'll tell you the truth. The three of us were watching over my father's cattle. We had driven the beasts to graze near some remote hills, far away, we thought, from other livestock. We were there for many days before we noticed a girl grazing a flock of goats. Every day she brought the goats to the hills and drove them onto the upper slopes. Day after day, we had only porridge to eat and water to drink, and our stomachs grew hungry for meat. One evening, a brother said, 'Why don't we take a goat from that girl's flock? We can slaughter and eat the animal in the evening, and when morning comes move our cattle away from here and never return. She'll think the goat wandered away and was taken by a hyena.' We all knew it was wrong, but we were hungry for meat and thought no one would catch us. So we found a goat to our liking and did exactly as we'd planned to do."

"Yes," said Masutwa, "Your story is like the others. But tell us truthfully, was this your idea? Were you the one who suggested the plan?"

"No, honored sir, I did not. It was the other two."

"I say, how would you answer us if we told you the other two agreed it was you who initiated the plan?"

"I'd answer that my brothers haven't spoken truthfully."

"Did you enjoy the meat?" asked another man teasingly.

"Yes," answered the youth, very earnestly, "the meat was fatty and delicious."

Musete's son landed squarely, though not with the agility of Ngipore's nephew. His light steps took him down the ellipse, but more slowly this time. He lingered before several of the maidens, rotating his body in close, tight circles, hoping to engage a set of eyes; but the maidens' downward stares did not yield. Twice more he hurled his body at the ellipse's ends, and then retired to his position on the side. A young girl emerged from a cluster of maidens. Her dance was lively and jostled the four plaits on her head. Encouraged by the clapping, she twirled and jumped, waving her arms and bobbing her neck and head until she tired and left the circle. Several others danced the line, but their efforts were not well rewarded.

Again a sharp *crack* was heard, this time forcing the taller of the two strangers into the middle. Quickly, he looked up and down the ellipse and found every eye upon him. His first steps were short and choppy, but as his confidence grew, his dance became graceful. He traveled the line much like Musete's son—though his eyes stared ahead and he hesitated before no one. Yet each time his steps brought him past Wondjoze, he turned his head and looked upon her—a movement that drew more attention than any other. His leaps were not as high as other dancers' and by his fifth landing his legs could no longer keep pace with the increasing rapidity of the clapping. Down the line his slowing body danced, each step requiring more time than the last. Near the center of the line he stopped and stood alongside Wondjoze.

"We've heard from each of you now," said Masutwa to the tall stranger. "Yet no one's told us who initiated the theft, and this we must know. Since each of you says the others are at fault, which simply can't be true, we've called you again hoping that you'll be honest with us. We're not here to condemn you, only to judge you honestly and to decide how best to restore the stolen goat. So, we ask you again to tell us whose plan this was."

"Honored sir," began the youth. "It wasn't I, but the other two who made this plan. I was with the cattle when they made it, and only after I returned to camp did I learn of the plan when they asked me to join them. Honored sir, that's all I can tell you."

"So that's all you can tell us, child?" responded Daniel. "Don't you realize that it's wrong to steal another man's livestock? Didn't this occur to you?"

"Yes," the boy replied, his eyes almost closed. "I knew it was wrong."

"Well, if you knew it was wrong," chided Solomon, "why did you agree to take part in the theft?"

"Honored sir," he said. "It's very difficult to explain why I did something I knew was wrong. It's true that we were hungry for meat, but that's not why I helped

*steal the goat. As we sat together making plans, my mind told me again and again,
'Suppose it were your goat and someone stole it from you?' But my brothers were
certain there'd be no problems, that no one would find out, so I kept my objections
to myself and agreed with them. I went along with it because I didn't want them
to think I was against them."*

The clapping ceased. The tall stranger lingered in place for a moment,
then turned his back to Wondjoze and moved toward his friends on the
side. The dance had begun in earnest.

Maidens and youths, one after another, took to the line with only occasional lapses. The fire had burned low, but the moon and stars were full
and bright. A light, steady breeze now blew across the valley floor, adding
its strength to the cooling draughts. Wondjoze and Wahona had danced
separately and together, and their brows were moist and shiny. Rikuta
stood with a strained expression and mimicked the clapping and stamping.
Her eyes darkened as she watched the dancers, her lips smiling only at
weakened steps or faltering leaps. As Vita's daughter finished her dance,
Rikuta's jaw was like stone.

The steady percussion of hands and feet beckoned to others, but the
ellipse remained empty. The beginning stiffness and reluctance had faded,
for now the heads and eyes of youths and maidens turned conspicuously
upon one another. Unexpectedly, Rikuta stepped into the ellipse and
moved cautiously down the line. Her gestures were sure and practiced.
And as her feet smoothly and flowingly carried her in reverse, her fluid
arms effortlessly imitated those footsteps; and in the beauty of her motion
every other sound and movement was lost. Her body and dance were pos-
tured to invite attention to the abundance beneath her rear skirt—that a
fuller, more pleasing appearance might win some temporary affections.
As she neared the ellipse's end her direction changed and her feet began
to bear her forward. Her pace slowed as she approached the strangers,
and before their eyes she twisted round and round, spinning a progressive
web as she moved toward the line's end. But the end was not reached, for
Rikuta danced but several more paces, then quickly turned and closed the
web. Every eye fixed upon her, puzzled, questioning, but fully knowing
her intent. Her breathing grew heavy as her movements found approval.
Finally, the lads began a swift clap and urged the full company to join.
Louder and louder, faster and faster they clapped, yet Rikuta seemed unaware of the burgeoning pace. As the youths cried, "*Mu-ni-ka, mu-ni-ka* (let

us see, let us see)," her expression changed. Her steps became rapid and powerful, and as she came to the end of the ellipse she leaped into the air to answer their petition. Rikuta's speed and agility carried her high; and as she turned her body and began the descent, teasingly, provocatively, she reared her left hip with enough force to lift her back skirt and, for an instant, reveal her wares before touching the ground. The company roared its approval. And Rikuta, her face and eyes looking downward, took a place on the side. Opposite her, the shadows moved as Musete's son and the two strangers found new positions.

"Most of our morning and part of our afternoon has been spent discussing your case, but we've reached a decision," said Masutwa. "And you three must stand before us to hear that decision—because it's one that requires explanation. Your case has been difficult because you haven't been truthful. Each of you has confessed to the crime, but the evidence against you was so compelling you could hardly have done otherwise.

"Being herdsmen, you know that stock theft is a very serious crime. And even though you may not have thought that taking a goat and roasting it to please your stomachs was stock theft, that's what it is. I say, the major question before us was not your participation in the theft, for that was beyond doubt, but whether or not you were equally guilty; whether or not one of you bears a greater responsibility than the other two. But as no one's confessed to being the originator of the plan, we have no option but to find the three of you equally guilty. The consequence of this is that you'll have separate and equal punishments rather than sharing a single punishment."

Solomon rose from his seat.

"I say, Masutwa, before you go on I must speak a few words to them." And turning to the accused, he said, "Children, I'm not so old that I don't understand what you did. I think if the truth were known, we've all had thoughts of doing this at one time or another. Yet, it's an action we must fully condemn. It is, however, one thing to commit simple stock theft, but quite another to commit it stupidly. As we sat here discussing the case, again and again your collective stupidity overwhelmed me. I actually hoped to have you punished for your stupidity as well as your theft!

"I can't understand how anyone could steal a goat, slaughter it, throw its skin onto nearby bushes, cook the meat, eat it, then leave all of the bones behind in the camp everyone knew that you and you alone were using, and fully expect to evade *capture. How could you act so stupidly, yet think you wouldn't get caught? I told the others that you deserve another fine, but Masutwa said we can only punish you for theft, not stupidity. And though I regret this, I see that Masutwa's right."*

The three received Solomon's chastisement knowing it was well deserved, and when he finished, they hardly dared to raise their eyes.

Masutwa hesitated slightly before continuing. *"When a man steals livestock, he must pay seven animals for each animal he's stolen. Because you three have chosen to hide the truth from us, we have no choice but to order each of you to pay Kupika seven goats of comparable size and value to the one you stole from him. These payments are to be made as soon as your arrangements are completed."*

The lads breathed deeply.

"Unless you have questions," finished Masutwa, *"you are free to go."*

Clapping and stamping began anew. Carefully, Rikuta peeked from beneath her deeply inclined face to observe her success. Her mouth broadened, and only when she could suppress its movement did she lift her head and fully join the others.

The moon had drifted well beyond its midnight apogee and the fire lay in ashes. Gradually, the dance wore down until the maidens and youths fell into groups and pairs and walked across the plain, some of them disappearing in the shadows of trees.

· 7 ·

The Path of a Man

. . . is not easy to define and more difficult still to walk. Though the frivolity of childhood and youth are left behind, the path of each man is slightly different. Wandisa and Katwerwa have made their ways along different tracks, and now that Dakata is to take his second wife, he must find his own path. Being a man requires a good heart and a good head—both gifts from Mukuru; it also demands an honesty acquired piece by piece, experience by experience.

If a man walks the narrow trail lying between the Kunene River in the north and the mountains of the east, after many days he comes to a beautiful river called Marombora. Not far from its banks stands a great tree, the greatest of all trees. We call that tree Omuzu, for it is the womb-tree that gave birth to people. Long, long ago, before human beings walked the earth, Mukuru set a man and a woman inside the Omuzu tree. They lived in darkness within the tree until a slit appeared in its trunk. The man and woman peered through the slit and were enchanted by the outside world. Every morning and every evening they watched the sun rise and set. One morning, however, the tree shuddered and shuddered and woke the pair from their sleep; but as soon as they looked through the slit, the movement ceased. As they settled down again another tremor rose, and then another and another, each tremor gaining in strength. The movement was bewildering, but finally the tree became still, and when the man and woman set their eyes upon the slit, they found the narrow opening had widened enough for them to pass into the outside world. Singly, they emerged from the great tree. As the man stepped to the ground he called himself Musisi (sacred bull), and when her feet touched the earth, Musisi named the woman Kamungarunga (creator of new life).

The sun had fallen beyond the mountains as the pair stood and looked across the land. Behind them, cattle passed from the same opening in the Omuzu tree and walked silently into the coming darkness so as not to be seen. The world was beautiful to Musisi and Kamungarunga, yet it was also frightening. They knew the darkness of the tree's belly, but the earth's darkness troubled them. A thought came to Musisi's mind that he should light a fire, and though he had never done this before, the work came easily to him. When the sun rose, the two left their beds and walked about the land, examining the plants and animals. In the evening, Musisi lit another fire. At the edges of the light animal visitors appeared, but the flickering light frightened the timid creatures and they retreated into the night. One evening, a strange, new animal came to visit. The man and woman expected it to run away like the others, but instead it crept closer to the fire and began lowing to the woman. Musisi built an enclosure and Kamungarunga led the cow and those of its kind through the gate. Several of the cows had calves, and by moonlight Musisi saw them drinking from their mothers. Curious, he moved closer and rubbed his hands on the teats, and when his hands were wet with milk he tasted it and then called for Kamungarunga to come and taste. From that day forward the man and woman drank milk from their cows. Time passed, and still the man and woman lived as companions, not as husband and wife. One day, Kamungarunga climbed a tree to pick berries. Musisi stood on the ground ready to catch them as Kamungarunga pulled them from the branches. Musisi raised his eyes and saw under Kamungarunga's skirt; when she came down from the tree they began living as husband and wife. Kamungarunga bore Musisi many sons and daughters and he was happy, for Kamungarunga had given him both children and cattle.

Dakata was to marry a second wife, a maiden who lived a day's trek to the north. His first marriage was a good marriage, but it was not fruitful.

As a youth, Dakata had been lured by the promise of good wages to join a special unit of the South African Defense Force and, against his father's advice, became a soldier. When he returned from service, he packed away his uniform and dressed as a Himba and began herding his father's cattle. Only rarely and after much prompting would he ever share his experiences of war, for they had drawn him into a world fully beyond his youthful imagination—an ugly and melancholy world he wished not to revisit. Shortly after his return, preparations were made for Dakata to marry Yapura, the daughter of Wandisa's second wife. Yapura was born without benefit of wedlock and came to live as a stepdaughter in Wandisa's household before she uttered her first words. As Wandisa and Dakata's father, Katwerwa, were cousins and shared the same ancestral fire, Yapura and Dakata had grown and matured side by side in Otutati, their friendship holding the promise of a satisfying marriage.

Since their wedding, Yapura had carried several children in her womb, but tragically her body expelled them before their time, and now many seasons had passed in unrequited want. It was a circumstance Dakata bore with sorrow equal to Yapura's, but it was she who finally suggested he might wish to take another wife.

The situation was uneasy for Wandisa and Katwerwa. Though each of them had several wives, neither had married in such close company or for the reason pressing upon Yapura and Dakata. Their children's union had further intertwined their own maturing lives, and while they both understood and agreed with Dakata's decision to take another wife, the prospect was tinged with sadness.

Wandisa was a middle-aged man of moderate height and build. In appearance he was his mother's son, with a fine, round head complimented by deep set eyes, full lips, and a flat, wide nose. His two wives and two families lived separately, though the tensions underlying the separation had greatly mellowed. Wandisa, too, had mellowed and seasoned over the course of his life. As a child he was said to have been loud and belligerent, as a youth, unruly and publicly disrespectful of his father. He was curious about the world beyond Kaokoland, and after testing the life of Opuwo, he drifted southward toward Windhoek. There he fell into company with other dissatisfied young men and eventually moved to Walvis Bay to work at a fish cannery.

Wandisa admired the vestiges of European life available at Walvis Bay. He never wanted for association, but like many of his colleagues, his evenings were spent in a blacks-only bar, drinking and carousing until his need for alcohol overshadowed every other sensibility. Wandisa's labor contract with the cannery was prematurely ended because of his drinking; and when his wages were issued, he journeyed back to his father's homestead. Wamesepa was relieved to have his son home, but Wandisa's long struggle with alcohol strained their relationship. Migrant traders from Vamboland were eager to furnish him with cheap wines, and for several years Wandisa sold and traded beast after beast, slowly depleting his father's herds. Wamesepa despaired and confessed his inability to help his son, yet he continued to encourage him. The persistent loss of cattle worried relatives and others whose well-being depended on those animals. They discussed Wandisa's affairs among themselves often enough, but it was finally decided they should meet with Wamesepa and ask him to take decisive action. Wamesepa led his son to a secluded thicket of trees along the riverbed and spoke to him. "I don't know why," reflected Wandisa, "but on that occasion I listened to my father. I knew it had to end—I had known that for a long time. But it was then, for some reason, that I decided to stop drinking." Wandisa did, and slowly began rebuilding his life and reclaiming his fallen reputation.

Katwerwa was older than Wandisa—just as his father was older than Wamesepa. His arms and torso were thick and well muscled, and his handsome face somewhat brooding in expression. He was tall, his voice boomed when he spoke, and his powerful chest was covered with hair—some of it black, most of it gray. His appearance was striking, even formidable, but it was also deceptive, for Katwerwa was a gentle and unpretentious man. He concentrated his life on fulfilling basic responsibilities and obligations, and his journeyings had taken him around Kaokoland. Two of his three wives and families lived together in the same homestead, the other wife and family—the youngest—preferred the solitude of a private compound not more than fifty paces from the other. Katwerwa was a fair man. He avoided contention in his private life and resided peacefully with his wives and children. He loved cattle and their herding and care, and took pride that his sons were eager to learn the skills and practices that bring praise to a man. Though physically vigorous, Katwerwa claimed he could no longer walk as rapidly or as far as he had the previous rainy season. It was a statement he made occasionally, and when he did, his meaning was clear. Eyes inevitably fell, discreetly, upon his left thigh where long, dark, heavy scars deeply partitioned the muscles of that thigh.

"I was a young man when it happened—many, many years ago. All day the cattle had been grazing in the bush, and as the sun began to drop in the evening sky, I awaited their return. In those days the wells were here, close to the homestead, and the cattle knew to come and drink before nightfall. But that evening they didn't return; I was concerned, but not worried. The next morning we saw vultures circling in the sky near the foothills and said to our young sons, 'Walk over there, where the cattle are, and see what those birds are eating. If it is one of our beasts, run back and tell us.' So the boys took their sticks and began walking toward the cattle. Just before high sun, they returned. They had been running and were out of breath, but told us that an ox had been killed. Because no bones had been broken, they suspected a lion and searched until they found its spoor.

"Four, five, six of us decided to band together and hunt the lion. We gathered knives and spears and walked swiftly to the site of the kill, leaving the boys behind. It was exactly as they had said—the ox and the spoors. We followed the lion's trail through the bush and over the sand. From the depth of the spoors and the broken grasses we surmised the lion was full-grown. We walked cautiously, moving our eyes from side to side lest the creature be lying in wait. Jarijo stopped and pointed with his eyes. In the distance we saw the lion resting in the shade, looking directly at us. An instant later it jumped to its feet and trotted into the bush. Our movements slowed as we pursued the animal; lions are not clever like leopards, but they hide themselves well and are very strong. No one spoke, and our footsteps became shorter and shorter as we listened for its sounds.

"Suddenly Tweirimba cried out. We turned and saw the creature lunge toward him. It bit him in the shoulder and quickly disappeared in the undergrowth. As we rushed to his aid, I thought I heard the lion charging again; I turned and saw it coming at us. I raised my spear to stab the lion, but it swerved and my spear hit the ground. The lion was nearly upon us, and without thinking, I grabbed its ears from behind and held them with all my might while Kujaitjiti cut open one of its hind legs with a short knife. The lion roared and bolted. I lost hold of one ear and the creature turned on me, tearing at my leg. I fell to the ground, but somehow Jarijo managed to seize the lion's mane and hold it back while Javirikiza sliced up its back. The lion was weakening and Jarijo slipped his hands round its throat and choked it till my leg fell free. The others closed in and killed the lion with their spears.

"After that, I only remember being in my house. My thigh was tightly wrapped in a skin and bound with long strips of ironwood bark. It was some days before I could get to Opuwo, and many days before my leg had healed enough to bear my weight."

Their ancestors, their families, their cattle, their duties, and their mutual respect drew their lives together time after time. But Wandisa and Katwerwa were as two leaves on a tree, distilling much from a common branch while remaining separate, independent beings. And nowhere was their separateness more evident than in their visions of modernity and the future.

Katwerwa's wives had asked Michelle and Katanga to help them grind maize meal in preparation for Dakata's wedding feast. Though the live-stock had long since been driven to pasture, it was cool as they walked the dusty path toward the large homestead situated well beyond the river-bed. Elspeth paused now and again, looking for stones, but never lagged too far behind. I walked in a different direction carrying the leather bag. Several days previous, Masutwa was chopping branches with his sons for use in repairing a fence. One of his strokes had missed, severing the tip of his left thumb. The elder son helped Masutwa to our tent where he lay down in the shade. To stem the flow of blood the youth tightened thin strips of bark around the base of Masutwa's thumb. When at last we arrived home, I cautiously looked over the thumb and then submerged it in a solution of water and bleach. After a painful soak, we bound the wound and hoped for the best. Three days had passed and it was time to air the thumb and change its dressing.

Masutwa's homestead was near Vita's on the northern edge of Otutati. As the small, somewhat forlorn arc of huts and shelters came into view, I noticed three men sitting in the shade beside Masutwa's house. Masutwa stood out among them because of the swollen bandage on his thumb, now considerably tarnished. One of the two remaining figures was Kavetonwa, the other, a man unknown to me. We greeted one another as I passed into the homestead and joined their small circle. Unfolding my chair and unlatching the bag, we exchanged news and pleasantries. And when the materials needed to air, cleanse, and rebandage the thumb had been laid aside, I carefully cut away the gauze and tape and removed the dressing. The shortened thumb appeared clean and the tip was beginning to seal. Masutwa held it for the others to examine. Kavetonwa winced and turned his head. Masutwa's wife—normally timid in such matters—rose from her grinding stones to have a look. When their curiosity was satisfied, Kave-tonwa, Masutwa, and the stranger resumed their conversation.

"Yes," stated Masutwa, "it is so. He's already left for Opuwo hoping to find his missing cattle—oxen, I think."

"Eh, eh, eh," said Kavetonwa, shaking his head. "What's happening to this world of ours? Who's stealing these animals—are there strangers among us? I say, when first I heard of that place in Opuwo where a man can take cattle and sell them, I thought there'd be problems."

"Ah," replied the stranger, "but a man must prove ownership before he can sell animals at the auction hall."

"Yes, yes, yes. But how does a man prove ownership? He says, 'These are my cattle and I want to sell them.' How should some Vambo or Boer know whether or not the beasts are stolen?"

The stranger did not answer.

"I say," lamented Kavetonwa, "such people have bad hearts."

The conversation lulled, but long moments of quiet were often part of serious talk. The mild disinfectant I had sprayed on Masutwa's thumb was nearly dry and the late morning air had improved the skin's pallor. I pulled the bag to my lap to search for a tube of ointment and asked the three quiet men what was meant by a "bad heart."

Kavetonwa raised his head. "Now," he began, "now you ask a question that's difficult to answer because we must describe something we feel inside of us, but never see." And looking toward Masutwa and the stranger he added, "Since I'm older than these two, I'll respond first, and when I'm finished they may speak."

Kavetonwa shifted his weight and pulled the snuff spoon from behind his ear. Nimbly, he unfastened the tube and shook it before inserting the spoon. His nostrils flared as he inhaled the powdery tobacco and passed the tube to the stranger.

"When I say 'heart,'" he continued, stretching his arms around both knees, "I don't mean the heart as it works in the body. We know the heart is very strong and forces the blood—and sometimes breath—through the body. But when I say that a heart is 'good' or 'bad,' I speak of its other purpose: through our hearts we think and decide whether something is right or wrong. And because they lead us to see things in one way or the other, decisions about what is good or bad are strong and must be made in the strongest part of the body."

Kavetonwa let his head sink forward slightly and itched a small welt on the back of his neck.

"But the heart doesn't act alone. To think, the heart and the brain must work together. The brain has a thought and sends it to the heart. Perhaps I see an ox drinking at the fountain one day—an ox very beautiful to me.

I look and look and look at the ox, and feel I simply must have it; yet I know it belongs to another man and the only way for me to possess the beast is to steal it from its owner. My eyes see only its beauty while my brain begins to lay plans for its theft. Then my brain sends these thoughts down to my heart and my heart looks at them and thinks about what the brain wants to do. Whether or not the brain's thoughts are truly feasible is not determined by the heart, but only whether they are right or wrong. When the plan to steal the ox is received by my heart, if my heart is good, it tells my brain, 'No, it is wrong to steal,' and I follow my heart's voice. This doesn't mean I'm compelled to do as my heart says; I could hear my heart and still decide to steal the ox. But a good heart is a good guide—it tells us what's proper, what Mukuru wants us to do."

Masutwa and the stranger listened intently to Kavetonwa, murmuring affirmatively though never looking directly into his face.

The ancient man closed his eyes and loosened his grip round his legs, his chest calmly rising and falling. "I think most people have good hearts, but there are some people whose hearts are bad. We don't know why one person's heart is good while another's is not, we know only this is so. I've also seen hearts change; a person with a good heart can, over time, come to have a bad heart. I think this is more common because I've known only one man whose bad heart became good.

"If my heart is bad and I stand at the fountain looking at the beautiful ox, desiring to have it, when my heart receives my brain's thoughts, my heart advises me to steal the ox. It makes the wrong seem right; it leads me to do what Mukuru would not do. My heart's judgment is then passed back to the brain and I plan the theft.

"Most of our hearts don't act so quickly," said Kavetonwa as he raised his chin. "When I make important decisions sometimes my heart doesn't speak clearly for several days. Often too we hesitate; we move back and forth trying to decide which voice we should follow—our brain or our heart. But if a man has a good heart and follows its counsel, he can rely on his heart to tell him what to do. If a man has a bad heart, its counsel is always bad. This is how I understand the matter."

Masutwa watched his thumb disappear beneath a white bandage. The sun had moved and turned the shade into light. Masutwa, the stranger, and I shifted our seats into the shadows; Kavetonwa remained where he was, claiming the sunlight felt good against his back.

"Do you wish to answer now?" asked Masutwa quietly.

"No," replied the stranger, "I'm not yet ready to speak."

Masutwa straightened his turban as a rough, muffled sound carried past the house. He cocked his ear, but heard nothing more.

"I say," he began, leaning forward. "I agree with *Tate*'s words. The head thinks first and is responsible for generating thoughts. Sometimes though strange ideas come into our heads and we wonder, 'What's this? Where does this comes from?' and recognize that such thoughts don't really belong to us. Evil people—doctors of *omiti* and others—have power to place thoughts in our heads. I don't understand how this is done, but we realize such thoughts are not our thoughts. They have been forced into our brains so that we should act upon them and bring misfortune to ourselves and our households . . ."

Abruptly, Masutwa stopped and turned around as two hungry dogs fought over a scrap of food near his ancestral fire. "Sik!" he yelled at them, throwing a cudgel at their legs to end the struggle.

"The heart itself does not generate thoughts," he continued. "A good heart only evaluates thoughts and tells us whether they are good or bad. A bad heart cannot do this. My father taught me that a bad heart no longer works. It doesn't endorse evil thoughts, but stands silent: a bad heart passes no judgment on thought. As *Tate* said, we all experience times when our heart tell us something is wrong, yet so strong is our desire that we pursue it against our heart's judgment. It isn't a battle between a good heart and a bad heart, but a conflict between the head's ideas and the judgment of a good heart. When we don't listen to our hearts, we follow our heads.

"Sometimes the heart no longer works because a man has rejected its counsel for so long. There are people who do evil things without any hesitation because their hearts no longer work. This is what I call a 'bad heart.' Whatever thoughts the head sends down to the heart return to the head without being properly judged. When an accused man stands before the council and confesses his crime, we ask him: 'Doesn't your *ozondunge*[1] work?'—because anyone who commits a crime shows very poor judgment. People whose judgment is repeatedly poor no longer listen to their hearts or have lost the capacity to judge between right and wrong."

---

1. *Ozondunge* denotes the mental process of judging, weighing, and finally determining the moral value of an object or idea.

Masutwa had finished. The stranger glanced at both men and then looked far into the distance. A light wind fluttered leaves and carried dust to his eyes. He turned his head and fanned his lips.

"I say, both of you are right."

He stretched a leg but otherwise made no movement. At last, he scooped a twig from the ground and drew a circle in the dirt.

"Both of you are right because both of you describe the feelings inside our bodies."

Carefully, he scratched a line through the circle.

"Sometimes," he explained, pointing to the eastern half of the circle, "this part of us thinks one way while the other part thinks the opposite way. And though no one else is aware of it, we struggle and struggle inside our bodies and finally reach a decision. If we follow a good heart, we follow Mukuru; if we don't, we fall into trouble.

"Now, how this looks inside our bodies I don't know. This is why I say you're both correct, correct because you both described the feelings of heart and brain."

He waited a moment and then cast aside the twig.

A new sun shone faintly behind the eastern hills. The valley was still and cool, and a light dew polished the leaves of low growing bushes. As he stood beside a work shelter, Dakata's body glimmered—his mahoganied limbs and loins, chest and back attracting the softest morning rays. His leather skirts were freshly reddened, so too was the groom's bonnet he wore over his turban: a leather cap that settled high on his forehead, tightly above his ears, and cascaded loosely to his shoulders. His father stood near him as they waited for Dakata's friends. They said nothing, but looked toward every sound indicating the possible approach of footsteps. At last three young men appeared, their shoulders covered with straps bearing leather pouches filled with provisions for their journey. Two large sheep—gifts for the bride's family—and a smaller goat were led by the tallest lad. Their animated greetings lasted but a moment and then Katwerwa stood alone, watching his son until the party disappeared from view.

Over the northerly hills and mountains and across three wide valleys they walked before reaching their journey's end. Dakata's bride, Penguka, came from a large and well maintained homestead and already gourds and pails of fresh evening milk hung from the tall circular fence that separated cattle from people. As Dakata was barred from entering the homestead until the morrow (indeed, his presence at his father-in-law's house had been unwelcome since announcing the betrothal), he sent his companions to convey greetings to the bride and her family. They entered cautiously. The feigned scowls of those who met them only confirmed their suspicions: their approach had been seen from afar and their arrival fully anticipated. Slowly, the friends walked across the homestead, drawn by the placement of spectators to the shelter where Dakata's father-in-law and bride sat waiting for them. Dakata's married friend conveyed the groom's greetings, while the seasoned man listened with a calm and solicitous expression. "We thank you for his greetings," he said. "And tell your friend I shall await his visit tomorrow afternoon." The three young men bowed slightly and took several backward steps before turning into the jovial crowd that mockingly dismissed them from the homestead.

Dakata pressed for every detail when his companions returned and joined him in building a makeshift hut. Again and again they recounted the brief interview, yet each time Dakata wished to hear more. Finally, the last skin was set over the framework and the floor laid with their bedding and provisions. One of them crept back to the circle of homes and returned with an ember. The weary day was closing and Dakata reposed with his friends around the growing fire as a light breeze chased the lingering afternoon heat. The tallest lad rose, untethered the goat, and led it to a nearby tree. Quickly, the small animal was slaughtered and set to cook. And under a waning moon—the moon of the running hare—the young men ate, their mouths and chins made glossy by the rich, fatty meat.

The bustle of Penguka's last night under her father's care was merry and festive, and its sounds spilled beyond the large circle of houses. Few words were spoken round the small fire as Dakata and his friends listened, often intently, to the growing yet unapproachable gathering of people. The moon lifted higher and the friends emptied the kettle. The ground surrounding the hut was clean and free of bones, as these, once broken and drained of their marrow, were thrown into the bush. When the last bone was pitched to the night, the friends settled back, their eyes pondering the softly dying flames.

"Are you nervous about taking a second wife?" asked one of them.

"No and yes," replied Dakata slowly, looking at his friend. "I say no, because I have learned to live with a wife, and I say yes, because I haven't yet learned to live with two."

Dakata's eyes returned to the fire.

"Is it," asked another, "is it good to be married? Or is it better to be free?"

Though the young man's voice was steady, it was also teasing. Dakata, however, responded with directness.

"For me," he said, "marriage has been good—and my wife hasn't made me feel like a goat in a pen! I can't even think of myself as a bachelor anymore. I say, I much prefer having a wife to not having one." Gesturing toward Mitakamwe, he asked, "What do you say, Mitakamwe? You married long before I did—how would you answer Karora?"

Without hesitation, almost as if he had been prepared for such a question, Mitakamwe responded.

"It's true I've been married a long time, but I married early at my father's insistence. Perhaps it was too early for both of us because we teased each other like brother and sister. We didn't behave with the respect a husband and wife should have for each other. And even after our first child was born I felt like a boy dressed as a man. I think my wife also felt this way, but we've matured, and now she has respect for me and I have respect for her. I never call her by name anymore. It's good to be married and to have children and cattle; and though there are problems, it makes my heart glad. When I was young, I liked being free. But now that I'm old, I like being married. I don't think one is better than the other— they're simply different times of life—and what's good at one stage isn't good at another. But this is only what I think."

The conversation waxed and waned many times before the groom and his friends retired to their shelter.

The small framework was so heavily laden with skins that the bright morning sun had no effect on the slumbering companions. Dakata's two sheep heard the nearby movement of other livestock and called and called; finally Karora stepped from the shelter. He wiped his brow and looked about, and when his eyes could bear the daylight he looked east and saw it was still early. Stooping low, he reentered the hut. Dakata lay on his side sifting through a leather pouch. The other two were awake and dressing, and knowing that a groom should not be hurried, the two companions took the sheep to drink and graze, leaving Dakata alone in the hut.

Methodically, he laid his necklaces, groom's bonnet, and knife upon the bed. From another bundle he drew containers of butterfat, *otjize*, ground charcoal, and dried herbs and set them on the floor where a gourd of water rested against the frame. He turned his head. His companions had pulled the skin away from the hut's opening for light, and he studied it briefly before kneeling at the edge of his bed. With his belt unfastened, Dakata removed his skirts and stretched them on the ground. His eyes swept over them as he found the *otjize* and began restoring their mahogany luster. He refreshed his bonnet and his belt and carefully checked his work. Leaning forward on his knees, Dakata reached for his knife and the water gourd. His rough and calloused hands moved across his face and easily detected the weak stubble growing on his chin, throat, and cheeks. Dipping from the gourd, he moistened his beard. Lightly, he drew the knife against the bottom of his thumb; pleased with its sharp edge, he began to shave. The strokes were long, and many were needed to smooth his face. With only his fingers as a guide, Dakata felt his skin and sensed he was clean. After looking over his chest and loins and touching under his arms, he reached for the knife and gourd and cleaned these areas as well, and when finished, laid them aside and rinsed his hands.

A few beads of water dripped from Dakata's fingers and disappeared into the ground. He inhaled deeply for a moment and then took the *otjize* and began polishing his skin. His toes, his feet, his ankles, and his legs he rubbed and rubbed until satisfied with their appearance. His thighs, hips, abdomen, and back were lustrously refreshed. And though the *otjize* container was deep, it was nearly drained as Dakata finished his arms, shoulders, and chest. He opened the bag containing butterfat and smeared some on his left palm. Delicately, he squeezed charcoal dust between his right thumb and forefinger and sprinkled it over the grease. After blending the dark with the light, Dakata lifted his palm toward the doorway to view the color's depth. Adding another pinch of charcoal, he watched the substance become blacker and blacker. Again, he held his palm toward the light, and this time he was pleased. His eyes darted around the hut searching for something to clean his fingers. But finding nothing better, Dakata simply wiped them against the soles of his feet. He added several pinches of dried herbs to the ebony mixture and his work was complete.

The two white-beaded necklaces—the one thin, the other nearly as thick as a woman's wrist—were lightly smeared with the blackened grease. Dakata worked to rub the blackness away from the beads and into the tiny spaces separating them. When he finished, he held the necklaces and admired the contrast of white and black. His neck and throat were polished with the mixture, and finally the hollows of his arms. Glancing quickly toward the opening for reassurance, Dakata smeared a bit of the ebony cream wherever he felt bodily odors might arise.

The sun had climbed high in the cloudless blue sky. Dakata stood outside the hut, beautifully arrayed, looking for his companions. He scanned the landscape to his left and to his right, but it was the sound of sheep that caught his attention. A tall boy was trailing a large white ram across the plain, moving in the direction of the hut. Dakata strained his eyes, but not until the lad had walked another hundred paces did he recognize the figure. It was his bride's youngest brother, and the animal he drove was a signal from the boy's father that the people of the homestead were ready to receive the groom and his party.

The ram was led by its ears from the hut to a group of soaring thorn trees quite some distance from the homestead. The three companions walked swiftly while Dakata lagged behind taking care not to sully his clean appearance. Karora fed a tiny coal until it began to flame and then helped the tall one chop green, leafy ironwood branches and lay them close together on the ground. Mitakamwe had borne water, but now he sat beneath a tree and sharpened his knife with a stone and a fistful of sand. Again the fire was encouraged, and then three pairs of hands skillfully reduced the living creature to a luxuriant fleece and heavy cuts of meat neatly laid across the ironwood. The carcass was divided into right and left halves: the left portion, the *evango*, was for the groom and his party; the right portion was for the bride's parents. Dakata managed the division of meat, taking the pieces as they were cut and setting them in place. He and his companions would have to carry the mutton to his father-in-law's home before greeting his bride. A three-legged pot was filled with water and meat, and set to cook. The shade was cool and peaceful, and Dakata rose now and again to turn the stew.

The afternoon was closing as Dakata entered his father-in-law's homestead, flanked by his companions and the two black-spotted sheep. The shelters and gathering points teemed with people laughing, visiting, gossiping, and lightheartedly contending. Dakata stopped inside the compound and haltingly surveyed the boisterous menagerie. The scope of it all was wholly unexpected, but more troubling still was Dakata's unacknowledged arrival. For how should a groom enter his bride's homestead if not by the chiding and mocking of her people? His companions forlornly stood behind him—the mutton gaining weight with each passing moment and the sheep no longer content to idly stand. Their woolly heads moved from side to side while their noses twitched wildly. Finally, the animals protested the unusual commotion with anxious bleating. The tall lad tried to calm the sheep, but succeeded only in their further aggravation. Dakata turned his eyes to them.

"I say," shouted a voice, "the pauper and his useless friends have arrived!"

Dakata turned back. Though the noise had lessened but slightly, many eyes were upon him; with his friends he pressed forward, walking slowly toward his father-in-law's house. The ground was dusty and strewn with the droppings of smallstock, yet Dakata trod solidly, his head and body erect, his gaze deflected, scouring the path. He changed direction and walked beside a work shelter crowded with women.

"Who are you that you should come and steal the daughter of this house!" roared one of them to peals of laughter.

Dakata recognized the voice as belonging to his bride's sister and lightened his expression. A cacophony of voices faulted every movement, every gesture, every article of clothing, every blunder, and every stride the groom's party took. Lesser tones though whispered the handsomeness of Dakata and the good fortune of his bride.

A large man stepped forward to meet the advancing lads. "How dare you parade those miserable looking sheep!" he chastened them. "Ondjiviro is giving you a beautiful and worthy daughter—and this is your gift to him? Ah, you must hide for shame!"

Dakata passed the man. A large circular house came into view, and adjacent to its southern edge, a newly built work shelter. The ground enclosed by the shelter was empty but for a man seated on a carved wooden stool. His face was clean. His thick eyebrows were nearly white, and the skin surrounding his eyes folded into wrinkles. Copper bangles covered the wrists of both arms. The man acknowledged Dakata's nearness by turning his head and looking away. Though a number of people moved closer to watch the encounter, the path and shelter remained free. Dakata carried a hind leg of mutton. Sun and wind had dried the raw flesh, turning its outer layer into a shiny, delicate crisp. His footsteps became deliberately slower until Dakata stopped before the shelter. He cast his eyes low and spoke.

"Father of my bride, I share with you the sheep you shared with me. My father sends his greetings and these two sheep for your hospitality."

"It is well," replied the man, "send your father my appreciation. Come now and sit with me."

Dakata laid the mutton on a pile of branches beside his father-in-law and sat on a clean goat skin. The temporary hush ended and their conversation was lost to everyone else. The two spoke for quite some time. Dakata's companions delivered the rest of the mutton and the two sheep to other members of the bride's family, and then merged with the greater company.

Quietly, three maidens and a woman left the large home and stood to one side. Moments later, almost unnoticed, Penguka emerged from the narrow opening and stood before the falling sun. Partially hidden from view, her caretakers inspected her appearance. Her body gleamed, every limb and joint, every pore and strand flawlessly gilded with *otjize*. Her bracelets, necklaces, anklets, and belts had been cleaned and refreshed. Her skirts were as mahogany as her skin. The maiden's head was crowned with her wedding bonnet, a long cap that fell to her shoulders at the back and sides, with a cluster of three long, stiff, triangular spikes, also of leather, fastened to the top. Draped about her shoulders and back was a long cape of mohaganied leather, and over the cape, suspended from her neck, hung thick panels of iron beadwork.

Without a sound, her graceful legs carried her forward. The heaviness of her cumbersome attire was not portrayed in her movement as she walked beyond the house to where she could easily be seen from the work shelter. Demurely, her head lowered—though her eyes actively surveyed the gathering. Her father gestured toward her with his eyes and Dakata rose to greet her. He walked to her side and spoke a few quiet words, but she made no response, and without touching her, Dakata took his place on her right. Behind them, her caretakers, joined by other maidens, began to sing:

Here in this house, here in this house
A maiden will marry her man.
Here in this house, here in this house
A maiden will marry her man.

Slowly their voices lifted and drew attention, yet the bantering crowd did no more than look at the pair. Again and again the verse was repeated. With placid expression, Dakata and his bride listened and watched the gathering, never once looking at each other. Then, sensing the time was at hand, Dakata broke from the chorus and began walking to the center of the throng, his bride directly behind him. More and more voices joined the chorus as the bridal pair strode from house to house, shelter to shelter, and cluster to cluster, to be received by everyone in the homestead.

As the bride and groom made their ambling round, their friends and relatives acknowledged both the frivolity and the seriousness of the occasion; their words of greeting or advice were sometimes sincere, sometimes amusing. Dakata and his bride seemed to enjoy themselves and advanced slowly, lingering here and there to visit longer with those who were more familiar or more loquacious. The bridal pair finished the circle where they had started. Without a word they separated, and the bride joined her friends while Dakata searched for his. Cooking fires burned on every hearth in the homestead. Great kettles and topless petrol tins filled with meat and porridge sat above the brightest flames. Livestock were returning and being milked, but on this evening it was sons and daughters rather than mothers and fathers who undertook most of the work. As twilight fell, Penguka and her group of friends disappeared into a house; Dakata sat with his friends in the company of others.

The low evening hours were spent feasting and chatting, and though a dance was suggested, the unusual generosity of food had imparted a pleasant lethargy, and few had any real interest in movement. The evening wore on and people grew weary. Dakata was quietly summoned by his father-in-law: Penguka and the hut were ready. Though they were not yet wedded, Dakata and his bride would spend the night together in a small hut near the ancestral fire. The hut was built of saplings set in a circle, gathered in the middle, and lashed to a willowly central pole. The frame was covered with blankets and the entrance faced the ancestral hearth. The ground was laid with many blankets and skins, for Penguka's father was a wealthy man and known for his hospitality. Dakata stood and waited for his bride. She emerged from behind a house and walked cautiously to his side. They turned and moved toward the hut, Dakata leading, Penguka following. There was laughter and talk, but many people had already retired. As they approached the hut, Dakata's companions stepped forward. Dakata entered first and immediately turned so that as he lay on his bed with his feet facing the ancestral fire, he was to the right of the central pole. Penguka entered, turned the other direction, and readied herself for sleep. All night the bridal pair would hold these positions without touching, embracing, or speaking.

Most of the spectators left the scene for their own shelters, but a vigilant few, including Dakata's companions, sat quietly, watching the hut and listening to the bridal pair. The moon was high and the sky filled with stars. After a while, Mitakamwe stood and found his walking stick. Silently, he crept toward the hut and raised the stick. Lightly, so as not to damage the frame, he dashed it against the hut. "Remember!" he cried. "The man who will not be separated by the pole soon finds himself withered and dry, like a sun-baked vine!" He struck another blow and then stepped away.

"We hear you in there!" called another. "And we shall sit here all night and catch you in your naughtiness!"

The watchmen laughed. From time to time other threats were made, but soon they unrolled their skins and blankets, and once enclosed by their bedding, fell fast asleep.

The first mild rays of morning drew Penguka from the hut. Quickly, she trotted among the morning shadows into the bush and then repaired to a house. Dakata made neither sound nor movement. The night had been late for all, yet the animals did not understand, and when their patience wore thin, they roused the people of the homestead with their concern. When he could no longer ignore the commotion, Karora sat up in his bed. He looked at a nearby work shelter post and saw the leather pouches hanging from it. As children began leading animals to pasture, he quickly fastened his sandals and retrieved the pouches, delivering them to the bridal hut. Unaware that Penguka had already taken leave, he paused on the groom's side and lowered his head to the framework.

"Dakata," he whispered. "Dakata, are you awake?"

"Yes," came the response, "I'm awake."

"I have your things. I'll leave them at the entrance."

"Yes. That's good—at the entrance."

Karora laid the pouches at the hut's entry and swiftly retreated. The patch of ground wherein the hut and ancestral fire lay was secluded by a border of silence and respect. The *omuvanda* was not a common thoroughfare, but a place for Mukuru and the ancestors, a place of deference and special visitation. But beyond its protective borders, the homestead was consumed in the tasks of morning. Pails of milk from cows and goats were carried to various households, children and youth chased after stubborn or reluctant animals, and many of the people who had gathered the previous afternoon were preparing to return home.

At the edge of this activity, a woman of some years walked toward the ancestral hearth and laid a smoking branch just beyond the hearthstones. Kneeling beside the branch, she blew on its smoky end till it faintly glowed and then set twigs where her breath spread heat and flame. Thicker twigs and broken pieces of ironwood were added as the fire grew. A small fire was her intention and its beginnings had been fulfilled. Though she was not her husband's senior wife, because it was her daughter who, this very morning, would approach the fire, it was her privilege to revive the sleeping flames. She was a tall woman with capacious but pleasing girth, and the youngest of her husband's wives. This daughter—her only daughter—was the first of her four children to marry.

Dakata followed much the same course as the previous morning in preparing himself to receive his bride. Activity in the homestead was declining. The milking was long since finished and the livestock discharged. A few visitors had taken leave; more were in the process of doing so. Though still low, the sun was rising and Penguka's father knew the journey to Otutati was long. But he also understood youth and realized the tyranny of hastening a bride's preparations, so he contented himself in readying the implements under his immediate charge. He walked to the ancestral hearth and noted the steady fire. He returned a few moments later with two wooden bowls, one filled with water, the other with *omaze* (cooked butter). He set them on the flat stones at the extreme left end of the hearth and then walked to the milking enclosure. His eldest son had filled a wooden pail with soured milk from cows sacred to their patriclan. The man took the pail and carried it to the hearth. There he stood, thoughtfully studying each piece until finding something amiss, he went to his house and returned with a bundle of firedrills.

Dakata sat on a blanket not far from the hearth. Penguka and her party of four walked in near unison around the back of her father's house before turning in toward the fire. She was beautifully attired, wearing the same garments as the previous day with but one addition. A veil of long leather fringes entirely covered her face. The bridesmaids were also veiled, and each lowered her head as they neared the *omuvanda*. Their pace slowed, and at the threshold of the homestead's sacred ground, the bridesmaids stopped. The bride herself hesitated and stooped low to remove her sandals. Then, with her whole body in a downward posture, Penguka approached the fire from the left, taking short, halting steps until she knelt at the fire-keeper's feet. Her father rose and stood on the stones gazing westward. Before him was the fire, and just beyond it, the pile of branches representing his individual ancestors. To the right of his feet lay the firedrills, set out in a deliberate sequence: one for each of the previous fire-keepers who, together with the bride's father, formed an unbroken chain stretching back to Mukuru.

"Fathers!" he called. "And you, Mukuru—come and be with us now!"

He bent down and took the bowl of water. He pressed the wooden edge to his lips and filled his mouth. Raising his chin, he inhaled deeply through his nose and then drove the water from his mouth, spraying it over the collection of ancestral branches as deeply as his powers allowed him.

"Fathers," he repeated, "all of you! And you Mukuru—come and be with us now!"

He replaced the bowl and knelt at the edge of the hearth near his daughter. Through the thickly hanging fringe she saw him gesturing for her to crawl forward. The keeper reached for the other bowl and dipped the fingers of his right hand into the grease. Leaning toward her, he smeared *omaze* over her stomach and then spoke to God.

"Fathers," he said, "and Mukuru, listen to this man. Here before you is a beautiful daughter of your house, a daughter of my loins and a daughter of your loins. She has matured and is ready to be married and to leave this house, your house, and be joined to another. She is to be given to Dakata, the son of Katwerwa, of the house of Ngombe. She will be joined to the house of Ngombe and bear children for that house, and be protected by its fathers.

"Fathers and Mukuru, I ask that you bless this daughter—your daughter and my daughter—that she will be a good wife, a good mother, and create a harmonious family. I say, this is our request. Hear us."

A small group of people—mostly the bride's menstrual sisters and close relatives—had gathered to witness the separation of the bride from her father's ancestors. They strained to hear, for the keeper's words were intended for Mukuru, the fathers, the bride, and groom. It was a solemn occasion for these participants, yet the behavior of onlookers varied.

The keeper motioned for Dakata to come forward and sit on the hearth. As he settled, his father-in-law lifted the pail of sour milk and laid it in his hands.

"This *omaere* is from cows sacred to our house. You are the first to drink of it, and by so doing, witness to our ancestors that you accept the responsibility of caring for their daughter. A long life to you both!"

Dakata raised the pail and swallowed once. The keeper held out his hands and retrieved it from the groom.

"You too must drink," he instructed his daughter as he set the pail in her hands. "Even though you are no longer under their care, you must witness that you'll not forget your fathers."

The bride took and drank; then the fire-keeper drank before rising to his feet. "May your union be happy," he said. "And now, it's time for you to go."

Dakata remained seated while Penguka stood and assumed a downward posture. Stepping backwards, she withdrew from the fire, not turning or straightening her back until she had passed from the *omuvanda*.

Retiring quietly from the hearth, Dakata walked to a tree at the edge of the homestead where his companions stood in filtered sunlight. As he drew near they ceased chatting and waited for him to speak. "You should go now, Karora," he said. "Tell them we ought to reach Otutati around nightfall and to make certain everything's ready." Karora stepped aside, took a long drink of water, slung a bundle over his shoulder, and left.

Penguka's mother oversaw the preparations for her daughter's flight; she knew it must be swift if the bridal couple were to reach the groom's homestead before sunset. In all, six people would accompany the bride: her older brother, four maidens, and a recently married cousin to act as escort and guide. As the groom and his companions stood in the shade awaiting the bridal party, Dakata peered over his bundles into the light. The air was still cool, but the sun was increasing in strength. A girl brought a pail of water to the three lads who drank in turn. Before long, Penguka's maiden friends joined them, and then her brother, but little was said. The bride's father stood hidden in the shadows, looking around the homestead. Two of Penguka's aunties walked toward the group with tightly packed bundles and pouches—an indication that the bride was ready to leave. A moment later, one of the maidens called out, "She is here!" And everyone turned.

Treading lightly behind her guide, her head and body engulfed by an immense cape that all but sheltered her from the world, the bride came into view. She was a dangerous person, and would remain so until she approached her husband's ancestral fire. For having been released from the protective care of her own ancestors, she stood alone in the world, possessing no shield against harm and evil. The journey to her new ancestral fire and the ceremony that would bind her to her husband's fathers would be long and require great caution as her condition was infectious: the bride's vulnerability could easily undermine the strength and well-being of others. She and her escort approached the wedding party, stopping five or six paces from them. When the lads and maidens had lifted their bundles and pouches, Dakata stepped forward and led them from the homestead. Once the party had moved into the bush, Penguka and her escort would follow. Long moments passed before the wedding party disappeared from view. The escort gestured to Penguka and she took the first steps that would lead her from the only homestead she had ever known. The bride had walked no more than ten paces when her father called her by name and rushed to her side. He took the sandal from his right foot and tucked it in one of her pouches, then he laid his own walking stick in her hands. These objects would always lead her back to the family of her birth. The bride said nothing; silently, she followed her guide out of the homestead.

Dakata's party had walked about halfway across the first valley when he halted and asked the others to wait. He wished the bride and her escort to walk with them, not behind them as was the custom. No one questioned his reasons for wanting it to be so, only agreed that it might be done if, after reaching the last descending hillside into Otutati, the groups separated and gave the appearance of complete propriety.

The wind cooled the sun's warmth, yet at so swift a pace the journey was tiring. As the groom and his party descended the final hill, leaving the bride and her escort to follow, the vanishing daylight gave way to dusk. The path was steep and littered with brittle stones. At the bottom of the path, where the hillside ended, stood a memorial to a man who had died on that path ages ago. It was simply a tree, a large ironwood tree, and every wayfarer set a leaf at its trunk to honor the unknown man and to plead for safe passage. Beyond the foot of the hill lay an enormous ravine, and then nothing but flat land.

Small cooking fires glowed as Dakata passed scattered homesteads and greeted people at their evening chores. Silhouetted against the dusky sky stood the three giant sentinels, and behind their protection, Wamesepa's homestead. As the party approached the dry riverbed, their footsteps grew lighter and the last several hundred paces quickly drew to a close. A small crowd, including Karora, greeted them with happy salutations. Dakata's father was among them. He came forward and quietly welcomed his son, and as they spoke, Dakata respectfully turned his eyes downward. Dakata's words, though, were strangely rigid and halting, for underneath his father's gaze, his own eyes swept over the darkening homestead. And only when he noticed the hut standing in the *omuvanda* did his manner ease.

Two men stood bickering about the color of a sheep Dakata's younger brother had brought to the homestead. The animal was tethered to a post nibbling on a tuft of fallen thatch, unaware of its role in the dispute.

"No!" said Solomon. "I'm telling you that an *ondu jondjova* mustn't be black! It must be white! Everyone knows that!"

"Well, I'm telling you," responded Katwerwa's brother, "that indeed it must be black. When I married, the *ondu jondjova* was black. When my son married, it was black. I say, I think I know what color the sheep ought to be!"

"Perhaps you're right," admitted Solomon meekly. "My father was a Christian, not as one of you, and reared me as a Christian. Still, I'm an old man and I've seen many a wedding; and at those weddings the *ondu jondjova* has been white. That's all I will say."

Solomon opened his tobacco pouch, filled his pipe, lit it with a coal, and then handed it to Katwerwa's brother for the first smoke. He turned his head to watch the reception on the other side of the homestead, his fingers playing with a beaded necklace a diviner had once given him to ward off evil.

Penguka and her escort had finally arrived and were cautiously greeted with words that were cheery but spoken in a flat, perfunctory manner. She lingered but a moment before her bridesmaids led her to a seldom used house on the right side of the homestead. Dakata walked with his father toward Wamesepa's day shelter to fetch the sheep. The black, woolly creature had small horns, but its body was thick and large with a long, bulbous tail dangling between its hind legs. Dakata untied the plaited leather rope and pulled the reluctant sheep toward the hut in the *omuvanda*. Set beside the blanket-covered shelter was a pile of dry wood, and next to it, a cooking pot Dakata recognized as his mother's. Securely, he tethered the sheep to a heavy stump, then lit a fire near the hut's entrance and waited for his bride.

The tethered sheep was an ordinary sheep, but in the hands of bride and groom it would become an *ondu jondjova*, their own "sheep of sin" to be slaughtered, dressed, and cooked by them under darkness of night. The proper handling of the sheep was a solicitation for purity, for a cleansing from the moral ineptitude and unnatural dalliance that otherwise make it impossible for bride and groom to approach Mukuru and the ancestors, and for the bride to be received under their care. Dakata had sharpened his knife and stood whittling the bark from a wide, flat stick he intended to use as a paddle. He looked up to see his bride approaching, her body fully covered, meticulously following her escort. The two received little attention as they walked along the eastern edge of the homestead to enter the *omuvanda* from the left. Penguka's guide led her to the boundary and helped remove her vast cape, then retreated, leaving the bride in the care of her groom.

Together, Dakata and Penguka slaughtered the sheep. After suffocating the animal, Dakata laid his knife deeply in its throat and cut a line from one end of the jawbone to the other and strung it from the nearest post. The dripping blood flowed away from the animal, gathering in a pool where hungry dogs disposed of it. Its entrails and vital organs were removed and some of them set to cook. As quickly as he could, Dakata reduced the carcass to manageable cuts of meat that he passed to his bride who fed the large, boiling pot. When all the meat was inside, she took the new paddle and stirred the heavy assemblage. The pot boiled and boiled outside the entrance to the hut. Inside, bride and groom worked on the fleece, preparing it for tanning and finally hanging it from the tenuous framework. The fleece of their "sheep of sin" was sacred to them and only for their use, never to be touched by anyone else. The animal's cloven hooves were set outside the shelter. During the whole undertaking, barely a word was exchanged as each watched the other, anticipating commands and requests for help.

Wearily, Penguka sat on a flat stone Dakata had brought for her, her beautiful face glowing in the flickering light of the fire, her eyes sometimes observing the cooking meat, but more often resting. Repeatedly, Dakata went to chat with friends who sat round Katanga's cooking fire, but never for long. The moon was now high and the mutton had been cooking since it was low. Dakata returned to his resting bride and stirred the meat. Some of it fell off the bones, indicating it would soon be finished. Quietly, he walked to several homes and announced the meat was nearly ready to be taken from the pot. Before long, most of those still awake gathered at the edge of the *omuvanda* to watch. Penguka set out a number of baskets to receive the meat and crouched beside the pot. Dakata also crouched, taking care not to block the view of those who had gathered. With the paddle, he began lifting the meat, piece by piece, from the pot. As he drew it from the water, each piece was brought close to their faces that he and Penguka might breathe on it, over it, through it, that their breath, their life, their soul—all so connected with this animal—should make its flesh safe to eat. The onlookers talked and visited as they watched the bride and groom fill the baskets. And then it was finished; every piece had been extracted and made safe. But none of it was for the people of the homestead, so they dispersed, leaving the bride and groom to themselves.

The shoulder blades and ribs rested in a single basket the bride had set inside their hut. But one large basket remained, and the two sat together outside the hut's entrance separating the meat from the bones until the large basket contained the bones of the entire sheep. The bones were a danger since they could easily be used by doctors of *omiti* to harm Dakata and his bride. Their *ondu jondjova* held a part of their essence; in some way, its flesh was like their flesh, its bones like their bones. And anyone wishing to injure them would have to do no more than injure a bone from their "sheep of sin" to inflict great damage upon them. Dakata lifted the heavy basket and placed it inside the hut. The meat was removed to an empty storage bin where it would be safe for the night. The next day, after Penguka had become Dakata's wife, her brother would be given the meat, along with the task of delivering it to their father.

It was now very late and a moderate wind blew ceaselessly through every corner of the homestead. Worn from the long journey and evening's activities, the pair crawled into the small hut. Together they feasted upon the delicious, fatty ribs and shoulders, scraping the bones to remove every morsel of flesh, for along with its fleece, the *ondu jondjova*'s shoulder blades and ribs would be retained by the bride and groom. "They keep a marriage together," whispered Kavetonwa's wife. "Each bone has a distinctive shape and use, yet they are connected like husband and wife." Following their meal, each lay down on separate bedding and maintained the rigid isolation of their previous night together. Sleep did not come easily to Dakata, knowing he should rise with his bride before dawn and bury the bones at a lonely spot in the bush. All night the hut trembled from the force of the wind, and when finally it ceased the morning was nigh.

Dakata stooped outside the entrance to the hut, sliding the basket through the doorway. Penguka followed the load of bones, her body wrapped in a blanket to keep away the morning chill. Dakata lifted and steadied the basket on his head with one hand and grasped his walking stick with the other. The two walked silently, not wishing to disturb the livestock. A few paces from the homestead, Dakata stopped. "I forgot the paddle," he whispered. "Will you fetch it?" Penguka returned quickly, and they resumed a southerly course, striding through the ironwood groves toward the foothills. It was still dark, the time of wandering, mischievous spirits, and every wayward sound was investigated by their four eyes. Along a dry stream that rarely carried water, Dakata thrust his walking stick and began digging a hole. The sand was deep and easily moved, and he crouched beside the growing depression and shifted the debris by hand. Looking at the basket, he judged the hole too narrow and tore at its sides with his stick. Penguka stood by, sometimes watching him, sometimes looking over the landscape. When his arms could reach no further, Dakata motioned for the basket and laid the bones, one by one, on the sandy bottom, setting the paddle in the hole last of all. The two of them carried several large, flat stones and put them down the hole to cover the bones. The sand was shifted backwards and compressed, the excess thinly spread along the bed. Lastly, Dakata swept the streambed with a leafy branch to disguise their footprints, and then stepped back to observe their work.

Soft light crept over the easterly hills as they reached the homestead. Animals were still resting and no human beings were about. Dakata returned to the hut, but Penguka walked around the homestead and entered a house on the other side. The long night of the "sheep of sin" was behind him and Dakata crawled into his bed and slept.

Dataka's beautifully refreshed clothing glimmered in the late morning sun as he knelt on a large sheepskin positioned on the left edge of the hearth. Opposite him, on the keeper's stone, sat Wamesepa with his wife at his side. The ancestral fire smoked rather than burned, but it was the best the old woman could produce. A crowd of sixty or seventy people of various ages ringed the *omuvanda* waiting for the procession to begin. Michelle and I stood with Katanga and Wandisa's wife.

The bride and her maids left the house and stood in formation. The escort studied every aspect of their clothing and appearance and then gave them the signal to advance. Each body was rich and glossy, every article of clothing perfectly detailed. Penguka, no longer encumbered by the menacing cape, led the way out of the homestead and walked southward along its border. The group's slow, deliberate steps and their heavily veiled faces invited scrutiny, and most people turned to watch the procession, commenting on its every aptitude. Dakata stood to view his bride and her maids, but Wamesepa and his wife remained seated. Penguka passed their house and three others before turning westward into the homestead—a large, uneven sweep that set a direct northerly course to the fire. The procession's already cautious movement slowed further as they approached the *omuvanda*. At its edge, the bride stopped and dropped to her knees, her maids following suit. The bridal party, each gaze lowered, began to crawl across the sacred ground into the presence of Mukuru and the ancestors. Their movements were graceful, almost enchanting, despite the marring of their feet, knees, and wrists by creamy dust. Seven or eight paces from the fire, the bridesmaids stopped. The last stretch of ground was for the bride alone to traverse. Lowering her body still further, Penguka crawled all the more deliberately until she came to rest upon the sheepskin beside her kneeling groom.

"You, Mukuru, and you, fathers," began Wamesepa in a weak, trembling voice. "I call upon you to listen and to watch. I am an old man, hardly able to stand, but I know you can hear my voice. Come and be with us here."

Wamesepa had been looking beyond the fire, toward the west, but now haltingly, and with great exertion, he turned his upper body toward the bride.

"You, Mukuru, and you, fathers, come and look upon your new child. This daughter is to be the wife of Dakata, the son of Katwerwa, the son of my brother. She is to become a member of your house and bear children who will honor you. She will be a daughter of this fire and you will be her fathers." He turned slightly toward Dakata. "This son is already of your house. You, Mukuru, and you, fathers, I ask that you bless them with a happy marriage, that your new daughter will bear healthy children, and that their lives will not be filled with want. Mukuru and fathers, I ask you to care for these your children."

Wamesepa lowered his head and closed his eyes. His body was still, as though deep in thought. His wife looked at him for a moment and waited. Then, hesitantly, she touched his arm and his eyes opened. The old man stared at her and then at the couple kneeling across from him. Again, the old woman touched his arm, gesturing to the bowl of *omaze*. Wamesepa sat up and dipped his right hand into the cooked butter. Several times he tried to lean forward, but could not. Dakata whispered to his bride, and they moved within arm's reach. Wamesepa's long, spindly fingers thickly smeared *omaze* on the bride's stomach; and when he finished with the groom's, he quietly declared, "My child, now you are a member of this house and this fire."

Wamesepa's wife handed him a necklace, a simple leather strap with four large, distinctive beads knotted in place. Fashioned from a piece of scrap leather and the hooves of the *ondu jondjova*, the necklace was called *okanatje* (children). With the help of his wife and his walking stick, Wamesepa stood and took a single step toward Dakata's new wife. With Dakata's help, Wamesepa pulled the necklace over Penguka's hair and veil, laying it about her neck, the beads resting above her breastbone.

"This, my daughter, is your *okanatje* necklace," he said, taking his seat. "We will give you a name for each of the beads, beginning from the left; and as children are born to you, these are the names you shall give them."

Wamesepa looked to his wife as she whispered something. "The first child is Mukuva," he said clearly. Then, taking his time, he recalled the second name. "Next is Ondjora." Again, he looked at his wife. "The third

name is Kusuko." And tilting his head back, "The last name shall be
Ndimbo. These are the names of your children. May it be so."

Wamesepa rose to his feet using only his stick. He turned and faced his
ancestors at the fire. "Mukuru and fathers," he softly petitioned, "bless
this new couple. May their life together be harmonious. May they be
granted many children and many cattle. And may they always live close to
you."

Wamesepa's frail, shaking body turned and he looked directly into the
groom's face. Dakata immediately shifted his gaze. "May it truly be so,"
Wamesepa added with great conviction. And then it was over.

Dakata now stood beside his kneeling wife. Through the privacy of her
veil Penguka whispered to him, and he bent low to respond. After hearing
his words she leaned forward and stretched her arms to the ground. She
dropped her head slightly to one side, lowered her torso, and began crawl-
ing backwards along a wavering course. The bridesmaids moved into position, and when their mistress drew near, they too crawled backwards over
the sacred ground. Once they passed into the space of the living, the crowd
moved back and the maidens stopped and waited for their mistress. At last
she crossed the threshold and was helped to her feet by her husband. The
bridesmaids also stood, but quickly retreated across the homestead. Husband and wife were alone, standing close, yet not embracing. Their ephem-
eral solitude, however, was swiftly and pleasantly broken as friends and
relatives pushed forward to greet them.

Two oxen had been slaughtered and dressed. The meat sat in an odd
assortment of three-legged pots and petrol tins, and cooked over a vast
fire burning near the *otjoto* (a wooden canopy inside the *omuvanda*). Not
only did the *otjoto* stand on sacred ground, but its limited environs were
further restricted. Married men alone were able to use its space, and they
tended both the fire and the meat. The selection of the oxen was not an
easy task, and Katwerwa had brooded over the details for several days. The
size of the beasts and the number of people to be fed were simple, almost
trivial judgments. Difficult was knowing who would likely attend and the
patriclans to which they belonged—for most patriclans had rules against
eating the flesh of certain cattle, with different rules applying to the twenty
or so different patriclans. Some were forbidden to eat livestock without
horns; for others, one color or another, stripes going this way or that,

large or small spots, were all decisive factors in eating or not eating the flesh of an animal. Some patriclans also forbade the consumption of specific organs or cuts of meat—the liver or heart, the left shoulder or rear shanks. Also, there was the general consideration of what to do with the blood and generative organs. These were powerful and sensitive bits of the carcass and had to be handled properly. Yet beyond this was the problem of contamination. If a forbidden cut of meat were cooked together with other cuts in a large pot, all of it was considered defiled, inedible to the members of the relevant particlan. These were the details Katwerwa mulled over prior to selecting the oxen.

Fires also glowed in the work shelters, as maize meal was turned into porridge, and other sauces and relishes were prepared. At the edge of the homestead two other fires burned, straddled by three-legged pots containing forbidden, defiling meat. Later, this meat would be given to those for whom it posed no threat. The gathering was festive and jovial, brimming with animated conversation and laughter. Dakata's wife enjoyed the company of women while he was surrounded by men at the *otjoto*. The afternoon sun was at full strength as the crowd gathered at several points in the homestead to see the pots and kettles pulled from the fires and their contents emptied into baskets and onto other makeshift platters.

While others continued feasting, Dakata put down his knife. A middle-aged man with long, graying eyebrows leaned toward Dakata and asked to use it. His lower incisors had been removed, making it difficult for him to eat politely without a knife. Resting in the man's left palm was a thick wedge of meat. As he lifted it to his lips, his molars quickly seized a corner while his fingers stiffened to hold the other end. Cautiously, he guided the knife along his cheek, and with a single stroke, freed a generous mouthful. The man chewed with vigor, unconsciously displaying every stage of the meat's disintegration; and when his mouth was empty, he began anew. Men sat here and there in small groups sharing the fattiest portions of meat, exchanging words without truly conversing. As the afternoon lazily fell toward evening, some left to attend to chores, but most showed no signs of pressing obligations. Dakata yawned as he rested against a post amid a group of men, most of them a generation older than he.

"Aha," said one, looking at Dakata. "With two wives you are truly a married man!"

Others laughed at this, but Dakata made no reply.

The same man spoke again. "Let me give you a word of advice. Perhaps you already know, but women are very jealous—far more jealous than men. Why Mukuru made them so, I'll never understand. A husband must be fair with his wives and divide his time equally between them, for if you don't then one thinks herself slighted and the other feels superior. And when that happens, life becomes difficult."

"I say," responded another, "this is precisely why men were never meant to live with women. It's simply too hard—their demands are impossible."

"What has your wife ever demanded from you," asked Mukuva, "except that she should have a child?"

Kuwiya had finished eating and sat beside Dakata.

"Ah," said Kuwiya, "let him alone. Your words mean nothing here. These situations can only be understood by a man who experiences them. And even then most of us fail to see what should be seen."

Hearing the voices, other men cast aside their lethargy and joined the small group. The first cool draughts of evening slowly crept across the valley and some of the older men moved into the fading sunlight. For a time the conversation was scattered, drawing attention from only a few, but eventually it fell upon a subject of great common interest.

"I was told he returned in the evening and found him with his wife— in the house he built for her last year."

"Yes, I heard that too—from his own mouth. He said he walked up to the house, very late at night, and was ready to knock on the door and call his wife's name when he heard her talking. He stood and listened, and when her boyfriend responded, he took his stick, pushed open the door, charged the man, and beat him till he ran away. Then, he started on her."

"And she had to be taken to the hospital in Opuwo."

"Yes, that's correct, she did. He was in a rage and she couldn't get out of the house."

"I can't blame him, though. If I came home and found my wife with a boyfriend I'd thrash him and then her. It's right that a man should be angry with an unfaithful wife."

"Ah, you think so?" answered Katere. "I say, now he'll have to convince the District Commissioner that a husband may beat his wife like that when he finds her with another."

"Why is the District Commissioner interested in this? It's our matter, isn't it?"

"It would have been had he not beaten her so badly, but he went too far. I've also heard that her father and brothers are making threats against him."

"And what of the boyfriend? What's happened to him?"

"No one knows yet. He should pay a fine to her husband, but some think the District Commissioner may overrule that."

"I say," remarked Katwerwa's brother, "I think women are always at fault. They're clever and wily creatures, always tempting us when we are weak. The only wonder is that so few of them actually get caught!"

"That's it," said an older man, "that's just how it is! Women lie in wait and then trap us. And if we're found out, they expect us to admit we've done something wrong! I say, in such matters women are at fault, not men. It's fine for us to have another woman, but it's wrong for them to take another man unless we've told them to!"

At this there was laughter and the speaker looked about, enjoying the amusement his words provided. Katwerwa listened without varying his silent expression, and then gently turned and walked away.

"Has the woman returned from Opuwo?"

"Oh yes, " said Katere. "She's staying at her father's homestead, and he's expecting her husband's father to pay him at least two milk cows for the beating."

"Two head of cattle for what she rightly deserved?"

"No one rightly deserves what she received," answered Kuwiya. "A mild beating, yes; but no man should ever handle a woman that way. Were she my daughter, my sons would have tracked him down and thrashed him. I suppose though, were she my daughter, I would never have allowed such a marriage. He's always had a brutal temper and everyone knows it. I say, he had every right to be angry and correct his wife, but not to attack her. That's no way for a man to behave."

The discussion persisted for a time, but no consensus was reached; the same conflicting opinions were rehearsed again and again. By the time Wamesepa's livestock had returned to the homestead and were ready for the night, the group had disbursed, many drifting homeward. Together with another of Katwerwa's wives, Dakata's mother entered the *omuvanda* and walked to the small hut where Dakata and his wife would spend their first night of marriage. Though it was dark, the two inspected the privacy of the overlapping blankets and skins forming the roof before they more comfortably arranged the chamber.

A steady wind had blown most of the afternoon and only now, in the deep of evening, did it begin to moderate. Across the way, Dakata's wedding hut stood abandoned—bare saplings, weakly lashed together, that no one dare touch. The tottery structure would simply collapse on its own and the mystical powers lingering in its remains should move whither they desired. Our tent flapped in the breeze but held the disturbance at bay. Inside, only a single lamp burned, but its glow was highly visible in the whirling night air.

"Odavido," a man's voice whispered. "Odavido."

Light footsteps ceased near the front of our tent. I opened the door slightly to the figure of Kuwiya standing in the light of a waning moon, his upper body wrapped in a blanket.

"Odavido," he repeated. "Please, you must come with me."

I found the medical bag and fastened the door behind me. Beneath the quiet of luminous starlight, Kuwiya led the way out of the homestead, yet not toward his own. It was difficult to know where he was headed, and for a time we walked a narrow path running between several gardens, well away from any houses.

"Where are we going?" I finally asked.

"Just over here," he replied, pointing with his head. "I have something to tell you."

We marched a bit further and came to an opening where the garden fences surrounded a large tree.

"Come, sit down," he said. "Nothing is wrong, Odavido—I only wish to tell you a story."

I sank into the old leather bag while Kuwiya carefully folded back his skirts and squatted on the sand, and when he had found the proper balance, he rested his stick against his leg. Though we sat in the light, well beyond the tree's shadows, it was difficult to see his face.

"Do you remember," he began, "three nights ago at Dakata's wedding feast when the men spoke about that woman?"

"Yes," I replied, "I remember it well."

"I say," he continued, "you must understand that some of those men spoke falsely—they said things no one truly believes. Among us there are always a few men who present themselves in one way, though everyone knows it's only talk. Such men are stupid, pretending to be something they're not—though I understand this well because I've also spoken falsely. It's difficult to explain, but as we grow up, we learn to speak about certain things in certain ways, and if a man's thinking differs from those ways, most often he says nothing because it's easier to say nothing than to be thought a renegade or a fool. But here, away from everyone else, I will tell you what I think about husbands visiting the wives of other men."

Not a single sound had risen from the shadows, yet Kuwiya stopped and cautiously looked about the clearing. Satisfied, he lowered his head and began his tale.

"Four years ago I was in Windhoek, staying in Katatura. I had brought my mother to hospital there because her heart beat too slowly. Most of the day I was alone, walking around town, looking at things, and sometimes chatting with people. One morning I saw a Herero woman drawing water at a tap—a beautiful woman with a full *omatako* [buttocks]—and every morning thereafter I walked to the water tap to see her. After a few days, she realized that I stood there morning after morning because of her and she began to work her wiles. She played with me, beguiled me, tempted me. She stayed longer than necessary, often looking in my direction yet pretending not to see me. All day my thoughts were on her; and in the evening, when my friends returned, still I thought of her. It was as if *omiti* had been placed in my head. But it was not really thinking, it was a struggle between my heart and my mind. What was inside me was divided in two, one part saying, 'Yes, it is good!' the other telling me, 'No, it is not right!' I couldn't understand this struggle because I knew it wasn't unusual for men to seek out other women. I had known of such things since my youth, yet my heart and mind struggled over my desire for the Herero woman. Finally, I went with her—not once, but many times—and the struggle was over.

"When my mother was well, I took her home and then returned to Otutati. As soon as I walked into my homestead my heart became heavy, like a great stone. It hurt me, and my eyes looked with sadness at everything I did. Day after day, my heart and chest were heavy yet I couldn't understand why. I kept asking myself, 'What's this hurting me? Why must I feel so heavy?' But at last I understood: it was Mukuru. I had followed my mind instead of my heart. I knew the Herero woman in Windhoek would do me no good; I knew I had turned from the promptings of Mukuru and my fathers. But I didn't know how to make my heart light again."

Kuwiya lifted his head slightly and looked at the darkened tree trunk.

"This was difficult," he continued, "and I must help you understand why. I knew this was a problem that had to be discussed at the fire with Mukuru and the fathers, but I didn't want to discuss it with my fire-keeper. I was ashamed he should know such a trifling matter was troubling me. So I said nothing. Then one day I could endure no more and sent everyone away. I told my wives I was ill and they must tend the animals and take the children with them. After they had gone, I closed the door to my house and barred it from the inside. I stood like a man at the fire and asked Mukuru and my fathers to hear my words even though I was going about it the wrong way. I told them about my heavy heart—that I knew they were cursing me and why. I said I would never take another man's wife and asked them to lift the sickness from me. Many times I repeated myself, and when I finished, I opened the door and walked to the groves. As I walked along, I could feel my heart becoming lighter and lighter as the sickness was taken from me; and I thanked Mukuru. That is my story."

Kuwiya's tapering words swiftly became part of the night, and after a moment of quiet he rose. I followed his lead and stood with my bag.

"It isn't easy to be a man," he sighed.

Reflection

It is late and the moon is sweeping toward the far horizon. Wind is blowing against the tent, sometimes gently, other times forcefully, and the sounds of rustling leaves and nodding limbs, of bothered livestock, of gourds bumping the walls of a nearby work shelter, and of scurrying nocturnal creatures all serve as reminders of the place where Michelle, Elspeth, and I have settled. Months have passed since our arrival and we are comfortable; we have learned how to live in Otutati. Our evenings now follow a basic routine: When the sun is down and our lamps are lit, Elspeth has her bath, a story, and then crawls into bed while I exhaust my repertoire of German lullabies and folk songs. Michelle washes, then I, and if no activities of note are planned across the homesteads, we withdraw back into our world and our language, and it is a welcome retreat.

On clear, brilliant nights such as this, when people are silent, when only a few unconscious elements of land and sky are maundering, if I am awake and listening, and if the smells of ironwood trees, *otjize*, slumbering fires, and huddled livestock are carried by the wind, mild apprehensions of this whole venture begin to circulate and I wonder what we truly know of the Himba—of Watumba, Daniel, Wandisa, Katere, and the others—of their world, their expectations, their experience, and what, precisely, we can hope to learn of them.

Entering their world was bewildering—entering upon their tongue, their manners, their rhythm, their ways of interpreting life, their modes of holding the body and positioning the eyes—and our blunders have amused them greatly. But much of this has passed; their world is now real. When Elspeth runs to play with her friends, shaping miniature houses and homesteads from sand in the dry riverbed, no longer are they interested in holding her arms to gaze at the veins beneath her skin or to touch her fine, soft curls. When people come to visit us at home it is mostly to visit, not to make requests. Women of the homestead call to Michelle when they need help in preparing communal banquets, and while she was told her first efforts at grinding maize were fit for nothing but dog food, she has now mastered the technique. To converse in the heat of the afternoon or the cool of the evening, not about what Himba feel or Himba believe or Himba think, but what Ngipore feels or Kavetonwa believes or Katanga thinks of the very subjects around which ordinary life revolves—marriage, child rearing, amusements, making a living, disappointments, entangling obligations, irritating in-laws and the like—is revealing, especially when our questions are turned upon us and our answers ring curiously familiar to them. And yet, despite all this nearness, there is still something that separates us. Precisely what it is and whether it is something deep or something shallow remains a bit of a mystery.

Few Himba have difficulty portraying their world in terms of what ought to be done and how things should properly be, and such patterns in their life are easily seen. Homesteads are configured in a certain way; the care of livestock and techniques of milking and butter-making are largely standard; ceremonies at the ancestral fire abide a steady course. Yet each pattern is deceptive, for no two ceremonies are identical; each woman's mode of butter-making and every hand's way of milking diverges from every other; in practice, no two herdsmen are in full agreement; and each homestead, no matter how well modeled after the ideal, has its own look. The same people who easily explain how things should be done are the same people hard pressed to point out a single example of absolute conformity. We have yet to attend a trial conducted identically to any other trial, or to see a parent disciplining a child or a woman sewing beadwork whose actions did not diverge in some way from previous or subsequent attempts. Neither have we heard a prayer or incantation uttered with genuine faithfulness to former prayers and incantations, or a piece of gossip retold without variation. Still, the eye sees and the ear hears and the nose smells and the tongue savors and the mind perceives more than a thread of similarity, of continuity, in all of this divergence. Each Himba is a person in his own right, though not without holding a special place within the Himba's culture. Each Himba is outfitted in this cultural world, yet to a degree moves about that world in his own time. And from all of these individualized movements, movements that in one degree or another stray from the expressed ideal, emerges a tenuous perception of continuity.

So, what sort of a thing is culture—this twisted morass of ideas and conventions in their various tangible and intangible forms—that has such hold over us? We may abandon our culture for another one, but once learned, no such twisted morass can ever be entirely forgotten and so is never entirely impotent. Sometimes, when I am visiting with Kavetonwa or Ngipore, my mind recedes from the conversation and I wonder what the two of us are doing. Here sits this man, Kavetonwa, who has thought a great deal about the world, about the plight of human beings and his own experience, and about the rising generation. I look at him and see a man arrayed in clothing, jewelry, and footwear very different from my own but essentially fulfilling the same purposes. Under his exotic dress, he is simply a man. As he talks, I understand him; I understand to a fair degree the world he believes to exist, with all its powers and causal forces. It is the world in which he moves and to which his words belong. Most remarkably, there is little question in Kavetonwa's mind that this idiosyncratic understanding of the world—an understanding partially formed through the strength of his own personal will, his desire to view the world in a particular way—is essentially correct; that it, more than any other description of which he is aware, most closely coincides with his own experience. For him, though occasional tensions may arise, and though he tells me of the dark spots and uncertainties he sees in his own understandings, he has settled into the overall correctness of his world, especially in these latter years of his life.

Opposite him, I sit with a very different conception of the nature of the world. He is aware that my conception is different from his, but he has no appreciation for the degree of difference. Yet could I possibly demonstrate that his conception is lacking while my conception is correct? Could he prove his correct to me? No! It is simply not possible; for it is within neither of our provinces to conclusively prove the one world while conclusively disproving the other. So here we sit, one of us old, the other of us young, in the grip of ideas about the *true* nature of the world with no facility to make a final judgment on that world. And what of human knowledge? What knowledge? At this level there is no true knowledge; there can be no true knowledge, only belief. What a remarkably deep and hidden capacity is the capacity to believe, yet all the while we are fooling ourselves that we do not believe. They, those people over there, only they believe; for we know that we know!

If culture separates us in a profound way, why do we feel we can understand one another? Why do Kavetonwa, Ngipore, Wandisa, and Mbitjitwa so often laugh and tell me, "I know just what you mean! People, we people, we're all alike." Is this merely a foolish deception, or is there a level at which human beings can understand one another despite the cultural divide? Is it even conceivable that as pervasive and inescapable as culture is, it remains only skin deep? It seems to me that culture does not significantly govern the affairs of the human soul—the experience of emotions: love, hate, jealousy, elation, embarrassment, indifference, and so on—perhaps not even the events that trigger them. And it would be very difficult indeed to assert that culture appreciably interferes or disrupts the basic course of human life, the movement from birth to death. Hence, it is not mere fancy to assert that common human emotions experienced in mostly common ways, coupled with the basic march of life and the anxieties that stem from the responsibilities attached to each stage, form the common ground of human understanding.

Why, then, is culture at once so meaningful and so meaningless? Why, at the funeral of a Hakavona woman, did all of her close kinswomen stand together on the north of her grave and smite their breasts with leafy twigs, cover their eyes with their free hands, and wail and shriek until tears coursed down their cheeks, while afterward several of them privately expressed to Michelle and me a profound lack of regret at the loss of their dear auntie. Were only some of the mourners constrained by culture while these few others were immune from it? These latter women certainly complied with the basic outlines of funeral behavior, yet did so without genuine feeling, without soul. Does culture strike at the inner core of whatever it is that makes us human; does it actually penetrate the human soul? Or is this great and wondrous morass so feeble it cannot induce true feelings, cannot foment deep passions? How often does the sheer force of personal will block the feelings of the human *soul* or stunt the directives of culture? And is any one of these three—culture, soul, or personal will—stronger than the others?

I doubt final answers to these questions will ever be found, instead, such matters will forever languish in the ambiguity of opinion. But these questions can steer one clear of simplistic conclusions. Why are we so willing to ascribe clarity and simplicity to the actions of others when our own experience should impel us to run from such reasoning? The other morning at Vita's, when his wife felt poorly, one of his daughters volunteered to fetch some water. "This daughter is always good to me," said Vita, once she had disappeared from view. But was this maiden truly dutiful and unselfish? Perhaps so, but later that evening Katanga's daughter told me Vita's dutiful maiden had wanted to go to the well because a youth she fancied would be there watering his father's goats. Perhaps it was duty and unselfishness, coupled with adolescent desire, that motivated her action. Yet, it remains possible that her motivations were even more numerous and entangled than this. Perhaps Katanga's daughter misread a fortuitous meeting or invented a piece of gossip out of spite. But now, several days after the fact, could Vita's daughter even be able to recall the complexity of her motives? Or were they simple after all?

Human life and human lives are rich and deep, defying every attempt at neat and tidy explanation. Every corner is filled with objects wanting to be seen and understood, things of merit and value, things of embarrassment and despair, things both odd and familiar. Perhaps it is this human yoke of ambiguity I find most striking—of uncertainty in the face of deeply felt certainties, a thorn quietly lying in wait to prick the heart at the most inopportune moments, and though mostly withstood, it is an experience that leaves one stripped of a degree of innocence and naivete that can never be reclaimed. And so, returning to the question of what we can know of these Himba, have I arrived at an answer? No, not yet. But this much I do know: I cannot hear the wind or see the shadows it moves about by blowing against the tent's fabric, for the wind has abated. Dying winds lead to a rising sun, or so we are told. But as the livestock have not yet begun to stir, I think there must be time to sleep.

· 8 ·

The Prophet Cometh

. . . as his children demand, and Katere believes he is in danger. The presence of a snake convinces him that people are jealous of him, of his position, of his relation to Wamesepa, and are calling on forces beyond his control. The prophet should be of some help, but only if evil is truly afoot and not simply the figment of a bothered imagination.

The colors of sunset were fading and pockets of shadows covered the ground. Several clusters of men walked across the dusty soil toward Wamesepa's homestead, their paths converging as they neared the circle of homes. Wamesepa had gone to Opuwo, taken there by Wandisa when he complained his lungs no longer held breath. Katere was walking alone. He stirred a bit of dust with his cumbersome gait, but his head moved calmly from side to side as he surveyed the familiar landscape. A lazy evening wind blew against the men, carrying the scent of returning livestock.

Mukuva walked and chatted with several friends and by chance turned his head. He noticed Katere standing off to the side with his body perfectly rigid and still. Mukuva stopped as Katere lifted his right foot and drew it backward, pausing slightly lest his movement arouse suspicion. "A snake," whispered Mukuva. He took the snake hammer from his belt and moved toward Katere, never lifting his eyes from the ground. His friends recognized the signs and followed him. Taking care with their footsteps, they formed an arc and cautiously swept downward. Mukuva closed in from the rear and spotted the creature—a small cobra rising to strike. He raised his snake hammer and took aim, but the serpent responded by lowering its head and quickly slithering through the dust. Mukuva lost the creature in the shadows and alerted the others. Together, they combed the immediate ground. Their search was frantic, for the snake was close to the homestead and each man investigated the slightest hint of movement.

Katere retreated a score of paces and leaned against his stick to watch the men search. When he broke his stare, he lowered his head to see the snake rising before him. He jumped in surprise and cried out. As it slithered forward, the creature parted its mouth and teased him with its long, black, ribbonlike tongue. Higher and higher rose the flaring head while its quivering tenon cast a spell on Katere. Suddenly, without warning, it fell, and a snake hammer lay beside its brilliant coat. But the serpent was only injured; slowly, it lifted its head and vainly struck the air. Mukuva and Katere stepped back, their eyes fixed on the broken creature. Another man rushed to their side and raised his right hand. With great intensity he looked down at the cobra and the creature's movement ceased. There was no sound, no motion, no breathing. The newcomer and the serpent were deathly still. They waited, each hesitant to strike. At last, the cobra's tongue flickered. "Eeyah!" cried the man as he threw the hammer with all his strength, lifting his knees to his chin to avoid a bite. As his feet touched the ground he jumped back, uncertain whether his throw had found its mark. The snake lay prostrate, its body slowly coiling. The man raised his walking stick and lowered his torso to his knees. Silently, he sprang from the ground and flung the stick with all the power his frame could muster. "It's dead," he cried. And the others closed round to bury the serpent.

"No," said one of Wamesepa's aging sisters. "If a man meets a snake, one expects it to threaten him. But should that snake move away and after a time return and threaten him again, something isn't right. I say, Katere was lucky not to have been killed."

Katanga was roasting fresh maize on a scrap of sheet metal set over the fire, attentively turning the ears to prevent their burning. "So what do you mean?" she asked. "Are you saying someone intends to harm Katere? Why should anyone wish death upon him?"

"I'm not saying that, only thinking it," the old woman replied, keeping her voice low. "But doesn't it seem strange—a snake seeking out Katere not once, but twice? Have you ever known of such a thing?"

"No," answered Katanga thoughtfully, "I haven't. But it doesn't mean that something is wrong."

"Then tell me why Wakamburwa has laid a circle of ashes around their home and why Katere hasn't left the house since he returned? Those aren't his regular habits, are they?"

Katanga turned to look at the line of ash, but darkness had settled. "Perhaps you're right," she said. "But what could it be?"

Wandisa returned later that evening with the news that Wamesepa was in the hospital and responding well to treatment. The next morning, after attending to chores, he fired up his old yellow truck. Already it was the scene of contention as people had arrived early to secure a place in its bed for passage to Opuwo. Unhappy latecomers milled about hoping for a seat, but no amount of protest or despair could loosen the people and bundles so tightly wedged in the bed. Among the fortunate was Katere, who sat astride his bedroll giving instructions to his daughter. And as the truck drove away, he called to his wife: She should expect him the following afternoon.

The line of ash round Katere's house was clearly visible and became an object of speculation. Katere was often at the center of whispering shadows, especially when Wamesepa's health turned for the worse. As heir to a vast cattle estate, it was only natural that he should anticipate his inheritance, perhaps even work to hasten its reception. His was a difficult position, and through his own misjudgments of community regard, Katere did little to allay the oft-voiced suspicions. In his view there was jealousy; but according to others, Katere was selfish, his eyes filled with greed, a man seeking respect and esteem yet poorly endowed to foster them. From time to time he was quietly accused of using *omiti* against his uncle, but those closest to him maintained he spoke ill of no one and was devoted to Wamesepa. When he returned the following day from Opuwo, he was rumored to be wearing a new protective necklace beneath his unusually thick *ombongoro*.

The afternoon was slow. Large, thin clouds drifted across the sky, occasionally blocking the sun. Men had gathered at the thicket of trees to watch a game of mancala. Kuwiya leaned against a trunk planning his next move while onlookers whispered to one another. Katere stood with several others but offered no advice. His eyes loosely followed the movement of pebbles from one small hole to another until attracted by an approaching shadow. Far to the east, a cloud of dust moved steadily across the valley floor; Katere's ears also detected an accompanying sound. He turned back and saw the group fully absorbed with the game and looked again at the stirring cloud. Moments later, the sound was heard by everyone: A motorcar was drawing near.

The players rose, and joined by curious children, five or six spectators began walking toward the tracks. Others resumed their conversations, watching from the thicket, but before long a crowd of thirty or forty stood to greet the passing car. Straightening his skirts as he walked, Katere ambled slowly toward the bystanders and pressed his way through a group of children to secure a frontline position. The dust cloud moved ever closer and at last an ailing blue sedan came into view. From a distance, the small, limping car appeared brimming with people and bundles. Apparently the driver noticed the crowd, for the sedan slowed to a crawl as it approached the onlookers. Katere walked toward the vehicle, straining his eyes, and then lifted his arm as if to greet a passenger. The engine continued howling as the driver pulled alongside Katere, and the two spoke briefly. A moment later, Katere lifted his stick and pointed across the flood plain, up the dry riverbed, and toward the large homestead. Slowly, the car left the tracks and drove to the edge of Wamesepa's house.

The Herero travelers remained in their seats as the curious walked in their dusty wake and gathered round the sedan. One by one, the doors opened, and amid a plethora of movement, three men and three women emerged from the car. Quickly, they formed a line and waited beside the driver's door. As it opened, a slightly built man approaching his middle years placed his feet upon the ground and rose before the congregation. The *Opropheto* had arrived! An unusual restraint fell over the people as they examined the Prophet and his entourage. He looked at them and smiled, displaying his large, white teeth, evenly set around a slight midline gap. The Prophet's smooth forehead, glazed with perspiration, enhanced his uncommon appearance. His suit, shirt, tie, and shoes were dusty and he glimpsed the world through gold framed spectacles secured on one side by a turn of black electrical tape. Katere's wife roused from a late afternoon slumber and poked a tentative head from the door of her house.

She recognized the visitors and retreated inside. The Prophet warmly greeted the bystanders, yet their demeanor portrayed no hint of surprise or further curiosity, and before long, the afternoon regained its slower pace. As people returned to their obligations, Katere stepped forward and extended his arm to each of the visitors. It was understood by all that he had summoned the Prophet.

The sun was low, almost sunken, when evening chores were finished. Katere showed his visitors to three lonely huts west of his own house and helped them settle. The Prophet had his own quarters, complete with a folding chair and a recently swept hearth. Its walls and roof were in good condition even if they appeared tired and worn. He arranged his things carefully, hanging his crimson vestments from the thatch and a small shaving mirror on the central post. His assistants unpacked their few belongings and gathered near Katere's house to chat. Katere knew the demands of hospitality required substantial meals and had earlier asked an elder son to fetch a sheep. The youth returned with an old, cantankerous ram that sought to injure Katere several times before a sharp knife brought it under control. Handily, the lad dispatched the animal and prepared it for cooking. As he sat near a large cauldron tending the mutton, Wakamburwa knelt by her grinding stones and filled basket after basket with meal. Her two older daughters had gone to draw water for their guests and the supper preparations, but were late in returning. When finally they did, Wakamburwa had them scrape the remains from two large pots, fill them with water, and set them to boil over a hissing, crackling fire.

Beyond Katere's corner of the homestead, and around the cooking fires of Otutati, people mused, pondered, gossiped, and debated the unfolding scene. Summoning a prophet—a man who draws upon the authority of Christianity as well as the powers of *omiti*—was an unusual occurrence, though not entirely unknown. But why had Katere done so, and why at this particular time? Was he afraid of supernatural attack, or was some other matter troubling him? Had he been using *omiti* to hasten Wamesepa's death? Was he now afraid his secret would be discovered and everything lost? And why did he deny wearing a new necklace—a necklace that bore all the markings of a protective amulet? Accusations, queries, and rumors circulated from ear to ear and mouth to mouth. Indeed, as Vita's wife observed, "Everything was as the wind."

Night settled over the valley, and the travelers finished the last of the porridge and the last of the meat. Though an entire ram had been eaten, their eyes scoured the cooking pots and serving baskets, searching for an overlooked fragment. The Prophet was more subdued, and when he finished licking the grease from his fingers, he called to his flock. The fire that had cooked the meat was relaid with wood and the six men and women assembled themselves around the growing flames. The Prophet signaled to them with his right hand and they began singing hymns to the accompaniment of clapping hands and stamping feet. Herero translations were sung to familiar melodies, and as one hymn followed another, people from across Otutati came to listen. So unlike Himba singing was the travelers' music that many had difficulty deciding whether or not it pleased the ear. The melodious hymns continued for a time, but as the evening deepened, the selections and performances became ever more dissonant. The once sober, primpish demeanor of the singers followed the music's path and their expressions intensified as their bodies swayed provocatively to the haunting monotony of repetitious words and tones.

The Prophet observed his sheep with seeming admiration as they persevered in their efforts. Interest in the performance steadily grew and a large group of spectators stood at different points in the homestead. Suddenly, one of the men of the entourage jumped from his place and ran a few steps to open ground. There, he roughly tore his shirt and flung it to the ground. His ill-fitting shoes he also kicked into the darkness. His colleagues quickly hastened the pace of their clapping, thus urging him forward. Heavy on his feet, he stood absolutely still, his chest rising and falling with irregular rapidity. His arms rose slightly and his hands became fists. These he turned toward his face, then viciously beat himself about the chest and abdomen. Abruptly, he stopped, and wrung his arms and hands and lowered his face. With prolonged firmness, he raised his stiff arms to heaven and began rotating his head. Faster and faster went its circular motion; louder and louder became his panting and gasping. Finally, the motion slowed, and then stopped altogether. The man opened his mouth and released his tongue. Placing one foot behind the other, he moved in halting steps that carried him backward, ever further from the light of the fire.

The man crouched behind a shelter, hiding himself from the crowd. Unexpectedly, he burst into vision, running at full speed toward the fire.

Not three paces from the leaping flames, Katere flung himself before the fire walker and threw his arms around him, restraining the possessed man who grunted with displeasure. Finally, Katere eased his grip and the man escaped, running to the edge of the homestead. Again, he hid himself among the houses, lurking in their shadows. The Prophet's sheep lifted their voices as the two remaining men stood on either side of the fire, and when the song was finished, the five looked bewilderedly at one another before the ladies started anew. Among the crowd there was anticipation and wonder. Suddenly, from the nether side of the homestead, came the sound of rushing footsteps, and three maidens screamed as the fire walker broke past them, running toward the hearth. Katere stood ready to inter-fere, but this time he was cast aside like a leaf in the wind. At the fire's edge, the crazed man leaped toward the blackened cauldron, but the Prophet's men saved him from embracing the steaming pot. He struggled against their grip, and nearly buried his head in the seething broth before they dragged him, against his will, to a vacant house where he might regain his presence. Moments later, fully clothed, he left the house under his own power and stood among his colleagues.

Wakamburwa had cooked another large pot of maize porridge and pre-pared a dark, rich, buttery sauce to accompany it. Katere was pleased with the fire walker's powerful display and touched hands with the Prophet and his players, bidding them to join him for refreshment. The spectators looked on, waiting for an invitation, perhaps knowing none should be made, and spoke quietly of the performance. It had been entertaining—of that there was little question. But was it real, genuine, authentic? The merits of the Prophet and his troupe would turn on this question.

"There are spirits that seize people," said Ngipore, walking with several friends. "But these days so many men and women claim to have such powers and hire themselves to solve the problems of others that it's a job to know whether they're thieves or truly blessed."

"I say, I'm not convinced this *Oropheto* is real," sighed Kupika, slapping his thigh. "I just don't understand where his power comes from. If it comes from Mukuru and the fathers, why doesn't he use the fire? If it comes from *omiti*, why should anyone hire him?"

"The only way to know if the *Oropheto* is real," answered Mbitjitwa, "is to see whether or not he solves the problem. If he does, his powers must be real."

"Perhaps," countered Masutwa, "but it might also be coincidence. And even if the problem isn't solved it doesn't mean the powers aren't real. How many times do we ask Mukuru and the fathers for something and it doesn't come? Does this convince us that Mukuru isn't real?"

The men stopped at the edge of the riverbed, knowing their paths must diverge.

"Ah yes," said Ngipore, before turning his way. "One thing we do know for sure: Katere isn't going to invite us to eat with him!"

A full sun had risen above the easterly hills, but the cool morning air was still to be felt. The morning's silence, however, was broken. The impatience of livestock and a distant chorus of well blended voices greeting the Sabbath day had seen to that. As children led the goats and sheep to pasture, their parents finished the tasks of morning. Already Katere had visited most of the homes in the area announcing that the Prophet wished to speak with everyone. An abandoned, partially dilapidated house some distance from Wamesepa's homestead was to be the meeting place. Many people accepted the invitation out of genuine interest, some for lack of better diversion, and others, like Katanga, out of respect for Katere's position as the next head of her matrilineage. The air was beginning to warm as people walked to the appointed place. Michelle and I strolled alongside Mbitjitwa and his young wife, noting how lush the surrounding pastureland was this far into the season.

The Prophet's entourage greeted the new parishioners as they trickled into the crumbling house. Nearly half of the wall timbers had been pilfered, and in their absence, the roof, now only partially thatched, sagged heavily in the middle. As the sun climbed higher and higher, light broke through the roof and began filling the structure. The indoor seating was nearly exhausted and new arrivals were directed to the ground outside. Wandisa, dressed in beige coveralls and a green, dusty beret, stood against an inside wall, his lively eyes hidden by black-rimmed sunglasses. The level of conversation was robust, and only when the choir broke into a hymn did the congregation settle.

The Prophet emerged from behind the house. He walked to the rear of the crowd and waited for the choir to finish before making an official entrance. His lean body was clothed in dark, neatly-pressed trousers and a clean, white shirt. About his neck hung a tie of unusual yellow hue (". . . like the bile of a giraffe," said Watumba), and draping his torso, from the left shoulder to the right hip, was a crimson vestment stitched in silvery thread. A light breeze ruffled the vast emerald cape fastened around the Prophet's collar, stiffening a bit as it touched the back of his knees. As he turned, a square of white satin, emblazoned with a large, golden cross, arose from the emerald sea. It was an uncommon sight, and as the Prophet walked to the center of the house, his shoulders and head firm and erect, he looked over the congregation and smiled at the whisperings his splendor elicited. Kakara's grandmother, seated just outside the house, coughed deeply, and without breaking his step, the Prophet turned and looked kindly upon her. Temporarily, she regained her composure but lapsed again as the Prophet took his final step. The man turned and stood before the crowd while a thin shaft of light struck his rhinestone brooch and carried the flash to Wandisa's hidden eyes.

He paused for a moment, demanding the respect of his position. To his left sat Katere, and beside him, his wife.

"I am here," began the Prophet, speaking in a moderate voice, "because there are problems. Some around here are envious; some are jealous; some of you withhold friendship. And because of these actions, people are suffering. I think of one man among you who has been wronged. I think of those who have wronged him. I think of the *omiti* used by those jealous of him, *omiti* that has brought him much affliction."

The crowd was silent, all attention riveted on the Prophet. Katere's head was almost motionless, yet his gaze moved quickly around the crowd, straining to discern facial expressions.

"Today," the Prophet continued, "at this very moment, we must do something. We must resolve this problem."

His words ceased, and the Prophet waited as if expecting a confession. Yet, his words were so veiled that the audience also waited, expecting him to speak more plainly.

Finally, Repuree called out, "I say, if you have something to tell us then tell us, for I don't understand the meaning of your words."

A general murmur of agreement wound through the crowd, and for an instant the Prophet appeared to lose his confidence. His glance fell momentarily upon Katere as he took a deep breath.

"The problem," he replied, "is that many of you have set your hearts against Katere. And at least one of you is using *omiti* to hurt him. This must end."

Again there was silence, but this time people began looking at one another.

Wandisa straightened his back and removed his glasses. Looking directly at Katere he asked, "Do you, Katere, do you truly feel someone here wishes to harm you? Do you truly believe someone here is using *omiti* against you?"

All eyes shifted toward the soft figure. A long moment passed before Katere opened his mouth. "I say," he began, "for a long time I've known that some of you are unhappy that I'll be inheriting my uncle's estate. It's clear to me that some of you would prefer that I not inherit his cattle." He lowered his head.

"I say," responded Wandisa, "is this all? You think someone hates you and wants to kill you simply because one day my father's cattle will make you a wealthy man? Is that what you're thinking, Katere?" Wandisa shook his head. "Ay, ay, ay, ay," he muttered. And then, looking over the congregation, he queried, "And am I that man? Tell me Katere, am I that man?" Wandisa shifted his stance. "When my father goes into his grave, his matrilineal cattle will go to you and his ancestral cattle will go to Katwerwa. This is our law and all of us know it. And I fully agree with our law."

Wandisa quickly reset his glasses, tipped his beret, and left the gathering without acknowledging the Prophet. His departure led to a surfeit of chatter as disbelieving men and women turned to one another. One by one, nearly half of the men slipped away from the meeting. Katere remained on the ground, observing the result of his words. At last, the Prophet took charge.

"This is no way to solve a problem," he said. "We must use the power of God and be truthful in our words." He paused slightly, lifting his chin. "I think I must speak with each of you if I'm to make things right." He looked over his congregation. "You there," he said, pointing to Katanga, "come over here and sit by me—it will be good for us to talk."

One of the Prophet's men unfolded his chair and placed it in the shade. Katanga crouched on the ground near the man's feet.

"Who are you to Katere?" he asked.

"I," replied Katanga, "I'm the daughter of his eldest sister." And looking into the sunlight she added, "Who are you to my uncle?"

The Prophet ignored her mild impertinence. "Do you find him a good man? Is he worthy of respect?"

Surprised by the unusual directness of his question, Katanga's eyes widened. "My mother's brother is kind to me and has given me one of his milk cows to use," she answered.

"Yes," acknowledged the Prophet, "yes." He turned his head slightly to the crowd. "I say," he asked, "have you lived here long?"

Katanga clenched her hands and began straightening her fingers one at a time. "Nine years, I think," she replied.

"And do you know the people living in these homesteads?"

"Some I know well, others I don't."

"Are there people here who've had a disagreement with your uncle?"

"Which uncle?" asked Katanga. "I have several uncles living here."

"With Katere," said the Prophet. "Do you know of anyone who's had a disagreement with Katere?"

"Women don't get involved with the disputes of men," she answered. "We have other things to do."

The Prophet continued, following several lines of inquiry, but they ended in frustration. Most of the afternoon was spent in fruitless discussion, though Katere seemed pleased with the content of the interviews— seeing in them a general confirmation of his amiable nature. As the day had passed without a meal, the Prophet's entourage had lost its pleasant exterior. He dismissed them to wash and prepare themselves for supper. And walking with Katere through the groves to an abandoned homestead, the Prophet entered a house to consult with him privately.

Baskets of porridge and steaming goat meat were served to the guests. Katere and his family, along with the Prophet and his flock, ate peacefully, quietly against the backdrop of a waxing moon. The meal was savored with a hint of reserve; absent were the greed and haste of the previous evening. Wakamburwa prepared coffee and sweetened it heavily.

In the morning, after the animals had been taken to pasture, Wandisa came to offer the Prophet several liters of petrol. As the two of them fed the hollow tank, the entourage swiftly loaded the car. Afterward, Katere invited the troupe to his wife's work shelter where four pails of soured milk were easily drained. The Prophet entered his sedan and turned the key. The sound of the engine drew a few spectators, as did the efforts of his men to secure two reluctant ewes among the baggage in the trunk. The hapless creatures were never entirely subdued, but their captors restrained them amid the many belongings. The doors opened and closed, and the Prophet, motioning for Katere, offered a final word of advice. Dust rose from the riverbed and meadow as the roaring sedan moved slowly toward the tracks.

Ngipore stood beside Kuwiya on the riverbank and carefully looked over both shoulders. "My heart is sad for your uncle," he said. "His only wish is to be a *muhona*, but he doesn't understand what that means." Discreetly, Ngipore gestured to Kuwiya as Katere walked through the settling dust toward his home. Around his wrist and about his neck were new protective charms. And though he had sought to tarnish their luster, no amount of *otjize* could disguise their freshness.

9

To Ripen and Dry

... is the natural course of maize, indeed, of all grains—to have their color, texture, and flavor set once and for all. It also seems true of human beings. Francisco lives among the Himba but is not one of them and has no desire to be. A continuing series of stock thefts calls for reflection on the source of human character. And, once again, Katere publicly spreads his character as though a vividly patterned fan, while Daniel prefers a patch of solitude in which to display his truer self.

The maize gardens were still on a windless, cloudless, colorless morning. The large, ravenous beetles that habitually rubbed their spindly legs together as they climbed the stalks in search of food had found some other home. Many weeks had passed without rain and the garden soil was turning to dust. Inside garden fences, maize was hardening and the stalks rapidly losing their fresh appearance. Yet beyond the gardens, many pastures were lush and green from the heavy rains that had fallen so late in the season; nearby grazing would be abundant for several more weeks. Fountains and wells were full of water, good pasture was still available, and the harvest would be sufficient: it was as much as one could ask of Mukuru.

For several weeks, the ripening maize had been left in peace while women and children scoured the countryside gathering fruits, nuts, herbs, and wild vegetables. Some were used immediately to compliment the unending round of maize porridge, while others were dried and stored for the coming season. Many times the earth had been dug around nests of flying ants and the delicate, fist-sized pouches of subterranean honey cautiously extracted. Each cache of the sweet, delicious liquid was shared among many. But the season of bounties was drawing to a close; the season of cold, the time of increasing want was eager to begin.

Sand finally gave way to rocks and dust on the path that led to Francisco's homestead. He and his wife, Wombinda, had lived most of their lives in this valley; their children knew no other home. Yet, among the Himba they were foreigners—people who maintained their own customs and identity. And like most of the other Hakavona living in Kaokoland, they had fled Angola hoping to find a more secure life among the Himba. As we emerged from a dense woodland, the cluster of three Hakavona homesteads came into view. Francisco lived in the farthest one. Wombinda greeted us as we entered through the gate and motioned for us to sit beneath a tree at the edge of her home. Her house stood at the end of a neatly arranged arc of homes, each twelve or thirteen paces in diameter. The roofs were heavily thatched and peaked in the middle, though exterior walls were shabbily plastered. The small entry doors were thick and heavy, made of one or two timbers suspended from a dowel inserted widthwise through long holes laboriously drilled through the timbers by burning and scraping.

The homestead was quiet except for several women chatting lazily in the afternoon heat. Their colorful skirts, their long, dark hair, their beaded jewelry, and the rich blackness of their skin impressed us with their difference from the Himba's costume. A handful of gray and black chickens pecked and clucked around the houses, occasionally stirring dust with their scratching. Just beyond the farthest house, Elspeth noticed three children playing with sticks and maize cobs, and ran to join them. A while later, from another direction, came Francisco, his hands shading his face from the sun.

"Oho," he called, "look who's finally come to visit!"

Francisco was a jovial man. His balding head, with traces of white hair, rested above a short but sturdy frame. His hands and fingers were thick and strong, and his voice firm and deep. Both the Himba and Hakavona communities regarded him highly, and though he had no true jurisdiction over the Hakavona, those living around Otutati looked to him for counsel and advice when difficulties arose. His ancestral home, a home he had

not seen since his youth, was a village set beside a stream five days' walk
north of the Kunene River. The journey that had taken Francisco from
his boyhood village to central Kaokoland was a strange one, a difficult
one.

"I came to Otutati as a youth," he said, "and found it was a good place.
I've grown old here in Kaokoland, near Wamesepa, but I've missed my
family, especially my mother. My father died before I left home and I long
to see his grave again.

"In the days of my boyhood, Angola was a good place to live, a happy
place, and I wouldn't have left except for the Portuguese. As a child, I
met a few of them as they traveled around, but it wasn't until my early
youth that they came to live among us. My father was an important man
with many wives and cattle and people who called him 'father.' But to
the Portuguese, he was no one. In time, a Portuguese farmer settled in
our area and began working on a house. 'Now, who is this man,' asked
my father, 'that he comes to our land and builds a house on it without
greeting us and announcing his intentions that we might decide
whether or not it is permissible? I say, who is this man?' Later, the
farmer's wife arrived with their servants and possessions; and after she
had settled they came to see my father. The Portuguese man spoke to
him through his servant, asking for a great number of men to help
build his farm. 'But where is this farm of yours?' replied my father. 'I
see nothing here that belongs to you!' The man then told him that our
land was his land now, and that we were required to work for him. My
father was angry and responded harshly. 'Who are you,' he asked, 'with
your dark hair and red skin; where do you come from? Who are you,
and what is this animal next to you whose breasts must never show?
Who are you that you may steal our land and then tell us we must work
for you? Who are you that you can do such a thing?' This, you see, was
our problem. The Portuguese farmer wanted our land—he said it belonged to him, but we couldn't understood how this was possible. We
hadn't given him permission to settle here; and if we hadn't, who else
possibly could have?

"Some time later the farmer returned and told my father if we worked
for him, there would be a place for us on his land. This time my father
was more cautious and told the man it was well. Still, though, he couldn't

understand what this meant. He sent all of the boys and youth of our village to every homestead within two days' walk to ask the men to gather at my father's homestead and discuss the matter. I still remember hearing the men talk back and forth, but I was young then and had little interest in their discussions. Later, though, I learned why my father had called the meeting. There were rumors that Portuguese had gone into other areas, and if laborers had not been provided, the police simply rounded up young men and led them away. My father thought it best to collectively decide the prudent way forward. The men of the area were nervous about the Portuguese, yet they concluded it was better to provide a few laborers than to risk a confrontation with the police. My friends began tending the farmer's cattle and working at other chores around his house. When I was old enough, I also took my turn. A few years passed, and then, before I reached marriageable age, my father died. His death was a bad death, for he died young—without any white hairs.

"I don't know why, but I seemed to work more and more for the Portuguese. Even though the farmer had little regard for us, I found him a fair and reasonable man. His wife, on the other hand, was insufferable; no one could tolerate her. Madam was an angry woman and would sometimes take her whip and strike us. When I think about it now, I don't understand why we stayed there and bore her punishment. Were we stupid? Why did we allow this woman to beat us without protest? It was a strange time. We were afraid to say anything, afraid we might get hurt, perhaps killed. The truth is we didn't actually know what would happen to us, and not knowing allowed our minds to play with terrible thoughts. During this time I decided to leave my ancestral home. To crawl about in fear is no way for a man to live. All around us were Hakavona, Zimba, and Ngambwe—even a few Himba—but these two Portuguese were more powerful than all of us standing together. Only they could force us to do things entirely against our will.

"Though I'd decided to leave, I didn't have a plan—it was really more of a wish than anything else. The seasons changed but the rains didn't come, and most of the farmer's cattle were taken to a fountain far away from his house where they could drink. About eight of us were left behind to help Madam while the others went with the cattle. One day, Madam approached us with her servant, an Ngambwe man who no longer knew his people. He helped Madam down the steps of her house, as she had become very fat, and left her standing under a tree. The sun was hot and we sat resting in the shade, waiting for the next command. 'You children over there,' he called. 'You children must come now and help Madam.' Sitting with us was a man very much older than I. He turned his head and asked, 'My son, there are no children here. Whom are you addressing?' Very skillfully the older man abused the Ngambwe servant with his words until the request was respectfully made. We rose and walked with him to the house where Madam's shay was kept. 'Madam wants to go to town,' said the Ngambwe. We stared at him and asked, 'How will Madam's shay be pulled when all of the oxen are gone?' With great contempt he turned and answered, 'Madam says to let you pull it.'

" 'How can we pull such a thing?' I thought to myself. But the servant was clever and positioned us in front of the shay. He wrapped long, leather straps around our chests and under our arms and had us draw the shay out of the house and over to Madam. It wasn't too bad until Madam climbed in. Her weight made us stumble a bit, but we found our balance. While she spoke to the servant, we stood looking toward the path—wondering, I think, how we could possibly do this. I heard a sudden crackle and felt my back sting. I turned—Madam was whipping us as if we were dumb animals. Immediately, all of us pulled forward, but we weren't oxen trained to draw wagons. I can't tell you how hard it was. As Madam sat there under a shade, we pulled and pulled and pulled. We had walked quite far, but since we'd had nothing to eat that day, we were weak from hunger. Slower and slower we walked until we couldn't pull anymore. Madam began shrieking at us, and again I felt her whip against my back. I was in front, in the lead, and I turned around and saw the whip coming at me again. I reached out and caught the end of the whip, and though it cut my hand, I pulled it from hers and threw it to the ground.

" 'I won't do this anymore,' I said to the others. 'I'm a man, not an ox.' I found the end of the strap that held me in place and loosened it. The others also untied themselves, and we left. I went back to my mother and uncle and told them what had happened. My uncle counseled me to leave. 'Visit your father's grave,' he said, 'and then go where there are no red people.' And that is how I came to Otutati."

Several times Francisco had invited us to see his garden that he might show us differences between Himba and Hakavona horticulture. As he and

Wombinda led us toward the southern flood plain, where most of their gardens lay, the two of them talked ceaselessly about the condition of leaves, plants, grasses, open fields, and soils before turning, more quietly, to a discussion of Wombinda's patients—for she was a practitioner of certain healing arts. The path narrowed considerably as it wound through a forest of scrub greasewood and ironwood trees. The singing and twittering birds resented our intrusion and hopped nervously from branch to branch in the dense canopy of their diminutive wood. The path began to widen and a dusty clearing became visible; beyond it stood the high wooden fences protecting the Hakavona's gardens.

Francisco pulled aside a number of heavy poles leaning upright against a brace and entered the garden, standing on a small plot of uncultivated ground. Wombinda stood aside and motioned for me to enter. A moment later, she and Michelle passed through the gate and walked along the westerly fence, leaving the two of us in the dusty forecourt. The large field seemed quite similar to Himba gardens as plants grew in clusters rather than rows. But unlike the casual dispersal of lesser crops among the clumps of maize, neatly defined beds of melons, pumpkins, and gourds lay at the edges of Francisco's garden.

"You can see," began Francisco, looking about the field, "that we are not Himba—we have no wish to be." He turned heavily toward the maize. "Himba food is for Himba," he said. "Hakavona food is for Hakavona."

Francisco moved through the towering stalks—a seeming endless stretch of drying maize. But ten paces into the field, the yellowing stalks disappeared; before us lay an expanse of copper-headed millet.

"This is what I wished you to see," said Francisco. "This is what we eat." He brought a curled finger to his mouth and whistled sharply to frighten away several blackbirds preying on the grain. "Himba eat maize, maize, maize. We also like maize, but for us it isn't a real food—it doesn't pleasure the belly like millet. If one cannot have meat and milk every day, then one must have millet!"

Francisco bent forward and laid a shaft in his hand.

"See how small and delicate the grains are? Its flavor is also delicate; but those who eat maize, maize, maize cannot taste that delicate flavor."

We walked through clusters and clusters of millet until we reached the fence.

"We've only begun to grow this again," he said, "but I think we'll be successful."

Francisco was pleased with the results of his planting—a garden filled with the grain of his childhood and youth.

"Will this flavor make you more Hakavona than you are now?"

Francisco laughed. "No," he replied, "it's not as easy as that." He ambled slowly along the fence, straining his mellow eyes at the crowns of seed on each plant. "It's not the flavor," he said, "that makes millet a Hakavona food. Hakavona make it a Hakavona food." Francisco stopped and peered through the fence. His expression became quite earnest and he lifted his right hand and forefinger. "A Himba man can eat millet porridge and say, 'This is nothing—it tastes like nothing!' And then ask, 'Why do you eat porridge that tastes like nothing?' But to him it tastes like 'nothing' because his mouth is crude, he doesn't understand the delicacy of flavor. The same man will drink millet beer and say, 'This is no beer—it tastes like water!' Why? Because he knows only what is strong, not what is delicate. I drink maize beer and enjoy its strong flavor, but I also know the delicate taste of millet beer and prize it for its mild flavor."

Francisco paused and looked across the field.

"Do you understand my words?" he asked. "Hakavona are not Himba, but it's not simply a matter of food. We may distinguish different flavors and prefer the delicate over the strong, but we're different from Himba because we see things and understand things in ways that Himba do not."

His lips tapered into momentary stillness.

"I say," he continued, pulling his body straight. "My thoughts are clearer than my words."

Michelle and Wombinda joined us and we visited two adjacent gardens. Each of them was a sea of maize with pumpkins, gourds, and melons growing randomly among the clusters of stalks. Our way home was slow, yet when we reached the homestead Elspeth said she had hardly known we were gone. In parting, Francisco asked us to convey his greetings through Wandisa to Wamesepa; then we left the circle of houses and found the homeward path.

Katwerwa walked through one of his wives' gardens, pausing now and again to open an ear of maize and test the hardness of its kernels. A light breeze gently shifted the drying stalks from side to side and whispered among the rustling leaves. The muffled sound of human voices drifted into the garden, and as Katwerwa became conscious of it, he changed his course and followed the trail of sounds. Through other gardens he passed until spotting a group of people sitting casually beneath a tree. Watumba's back rested against its trunk, and her infant son slept in the cradle of her thighs. Katanga sat nearby, as did the wives of Vita and Masutwa, and the four of them chatted as they prepared a meal of porridge. The men sat at the edge of the shade. Katwerwa entered the garden and Daniel was the first to turn and acknowledge his greetings.

The morning had brought important news to Otutati. Several travelers heading northward to Etengwa announced that police in Opuwo had rounded up a number of stolen cattle and were holding them for their rightful owners to claim.

"Yes," answered Katwerwa, joining the conversation. "I heard from a friend that two of my beasts are there—though not in the hands of the police. A boy was driving a few head of cattle toward the auction hall when my friend noticed several of their ear cuts were precisely like mine. He told the boy to stop. 'Whose cattle are these?' he asked. 'And where do they come from?' 'They belong to my uncle,' replied the boy, 'who lives near Kaoko Otavi.' My friend stopped the two beasts for a moment and examined them closely before letting them go. When he reached me last night he said, 'The cattle are yours. I know they're yours.' So early this morning, Dakata left for Opuwo. Tomorrow, I'll bring them home."

His words provoked a moment of quiet, for it was a serious matter.

"Ah, I see," murmered Repuree, stretching backward. "But there's something I don't understand: How are these cattle stolen? I see no strangers among us, so how do our cattle end up being driven to the auction hall by children from Kaoko Otavi?"

"I say," answered Masutwa, "I don't think stealing cattle is difficult since most of the day they graze in the bush tended only by our sons. Suppose I find a beast I want to steal. Quietly, I lead it away from the others, perhaps guiding it along the foot of the mountains where no one will see me. At night, I hobble its hind legs so it can't roam far, and early the next morning, before the sun rises, I drive it to Opuwo.

"If we notice a beast is missing," he continued, "we assume it has strayed and go in search of it. Even if we don't find it straightway, it doesn't occur to us that it's been stolen. It's simply missing. So we alert our neighbors, but by then the animal could easily be on its way to Vamboland or a white farm."

"Oho," said Kavetonwa. "Now we know who's masterminding these thefts!"

The men laughed, and then turned slightly to hear another voice.

"It isn't possible," stated Watumba, speaking softly lest her baby wake, "that a man living here would steal from his neighbors or kinsmen, is it?"

"I say," replied Repuree. "Perhaps your husband was away, but not too long ago a youth from Otutati confessed to stealing a goat."

"Yes, yes," said Vita, "but there's a difference between a teenage prank and outright cattle theft."

"Do you think so?" questioned Repuree, his eyes following the movement of children in the garden. "What precisely is that difference?"

Vita lowered his head for a moment to consider his response. But scarcely had he done so when Kavetonwa lifted his voice.

"I say," replied the old man, "the two thefts are very different. The boys stole a small goat—not a large, beautiful animal—and ate it themselves because they were hungry for meat. The man who stole Katwerwa's cattle didn't steal them because he was hungry; he stole them because he knew he could sell them in Opuwo. The boys who took the goat were hungry and stupid. The man stealing Katwerwa's cattle is neither; he is clever, but a cleverness that comes from a bad heart. I doubt the boys pondered the consequences of their theft, but a man can't steal so many cattle without knowing he's jeopardizing another man's livelihood. And this is the difference between the two thefts: the boys were merely stupid, but this man is malicious."

Kavetonwa glanced over the company, noting the bowed heads of the men, and further in the shade, the women struggling to pull a heavily laden kettle from the fire.

"*Tate* [father] has spoken my thoughts," said Vita quietly. "Even though one misdeed may appear like another, appearance doesn't tell whether the cause is stupidity or a bad heart."

The porridge was announced.

Kavetonwa rose to his feet and smoothed his skirts. "I must be off," he said. "I told my wife I'd meet her in our garden." Steadying himself with his walking stick and raising his free hand to shield his eyes, he leaned toward Vita. "It doesn't surprise me," he lamented, "but it saddens an old man's heart that so many of our children learn to love wealth more than people."

Slowly, his ancient legs carried him down the garden and through a break in the fence and his tall, lanky frame disappeared from view.

Porridge was turned into serving baskets and the children summoned from their play. The generosity of food seemed to lighten the somber mood as hands, small and large, dipped thick, steaming fragments into a buttery sauce and conveyed them to hungry mouths.

Katwerwa returned with his cattle. Vita had also walked to Opuwo and found two of his missing heifers; by now the other one was likely grazing in a very distant pasture. The thief or thieves evaded capture by hiring local boys in Opuwo to drive the cattle from their lairs on the outskirts of town to a point where the new owners took possession of them. Rumors that the thief was well acquainted with the households of Otutati and the residents' grazing practices were no longer dismissed. Yet it was difficult to believe anyone from Otutati was involved in cattle theft. Cattle sometimes die unexpectedly—either from natural causes or, more rarely, mystical attack. If a healthy beast is found dead, a diviner can discover the malicious person responsible and offer protection against further misfortune. A thief, however, remains invisible; no diviner can uncover his identity. Yet over time a bad heart always reveals itself.

To be afflicted with a bad heart is a terrible thing, for a bad heart is a selfish heart, a malicious heart, a sorrowful heart. We teach our children to love and respect other people, and even though we cannot always love at first, we can show respect. Perfunctory respect leads to genuine respect, and genuine respect becomes love, whether moderate or strong. Children learn respect from their parents. If their parents shun abusive language, children will learn to speak respectfully. If parents are not miserly but prudently give their children gifts of livestock and apparel, children will learn regard for those who give and those who receive. If parents restrain their anger, children will sense their respect. Children honor their parents if they are good stewards, caring for flocks and herds, their own possessions, and the possessions of others. Children respect their parents if they are truthful, if they are compliant. To learn respect and love is a long, difficult labor. Easily acquired, though, are their opposites, carelessness and jealousy—spirits that dwell wherever welcomed. Being a child is not simple. But being a parent is more wearisome still, especially when a child is afflicted with a bad heart. A child may pretend for a time, but as a child grows, the pretender's heart reveals itself, for a pretender never truly loves, never truly respects. And despite all of a parent's concerns and efforts, a pretender's heart remains selfish and deceitful. Such a child brings a heaviness to his parents' hearts, a grief that never lifts.

The maize was nearly ready to harvest. Around Otutati, grain storage bins were being dusted and repaired in preparation for the days of tedious work to follow. It was not the actual picking, but the hauling, shucking, and storing that required so much effort. It was, however, a familiar labor, one that required every able set of hands.

Ngipore had taken some pride in the success of his planting, but now that harvest time was upon him, he dismayed at the thought of having no wife to share the burden. His son and daughter would help, but they were still children. His nephew, he decided, would assist him best by tending the flocks and keeping a safe distance from Otutati. The relationship between them had been difficult for some time, and Ngipore faced the dilemma of all Himba men: a divided loyalty, a divided love, a divided obligation. For upon his death, Ngipore's nephew—the youth who threw stones at his uncle when angry—would inherit the greatest portion of Ngipore's cattle. This was not only expected, but morally correct as secular wealth is transferred matrilineally, from a mother's brother to his sister's son. The obligation of a man to enrich his sister's child while bestowing comparatively little upon his own is thought good and proper—though actually doing so can be trying. A man's own sons receive his ancestral cattle and the honor of supplicating their father for blessings and assistance as an ancestor, though for many fathers this is not enough.

Despite the looming maelstrom of work and the shortage of laborers, Ngipore was greatly relieved with his abundant crop. The anticipated yield, however, was the source of a further problem. The harvested ears of maize would have to be sun-dried for an additional number of days or weeks prior to shucking, and the roof of his only work shelter was simply not broad enough to accommodate the full crop. Another shelter would have to be built and Ngipore engaged a Zimba man to do the heaviest work. The gray haired man spent two days felling nine large timbers and a host of other beams and poles, and another day hauling the lumber to the homestead. Each of the nine timbers was taller than a grown man's up-permost reach, and in thickness, slighter than a man's thigh. At the top of each timber was a natural joint so that a beam might rest securely in its fanned cradle. On the following day, the timbers were set upright in holes nearly an arm's length deep. Three parallel rows of three timbers each stood in the dusty ground. The rows were spaced about four paces apart, so that a roof of four paces width and ten paces breadth could be laid. Heavy beams were placed along the joints and lashed to the timbers with thin strips of ironwood bark. Long, narrow poles were laid widthwise and lengthwise across the sturdy frame and patiently lashed together to form a dense latticework.

Ngipore stood with the Zimba man admiring the quality of workman-ship as the late afternoon sun warmed his back. The man was finished, waiting for his wages. During their brief conversation, Ngipore hospitably asked him to stay and share an evening meal, but the man politely de-clined, saying his wife and children would be looking for him. Pleased that his work was so well received, the man accepted his payment—three large but wary goats—and began driving them eastward toward his home. The new charges balked at the stranger and ran from him, but he gathered the wayward animals, and with his rope and stick, brought them under control.

Plastering the flat roof was the sole remaining task—a labor reserved for women. Wandjoze intentionally stayed near the homestead after their midday meal knowing if the man finished in time her father wished the plastering to be done before nightfall. Occasionally she strayed to nearby gardens and homesteads, but as the last poles and reeds of the latticework were tied in place, she and Rikuta scavenged nearby cattle enclosures for fresh dung, carrying basket after basket to the work site. Both maidens had plastered before and knew so large a roof would consume skins and skins of plaster. The shadows of late afternoon grew as Wandjoze and Rikuta finished collecting their supplies. Rikuta had drawn water and car-ried it to the homestead. Now she lay resting as Wandjoze gathered several baskets and a leather pail and hastily departed. From home to home she went, sweeping clean their hearths and filling her containers with the pow-dery ash needed to produce a fine, watertight plaster. As she returned, Rikuta was emptying the last of eight baskets of dung into a slight de-pression near the shelter; carefully, she dusted it with a pail of sand. Wand-joze added a basket of ash and a large tin of water, removed her sandals, and stepped into the depression to mix the plaster. Her heavy, plodding footsteps eventually broke the distinct colors of dung, sand, and ash, turning them into a tawny stew.

Ngipore took a handful of plaster and ran his fingers through it, examining its consistency. More sand was needed, and while Wandjoze mixed in another basketful, he spread an old goat skin on the ground beside her. Rikuta followed Wandjoze up a spare timber and onto the latticework. Together with his son and one of Mukuva's daughters, Ngipore drew the corners of the goatskin upward while another maiden filled it with plaster. All four of them raised the loaded skin, placing its corners within easy reach of Rikuta and Wandjoze. The skin was emptied and passed downward. Soon, four heavy loads of plaster were being pressed among the poles and reeds of the latticework. Below, Mukuva's daughter quickly mixed another batch and the effort began anew. Load after load was smoothed into the crevices, and after a workable area had been filled, a final layer of plaster was laid on top and another section begun. A few men gathered round to watch the progress and offer unwanted advice while admiring the plasterers' speed. Section by section the empty framework was filled, and as Wandjoze stood on the spare timber, plastering the final corner, her hands felt what her eyes could not see, for twilight had settled and the whole world lay in shadow. "It looks very nice," said her father as Wandjoze stepped from the timber. Ngipore stood quietly, straining to follow the contours of the plaster, while his daughter wiped her ankles and feet on the goatskin. A few days of sunlight and the roof would be ready to hold its load of maize.

The bustle of the season had come, and once Masutwa, Vita, and Katwerwa declared their crops ready to harvest, others followed suit. Within a few days the rush to pick the maize, bear the crop home, remove the outer casings, and spread the ears to dry, had swept through Otutati. The morning cool had lifted and the sun shone brightly through the still air. Wandisa and Katere stood in their adjoining gardens, separated by a heavy, wooden fence. Wandisa's wife moved among the clusters of plants, swiftly pulling maize from the stalk while overseeing the efforts of her younger daughters. The ears were taken to Wandisa who loaded them in large baskets and pails, or bound them tightly in blankets. The loaded vessels were strapped to the back of a donkey which the eldest daughter led home. It was a tiresome and monotonous round, especially as the donkey could not keep pace with the harvesters.

Katere's lips pursed as he surveyed the tall-standing plants. His gaze was soft and easy until he turned and peered over the fence. In the distance, he saw his wife walking toward the garden. Through motionless plants, Katere trod a path leading to the opposite side and passed from the field, hesitating a moment before turning homeward.

Katere had engaged Solomon to haul the maize from his garden to the work shelters by sledge. As the two had known each other for many years, Solomon was very explicit about the terms of their agreement, asking Mukuva to witness the covenant. He arrived midmorning at Katere's garden and tethered his donkeys to a thorny branch. His eyes fell over the careworn sledge and the new bark lashings that should keep its rear from dragging. A moment later, he entered the garden and saw Wakamburwa standing in the far corner. She turned at his footfall, but waited for him to approach.

"This is where you're to begin," she said, after greeting him. "I want all the maize in this corner picked and brought to the work shelters. Once this is done you're to harvest along the fence and up to the next corner."

Wakamburwa paused, waiting for acknowledgment. Her pungent words were perfectly understood, but Solomon continued looking about the garden before answering.

"I see your crop is ready to be harvested," he replied, taking care to avert his gaze. "But I was hired to transport your maize, not to pick it. You bring it to my sledge and I'll gladly haul it to your work shelter."

Solomon turned away meekly and left the garden. Wakamburwa raised her incredulous eyes as the slight figure walked to his sledge. Rarely were her commands rebuked, and never in this manner. Her composure suffered and her lips set tightly against each other and her long, delicate brow sharpened. A moment later her sandaled feet bore her swiftly through the garden, across the riverbed, and up the embankment toward home. Katere stood beside their house, noting his wife's hasty advance.

Wakamburwa's voice pealed with acidity as Katere acknowledged the details of his agreement with Solomon. His earlier assurances were false. Solomon was only engaged to convey the maize from garden to homestead; the picking, husking, and drying remained her tasks. The sharpness of his wife's words soared and drew attention from those loitering in the homestead, yet Katere leaned on his stick looking westward, not daring to restrain Wakamburwa until she was finished. When her words ceased, the woman was breathless and panting, her brow glistening with perspiration; all around her was silence.

"Wife," said Katere at last, "go to the field and begin picking. I'll find the girls and then come to help."

Wakamburwa stood a few moments, allowing her body to cool.

"Yes," she replied acrimoniously, "I'll go and begin. But you must be there to help, not just our daughters!"

"It is agreed then," nodded Katere.

Wakamburwa turned. A turbulence settled round her as she began walking to the garden, mumbling unsavory oaths against her husband. Katere also turned and gathered his three older daughters. Scarcely had the first basket of maize been filled when the daughters arrived, fully aware of the circumstances, and began a silent work. Katere entered the garden and walked to an opposite corner. He picked and filled his basket; and though he was upsetting the order in her garden, Wakamburwa only glared from a distance, too angry to correct him. The five harvesters slowly filled Solomon's sledge. And when the first load was ready, Katere walked beside the donkeys as they pulled the assemblage of maize across a dusty pasture, through the riverbed, and along the path leading to the homestead. Katere's eyes moved rapidly across distant images. Unexpectedly, he marched ahead and spoke to a young man, a nephew, and pressed him into offloading the maize. Solomon sat in the shade watching Katere and the young man empty the sledge; when they were finished, he returned to the garden with a message for Wakamburwa: Katere had strained his weak back and he would have to rest. Wakamburwa's fury grew all the more intense. But by midafternoon, Katere's back had somewhat recovered and he helped load the sledge four more times.

The afternoon sun was high, but a light breeze swept down the northerly hills, tempering its warmth. We passed a small homestead belonging to a young man and his family. He was tall, handsome, strong, and able-bodied, yet he had no livestock and his family lived in poverty. They were *tjimba*

(aardvarks), people who scratched in the dirt for a living, eating nothing but maize and wild foods—a deeply humiliating condition.

Their homestead consisted of a mud hut, a work shelter, and several raised grain silos; their nearly two years of residence in Otutati had passed in unusual isolation. The *tjimba* knew their neighbors by sight and name and greeted wayfarers politely, but never did they share meals or attend local festivities and gatherings. Instead, the *tjimba* kept mostly to themselves. Vita, who knew them better than anyone, was baffled by their loneliness and pitiful livelihood. "I don't understand how a man can be satisfied with nothing but porridge, day after day. Just look at him—he's twice my size, yet he does nothing, he has nothing, he is nothing. He has no animals, though he could easily go to Wamesepa and ask him for the loan of a cow or two and begin a herd. But he prefers to sit and do nothing." Vita's opinion was shared by the men of the area. The *tjimbas'* poverty lay not in lack of opportunity but in the lack of livestock and ambition. Feelings quietly voiced against them from time to time echoed the bewilderment of men who saw a fellow of theirs passively accepting a state of affairs that could so easily be remedied.

We continued along the path through a shady woodland toward Vita's homestead. The houses and shelters were still and deserted except for the presence of Daniel, who sat beside a modest cooking fire tending a kettle of simmering meat. As we approached, he lifted his head and peered through the shadows to see who was encroaching upon his solitude. He greeted us kindly, and we returned his salutations.

"Yes," he replied, "yes, I am well."

Then he gestured to the growing hillocks of maize atop the work shelters. "The others are working in the gardens. But as you can see, they've left me behind to prepare this meal." His eyes drew our attention to the three-legged pot.

"Are you expecting guests?" asked Michelle.

"No, Mikila. I've already had a guest—last night Muwandjesa visited me. And now I must feed him."

Muwandjesa was a spirit that occasionally took possession of Daniel's mind and body. The two had been sometime companions for about seven years, first meeting as Daniel traveled in the far north of Kaokoland near the Kunene River. All morning he had walked on an empty stomach and by noon his limbs ached and the need for water pervaded his every thought. The unfamiliar countryside seemed strangely barren of humans and habitat as Daniel stood on an outcropping of rock, his eyes scouring the landscape for the merest hint of water. Growing on a stony hillside was an enormous baobab tree. Immediately, and with renewed strength, Daniel lifted his bundle and stick and headed for the tree, believing one of its numerous cavities would surely hold a bit of water. As Daniel approached, he was humbled by its greatness and walked around its mighty trunk searching for an avenue to its top. He paused on the northern side and found, carved in its trunk, a series of shallow, recessed steps leading to its upper heights. Though he knew the ascent would be laborious, his thirst overshadowed his fears and he laid his things at the base of the tree and took his first climbing steps. His feet, legs, arms, and hands reluctantly conveyed him upward, and as he scaled the massive trunk, a recognition of the bodily strength needed to reach the pockets where water might be found weakened his resolve. He took a few steps and rested, and then took a few more. Half the tree's considerable height had been covered when his muscles rebelled; Daniel's feet and hands quickly lost their grip and his body slipped from the trunk and fell to the ground.

He was dead; Daniel was dead. His body lay in the warm soil, his tongue covered with dust. He saw nothing—not even darkness—as the sun crossed the highest point in the sky. Mysteriously though, Daniel began feeling the weight of his hands and feet; slowly, his eyes opened—like those of a newborn baby—and he rolled onto his back. He could feel his eyes darting around, looking at things, yet his mind was unable to recognize the images that passed before his eyes. Then, all of a sudden, awareness returned and Daniel looked into the sky and knew the sky. His eyes caught the dwarfish branches of the tree that had claimed his life, and he knew them as branches. But just as suddenly, the sky and the branches blended and separated, joined and divided, and his picture of the world spun round and round. "It was like the early morning after a long night of heavy sleep—waking, sleeping, but then neither waking nor sleeping. Finally, I came awake as pain began creeping through my body, and when it reached my throat, I lost my breath and died again." Twice, Muwandjesa attempted to enter his body and restore his life, but this time the attempt met with less resistance and the spirit penetrated the renitent flesh. Several hours' walk from the site of the fall stood a small clinic operated by the South African army.

Eventually, he awoke and found himself lying in a hospital bed, not knowing where he was or how he had come there. Only later did he vaguely recollect how the spirit had entered his body and carried him thither without pain or exhaustion hampering the journey. "But as soon as I found myself in bed, Muwadjesa left me and terrible pain began filling my body."

Daniel recovered and traveled homeward. He shared the experience of his death and resuscitation with his most intimate friends, and two full seasons passed as the memory of Muwandjesa lingered in his mind. Daniel and Watumba had driven their livestock to a highland pasture that bordered on one used by Vita and his family. On a dark evening, when both moon and stars were reticent in sharing their light, Daniel sat on a flat stone, leaning against a post. The flickering, sputtering glow of a weary fire dimly illuminated the faces of Watumba, Vita, and Vita's wife as their conversations began to wane. Suddenly, Daniel's head fell to his chest, and then snapped furiously backward, knocking against the post. His entire body shuddered and his chin dropped against his neck. Daniel's face shifted toward the night sky, the brown of his eyes concealed by the surrounding whiteness as they strained ever upward. His countenance wavered but little as the others stared in wonder. A moment later, a burst of spirit renewed his being and a deep, rich voice—so unlike his own—speaking an Angolan tongue, announced itself as Muwandjesa, a friend of Daniel. "But now I'm hungry!" shrieked the spirit. "I'm hungry for meat!" Daniel's face lifted and his eyes reflected the fire's light. "Feed me!" cried Muwandjesa. "I am Daniel's life: He is good to me and I am good to him!" The spirit continued its petition until a beleaguered Watumba promised to fulfill its wishes.

Daniel's rigid body gradually loosened and slid to the ground. Moments later he awoke from his sleep and was told of the spirit's visitation and ardent request. His eyes widened as the three witnesses recounted the experience and imitated the voice of Muwandjesa. "Ah," replied Daniel, "so that's how he sounds." The following day, a large ram was slaughtered and cooked. But Muwandjesa was never satisfied for long.

"Yes," continued Daniel, "he came last night and told everyone he was hungry for meat. Today I was to help Watumba in the garden, but since Muwandjesa demanded to be fed, what else could I to do? So I've slaughtered a goat, and by the time they return it'll be ready to eat."

Daniel seemed anxious to regain his interrupted solitude. We left the homestead and walked north to Masutwa's gardens.

The harvest lasted nearly a fortnight. And as it was a labor-intensive work, everyone—aside from the aged, the infirm, the very young, and the inattentive—helped to drain the gardens of the maize that would keep them through the coming period of dryness. When people finished with their own gardens, their hands generously turned to others, and garden after garden was harvested and left open for grazing. When the maize arrived at the work shelters, the golden brown husks were torn from the ears and thrown to the ground. The ears were tossed upon the roof, first congregating in the middle, later spreading to the sides. Cobs tenaciously held kernels of red, purple, white, and yellow in every conceivable pattern and configuration. Day after day, the sun bore down upon the rooftops, drying the maize till the lustrous colors began to fade. Some turned their maize for more equitable drying, others began construction or enlargement of grain silos to hold the bounties of Mukuru's season. Inside the high wooden fences of the flood plain, the land stood lonely and forlorn; the once luxuriant gardens were lifeless, empty, stripped of their abundance. But the soil had earned its rest.

10

A Spirit Must Be Driven

... because it does not willingly leave its abode. When Dakata's new wife is unable to shake a recurring illness, Wombinda is called to diagnose and treat the young woman. A spirit familiar to Wombinda has invaded the woman's body; fortunately, Wombinda holds considerable sway over that spirit. Still, all of her powers must be fully mobilized to finally break the spirit's grip.

Wamesepa was the father of three sons, each born of a different wife. One of his sons lived in the north where he tended his father's cattle. Wandisa lived beside Wamesepa in Otutati; but the old patriarch's youngest son, Zorondu, was a journeyer, a wanderer, a lad who never stayed beyond his welcome. Zorondu was tall, lean, and jovial. His name meant "dark" or "black"—a simple recollection of the deep ebony color of his skin at birth. As a baby and toddler, Zorondu developed as all other children; in time, though, spirits entered his head and began restricting the workings of his mind. At first, Wamesepa believed his son's affliction was temporary, a malady to be outgrown, but as Zorondu passed through boyhood, the hope of recovery faded. Still, Wamesepa arranged a suitable marriage for him. The future bride and groom remained as strangers until the time of budding maturity. And when the families met to settle the wedding plans, the young bride insisted on meeting her groom. Their encounter was brief; for upon seeing Zorondu, the maiden fled, boisterously refusing the marriage and doubting her father's regard. Her refusal surprised no one, least of all Wamesepa; though he desired his youngest son to receive the care and comfort of a good wife, he also knew he would never allow a daughter of his to marry such a man.

Zorondu had returned to Otutati during the harvest and laid his belongings in a shabby hut to the left of his father's house. His hair had grown thin and gray, and his eyes were often filmy. About his neck lay the heavily beaded choker of a youth, for his mental condition prevented him from advancing socially into adulthood. As he walked from house to house and homestead to homestead in search of people to visit, he amused himself by telling lengthy stories, repeatedly laughing at his own narrative. Sometimes his words could be understood, often they belonged to a realm no one else could enter. Zorondu was harmless and gentle; he was free and well received. Older women occasionally put him to work churning butter, fetching water, or building a fire, but his concentration easily lapsed and he rarely completed a task. His enfeebled mind remained a mystery—something only Mukuru could explain.

After their wedding, Penguka returned home with her escort and bridesmaids to gather all of her intimate and domestic possessions and bring them to the new house Dakata had built for her in his father's homestead. The seasons had changed since Penguka had approached Dakata's ancestral fire and their life together was one of contentment. Yapura welcomed her husband's second wife as cordially as anyone in her position could. And though both were passing through an awkwardness known only to plural wives, they also seemed largely unaware of Dakata's sensitivity in caring for them without provoking jealousy. Penguka had become an immediate member of the extended household and given charge of a sizeable portion of her mother-in-law's garden. Dakata's mother had broken the soil and planted it for her new daughter-in-law, knowing it would be too late in the season for Penguka to do it herself.

The maize was growing well, as were the weeds, and for several days Penguka worked to clear them from around the stalks. Late one afternoon, she arrived home visibly drawn and fatigued. Her mother-in-law took the hoe and bundles she was carrying and told Penguka to rest. She awoke the next morning without appetite, visited the bush, but could do no more than return to bed. By the third morning, her vigor had increased and she dressed and joined others sitting round a smoky fire waiting for the porridge to thicken. Dakata's mother offered her a gourd of soured milk and Penguka drank. Yet before the sun reached mid-sky, her strength was on the wane and her mother-in-law had to steady her as she walked across the homestead to her house. Penguka slept deeply that evening, rising the next morning to find her body fully restored. She was relieved. But scarcely had four days passed when her chest became heavy and she could no longer stand without support. Days later, the illness lifted, leaving in its wake a continuing pattern of sickness and health that plagued her throughout the growing season.

Katwerwa discussed Penguka's health at the fire with Mukuru and sacrificed a large sheep to his ancestors; Dakata took his young wife to the clinic in Opuwo. But the relief afforded by these treatments was fleeting and each time the illness returned with greater intensity. Its recurrent nature suggested the presence of an independent spirit. For had the illness been caused by the manipulation of unseen forces, the ancestors' power would have neutralized it. But an independent spirit could enter the body and leave at will; it could also shroud the sleeping mind with frightening dreams. Penguka suffered from such dreams, remembering neither detail nor storyline, only the fearful images they roused—images that lingered for days afterward. Her illness, however, was not unknown. In the recent past, a number of local women had encountered similar afflictions. The cause was thought to be one of several wandering families of spirits that had followed Hakavona, Ngambwe, and Zimba as they crossed the Kunene to escape the bloodshed of their own land. It was a troubling situation, for these powerful spirits were impervious to Himba medical practice, and afflicted Himba had to seek practitioners of a different tradition.

Dakata's mother arranged for Penguka to be seen by Francisco's wife, Wombinda. She arrived early one afternoon, wearing, by right, a thin, twisted fiber sash that hung loosely from her left shoulder to her right hip. The light-colored sash was a sign of Wombinda's expertise in dealing with a family of spirits called *ondundu*. Her connection to the spirit was bittersweet, for though she profited handsomely from *ondundu*, the spirit had claimed the life of her mother. Her very name, Wombinda, was a constant reminder that her mother had suffered traumatic illness in bringing her to life—an *ondundu* affliction that weakened and exhausted her entire body. The moon had twice completed its circuit since Wombinda's birth when her mother collapsed and died. At last, the powerful spirit withdrew from the household, leaving the family to bear its sadness, the memory of a bad death never entirely fading. As Wombinda blossomed and approached the time of her womanhood, the dreaded spirit returned and seized her. This time, though, her father called in a wise and experienced healer who forced the spirit's removal, and later, under careful tutelage, Wombinda acquired proficiency in driving that spirit from other afflicted persons. No other healer around Otutati was as highly regarded as she.

Penguka seemed reluctant as Wombinda stepped forward to greet her. Her voice withered as she was asked to describe her afflictions in detail. Wombinda had already made preliminary inquiries, visiting many of Penguka's associates to form a picture of the illness. As different families of spirits were associated with different symptoms, Wombinda's first task was to determine whether or not she was plagued by *ondundu*. Penguka's answers were brief and vague, but Dakata's mother, sitting at her side, offered the detail needed for certain diagnosis. As the lengthy interview finished, Wombinda was convinced she could drive the malicious *ondundu* spirit from Penguka. The young woman was dismissed and Wombinda discussed preparations with two of Katwerwa's wives, hoping to begin treatment the following evening. Her practice was not one of direct intervention and removal, but of creating an atmosphere in which the spirit could be persuaded to leave. Wombinda's presence was authoritative, and because the spirit knew her and recognized her abilities, it would eventually submit to her desires.

The warmth of the late afternoon sun filtered down through high, wispy clouds that dropped shadowy circles upon the valley floor. Dakata stood beside a large work shelter in his father's homestead. The old structure had fallen into some disrepair, but its westerly placement, well beyond the ancestral fire, made it the most suitable corner of the homestead for such a healing. Several goats and a sheep from Dakata's flocks had been slaughtered and the meat laid on freshly cut ironwood boughs—all but a hind leg of goat that dangled from a nearby tree. Beside the branches sat two large kettles and a number of smaller pots, all filled with water, waiting for evening. Skins and blankets hung securely from the roof along three sides of the work shelter, enclosing the space where the spirit would be drawn from Penguka. And as the sun fell below the hills, Dakata's younger brother arrived and set a box of distilled spirits behind one of the curtains.

Darkness enfolded the homestead and evening chores drew to a close. Cattle, sheep, and goats were safe in their enclosures; pails of fresh milk had been taken indoors and hung from the rafters. People began to collect near the work shelter, men gathering round the heavy cooking fires, women pausing in their flickering light to greet one another before stooping to enter the shelter. Children ran freely through the homestead, playing in the shadows, though some of the youngest had already made their beds in an open house. Beneath the work shelter's sagging roof burned three small fires. Heat emanating from the temporary hearths drifted to a single corner where makeshift seats had been arranged in a circle. Light from the rising moon penetrated the open wall, yet the interior remained dusky. The shelter's air was thick and pungent, heavily scented by wood smoke and perspiring bodies freshly anointed with *otjize*. Nearly a score of women sat chatting by the fires, their faces dimly illuminated by the quavering light. An older woman from Oritjitambo took a bottle from her cape and removed its cork. Before passing it on, she raised it to her mouth and drank. The clear vessel traveled from one woman to the next until it regained its owner's hands—though by then the liquid had vanished.

Bending near the fire, Vita and Dakata lifted steaming pieces of meat from the caldrons and set them in baskets to cool. Thick porridge was turned into shallow containers and men stepped forward to serve themselves. One by one they settled near the cooking fires, pulling baskets of meat toward their widening circles. Women and children also congregated, and meat, soured milk, and porridge were shared among them. In the work shelter, conversation waned as food passed beyond the curtains. Away from the crowd, Dakata's mother filled a small, broken pail with milk and porridge, and carried it through the darkness to a hut where Penguka and Wombinda waited for the healing to begin.

Baskets emptied and soon children resumed their play. Katwerwa's second wife knelt beside the cardboard box and began circulating bottles of alcohol. Round after round was made, but the bottles were few in number, and a swallow here, a swallow there was as much as anyone enjoyed. The internal fires were refreshed with ironwood branches to raise the shelter's warmth, for warmth would be needed to encourage the spirit's retreat. Insects flew about the firelight, resting now and again on a warmed blanket or timber. The level of genial conversation had grown, and few observed a tall, stocky man enter through the open wall, carrying a large drum under one arm. He was a stranger, a resident of a neighboring valley hired by Wombinda to lure the afflicting spirit through his artistry. The man walked lightly toward the corner, stopping at the backs of several women blocking his passage. He waited silently until noticed, and when the women had drawn aside, he moved forward to begin his work. With conscious design, the Hakavona man rearranged the seating to form two parallel rows enclosed at one end by a third row of seats.

The drum he had set on the ground was no ordinary percussive instrument, but one whose echoing sound was generated by a firm hand rubbing a moist wooden dowel. The man looked across the work shelter, then turned and took the only seat outside the configuration. After placing a bowl of water at his right foot, he eased forward and lifted the drum, blowing the dust from its shell before laying it across his thighs. The drum was metal, made from an old paraffin tin that had lost its top and bottom. A tightly stretched piece of goatskin covered one end; within the drum, a short leather thong, tied and knotted to the center of the goatskin, held the top of the dowel. The bottom of the dowel was secured to another thong fastened to the sides of the drum. The man dipped his fingers in the bowl and moistened the smooth twig. Twice more he dampened the thirsty wood and then pulled his thumb and forefinger along its length, producing a deep, resonant sound. He judged the moistness inadequate and returned his hand to the bowl. It was shiny as he rubbed the dowel again; and a moment later, friction and dampness joined, causing rich, dark sounds to emanate from the drum—sounds that varied only in pace and resonance. As his nimble fingers urged the instrument to sing, its mellow roar filled the shelter's stillness. *Tu, tu, tu-tu-tu-tu; tu, tu, tu-tu-tu-tu*: the haunting tones announced that the healing would soon begin.

The moon was now high and the shelter filled with people, though the drummer was the only man present. Wombinda sat at the head of the congregation with Penguka at her side. Already her body had warmed and heavy beads of perspiration trickled down her brow and underarms, forming tiny rivulets that dulled the luster of her skin. Around her torso, just below the fall of her breasts, Penguka wore a blanket. She was visibly weak and nervous, an appearance that left some wondering whether the spirit was tormenting her or if it was the effect of the spirits she had drunk. As she sat in her father-in-law's chair, her buttocks pressed firmly against its back while her upper body slumped forward, relying on her arms for support. Wombinda's posture was stiff and rigid as she brooded over her coming labors.

The small gallery of participants flanking Wombinda and Penguka was watchful—waiting for a definite sign that things should begin. The rest of the crowd was less earnest and chatted gregariously, some even mocking the drummer's beat. But as the moments rolled forward, voices became still and the festive mood grew increasingly sober. Hands rose to clap with the drum, repeating the lone man's pattern again and again. Many swayed to the rhythm while their breathing unwittingly succumbed to the drummer's spell.

Wombinda lifted the rattle in her right hand and shook it. Slowly, her head fell backwards and her lips pursed. They trembled for a moment and then burst open with a low, forceful moan. Her hand lost control and the rattle dropped to the ground. Penguka also began to stir, carefully following Wombinda's movements. Hesitantly, she raised her arms and extended them forward in imitation of her mistress, bringing them down gradually while her fingertips moved in circles. As the two became more entranced in their work, the tempo swelled, demanding ever swifter movement—a rapidity that would attract the unwanted spirit. Wombinda rose above her seat and lowered her torso; the drummer slowed his pace. Gracefully, she began swaying from her ankles in soft waves that stretched her body, teasing it upward. The waves became more forceful as they traveled from her ankles to her knees, through her hips, along her waist, above her shoulders, and into her head. She lifted her arms as before, yet now their movements crowned each growing wave. Penguka watched her flowing mistress for a time and then shifted to the edge of her chair. She rolled her shoulders and head again and again until she captured her mistress' flow. The full length of her body fell into motion as the two stood side by side, their movements the object of everyone's gaze. Wombinda turned her head slightly. "No!" she whispered, "you must bring the spirit up, not down!" Penguka watched again; finally she grasped Wombinda's rebuke and her body began an upward swell.

It was important that Penguka follow Wombinda's movement with exactness. The *ondundu* spirit had entered her body through its lower regions—most likely through a natural orifice or break in the skin. And so long as the spirit remained low, entering and departing the body from its nether regions, *ondundu* could practice its mischief unrestrained. Wombinda had learned from her teacher that *ondundu* was a low-moving spirit, wending upward through the body toward the head where it would cloud the mind. After taking its pleasure the spirit traveled downward and escaped the body. If the spirit followed this pattern, its movements remained free. But if *ondundu* were compelled to leave a body through the crown of the head, the spirit's ability to gain entrance would be lost, all of its malicious effects carried away, its activity forever distanced from the body. Penguka's health could only be restored if Wombinda enticed the spirit to enter Penguka's body, and once inside, drew it upward into her head, hindering any downward retreat. The enabling warmth, the throbbing drum, the tumultuous claps, a forceful mind, the upward swelling motions, and a knowing guide would lure the unsuspecting *ondundu* and then drive it from Penguka.

The drummer paused to rest his arms, but his silence was filled with soaring claps, a great pealing of hands that swiftly blanketed all other sounds. As the two shimmering figures continued to purl and sway, their fingers brushed against the ceiling and whispers of dust fell to the ground. Penguka opened her eyes for a moment and saw her mistress placid and deeply withdrawn, seemingly unaware of her surroundings. Penguka's eyes closed and her movements regained their former steadiness. The evening deepened and the dancers began to slow. The drummer, sensing a growing lethargy, returned his hand to the dowel and brought it to life, carefully steadying the tones before increasing their pace. Penguka responded by sharpening her posture and livening her gestures. Her mistress, though, remained aloof, unaffected by the world beyond her mind.

Some in the congregation had grown weary, but others responded to the drummer, hoping, perhaps, to witness the spirit's visitation. The shelter had filled with heat and noise and desire. Stirring ever so slightly, Wombinda turned her head from right to left. Though she appeared to observe the gathering, her eyes were fixed on some imperceptible vision, and the activity before her passed without acknowledgment. Her mouth opened calmly as Penguka's form came into view. Immediately, Wombina's head shook and a shuddering howl escaped her lips. Something had seized her body. She convulsed and waved her arms violently, striking those closest to her. Her breathing became heavy as she struggled against the unseen force. Stupefied, the crowd looked on until awakened by the drummer who urged them forward; the intensity of Wombinda's exertion was met by clapping and calling. The drummer's beat surged, his sounds reverberating faster and faster. The hand clapping was in crescendo, drawing curious onlookers toward the open wall. Louder, faster, louder, faster: The shelter was ablaze, moving at a pace that could not long endure. The spirit would be subdued.

"No!" shrieked Wombinda as her body slumped into a chair, "No!"

But it had vanished. The *ondundu* had merely played with her, enticed her, and then withdrew. Instantly, the shelter fell quiet. Penguka collapsed in her seat, exhausted from the dancing, not realizing the spirit had eluded their trap.

Only one of the cooking fires burned luminously. The others, still warm to the touch, had exhausted their fuel. Six or seven men sat round one of the dying fires, exchanging news and opinions. A larger number of maidens and youths had collected beyond the firelight, occasionally dancing, but finding greater amusement in earthy conversation. Both groups shared an interest in the healing and dispatched messengers from time to time to report on the progress. From the quiet work shelter, women stepped into the night, stretching their limbs and rolling their shoulders and necks. But the evening was far from over—Wombinda simply needed to compose her thoughts and prepare herself for the strenuous labors to follow. Pails of water were passed around and most of the women drank. A few sleeping children awoke, disturbed by the sudden clamor, and called for their mothers.

Wombinda and Penguka repaired to a corner of the shelter to refresh themselves. A night breeze drifted inward, cooling the once warm air, and both women laid cloaks about their shoulders. The drummer returned with his water bowl and rubbed his eyes. Noticing the low fires, he gathered several armfuls of branches and revived the sleeping flames as women, scattered here and there across the floor, quickly yielded to his footsteps. When he finished, he brushed the dust from his instrument and then leaned against a post to wait for Wombinda's signal.

The moon was still high overhead as the congregation found its way back to the shelter, heeding the drummer's call. The recess had been long, long enough for Wombinda to stroll across the darkened land and summon her powers. Though the shelter steadily regained its warmth, many sat with blankets draped around their bodies. Stroking her long, dark hair while silently greeting many of the assembled women, Wombinda took her place at the head of the inner circle. Penguka was already seated, her eyes tightly closed and the muscles of her jaw stiff and tense. After a moment, Wombinda lifted her rattle. Those closely flanking her followed her lead and raised their pebble-filled gourds. As the rattles converged to beat a measured pace, Penguka searched for hers, and when she found it, she blended its movements with the others, placing her body within the steady rhythm. The drummer invigorated the tempo, yet Wombinda's rattle had already fallen to the ground, and a series of long, tedious moments passed before she stirred. Gradually, Wombinda yielded herself to the enveloping beat, her body rippling forward and upward. Penguka observed her mistress and imitated the soothing movements—as did the circle's other members, their bodies' motion echoing the sound of the groaning drum. Thunderous clapping rose from many hands but never threatened the drummer's sonorous tones.

Within the circle, flames leaped from the glowing hearth, and heat trapped beneath the plastered roof cast a reddish hue upon Wombinda's glistening face. The mistress moved her arms in small, tight circles, intensifying her efforts to lure the spirit to Penguka. The drum roared louder and faster, and each wave of sound was met with a greater agitation of body. Gasping for breath, Wombinda and Penguka labored to sustain the furious pace, their hair swaying from side to side. Penguka twisted slightly and began trembling.

"Upward," cried Wombinda, "drive the *ondundu* upward!"

Penguka strained her chest and arms and turned her face to the ceiling. Now drawing her breath in shrieks, her body rippled with extremity and the blanket tumbled from her waist. Undulating ever upward, Penguka rose from her seat till her hair brushed against the rafters. Her strength was declining and she began to flail her arms—a desperate attempt to force the spirit's entry. Slowly, her mouth widened, but suddenly closed as her quavering body slipped to the floor. It was only exhaustion, for the spirit was not easily deceived. The inner circle broke and the congregation eased backward. Wombinda crouched low and helped the ailing Penguka to her seat.

It was still, and though several had forsaken the shelter's warmth, most of the congregation remained in place. Penguka rested beneath a large cape. Wombinda stood alone near the fire and spoke to no one. A northerly wind blew softly against the shelter's makeshift walls, causing them to swell. Dakata peered into the fire-lit darkness and caught his mother's attention; she rose to meet him, and beyond the ears of the congregation told him of their difficulty in trapping the spirit. Eventually Wombinda returned to her place, and once settled, the women of the inner circle took their seats. Wombinda's eyes pointed to the ground and the women lifted their rattles. One of them shook a sand-filled gourd and the others quickly followed suit. The drummer joined his strength to the growing rhythm and became its leader. Hands clapped to his pace, sometimes faster, sometimes slower, as he followed Wombinda's instructions. Outside, a luminous, orange moon began its decline toward the western horizon.

The central fire had burned low, yet beads of sweat trickled down many faces. A younger woman of the inner circle lifted her head and set her gaze upon another woman sitting in the opposite flank. Without parting her lips, she moaned deeply, and in her eyes stirred the reflection of a rising head. The two women stared intently at each other, neither one blinking, only patiently searching the other's unwavering expression. Somewhere in the homestead a bottle shattered against a stone and the pair jumped from their seats at the sudden noise. A stuporous laughter rose from without, weakening as it reached the interior. Averting her eyes slightly, one of them regained her place, squatting above a rusted tin. Stretching her arms low, she set her fists along the edge of the tin and then compelled her twitching limbs to support her upper body. The other woman leaped to her chair, turned, and snarled. Deep within her throat resonated a low, vibrating growl, for she was now a lioness, and her prowess and authority were being challenged by the lioness across the way.

As the growling lioness engaged the other, both appeared deeply entranced. Cautiously, they jumped to the ground. Their eyes rounded ever larger until the growing tension broke with a fervid roar—the contest had begun. The congregation looked on as the two women, enchanted by lion spirits, made their threatening overtures. Suddenly, they bounded from the shelter into the open homestead in pursuit of something known only to them, their hands and feet carrying them with remarkable speed and agility. Not thirty paces from the shelter, they stopped at the base of a tree and sniffed upward, spotting the fresh meat hanging from its branches. They leaped and jumped, batting wildly at the meat, but all their efforts failed. The drumming and clapping never ceased, though one of the work shelter's walls was removed so the congregation might observe the feeding animals. Their desperate frenzy attracted an older woman who neared the tree and raised her walking stick. Her toes held the weight of her body as she stretched her arm and ran her stick along the sagging branch to loosen a leg of goat. As the meat fell, she pulled backward, away from the beasts; immediately, the dominant lioness pounced on it. She bore her teeth and tore a ribbon of dripping flesh, her tongue drawing it into her mouth. The other lioness stepped back, biding her time; and when her superior followed the sound of a distant passerby, she lunged forward, seized the meat, and quickly disappeared into the bush. The other lioness roared and gave chase; an instant later their movements were invisible. Alone in the bush, they challenged each other till their voices grew hoarse. Finally, they settled and shared the meat, panting heavily while they ate to encourage their stomachs to fill with air. The air would help disgorge the meat, and only then would their bodies be free of the lion spirits.

The draperies had been rehung, leaving the shelter's congregation wondering at the lionesses' fate. The drummer paused to rest his hand, and as he laid his fingers in the water bowl, Wombinda looked his direction, her eyebrows raised as though hoping his percussion might break her lethargy of spirit. The dowel was parched, for three times he dipped his fingers before it would release its sound. Immediately, Penguka's dance sharpened, but Wombinda's movements continued depressed, her arms swinging in urgent, though erratic, circles. She was tired, and so was the congregation. Every clap, every twist, every gesture had slowed—only the drummer's beat remained constant. Wombinda's mouth and lips moved, yet her voice was entirely lost amid the trembling cacophony. She continued her supplications, enticements, and pleadings to force the *ondundu*'s presence, but no visible signs of the spirit's compliance followed her words. Penguka bent forward, the motion of her head following the drummer's rhythm, her skin glistening, and her breathing steady and deep. With half-closed eyes, she appeared but dimly aware that her body's motion had succumbed to the drummer's charm—the sweep and the sway of her torso and arms falling to its measured course. The mistress rose to her feet. Her dance intensified as her whole body slithered upward with greater and greater force. Her weary chest rose and fell more quickly, her inaudible speech became vehement. At last, those of the inner circle lifted their rattles and shook, urging their mistress onward.

"Up!" shouted Wombinda. "Stand!"

Penguka obeyed and pressed her body into Wombinda's pattern of smooth, upward waves. The two became mere silhouettes against the heat, the smoke, and the clamor—lone figures moving within a billow of confusion. Mistress and her client willingly drew upon this collective might, hoping its summoning power would prove irresistible to the *ondundu*. The tempo steadily increased and many of the outside crowd gathered near the shelter and clapped. The two dancers extended their arms and hands, then dropped and raised them in vigorous swells, imitating the drawing and releasing of the malevolent spirit.

In this flurry of movement, Penguka's form suddenly reposed, her body standing motionless. A shiver overtook her, and then she relaxed into utter stillness, except for her eyes which trembled beneath their lids. A moment later, she danced beside Wombinda who saw in Penguka's complexion the unmistakable signs of entry. The *ondundu* was present. The drummer quickly recognized the signs and strengthened his efforts, forcing the drum to sound louder and faster. Penguka's body surged upward, ever upward, driving the *ondundu* toward final expulsion. Mistress tipped her head backward as far as it would go and gaped her mouth as if to scream, her tongue falling over her upper lip. Her cheeks were flushed, and the taut curvature of her straining throat purled as it sought to convey breath to her lungs. Penguka's dancing slowed, for the beat had become too rapid, too difficult. Soon, her posture slackened, her hands fell limp, her legs weakened, and she tumbled to the ground, unable to move. Tears streamed from her tensely closed eyes, forming a tiny pool of moisture on the ground; finally, a blanket was laid over her shivering body.

Most eyes were upon the mistress, awaiting her direction. A few of the congregation strained to their feet and crept toward the shelter's opening. The moon was now less than a quarter sky from the western horizon. Wombinda turned and faced the spectators. She lifted her hand, then turned aside to search for her blankets. Most of the congregation followed her lead and, moments later, the floor was strewn with blankets, skins, and wooden pillows.

Morning came early as several young children wandered through the shelter looking for their mothers. Though the sun was rising beyond the eastern hills, within the walls it was dark, and most of the congregation ignored the children's searching. Penguka lay on the ground, sleeping on her side with her knees drawn toward her stomach. Wombinda also lay on the ground, beside a hearth, wrapped in several blankets, breathing deeply. The livestock had been driven to pasture when the first of them began to stir. Gradually, the heavy slumber lifted and Wombinda's eyes hesitantly opened. When she came to herself, she pushed aside her covers and sat forward, carefully looking over the assemblage. At last she spotted Penguka and crept to her side. Though Wombinda was certain *ondundu* had entered Penguka's body, the facial quirks and bodily spasms that indicate the spirit's movement had not been evident, and she wondered whether expulsion had occurred. As others arose, their movements and whisperings roused Penguka from her sleep. Her neck stiffened as she turned to look about, relaxing again as the mistress came into view.

"Does the morning treat you well?" whispered Wombinda, bending near Penguka's ear.

"Yes," replied Penguka in a low voice. "I slept very well." She wavered for a moment and then turned her eyes from Wombinda. "But the spirit isn't gone," she said. "I felt it earlier this morning and recall another of its dreams."

"Ah," said Wombinda, "it's exactly as I thought—but you mustn't worry. Rest now and collect your strength. I'll go speak with your husband and make arrangements for this afternoon."

Dakata's undertakings were few and easily laid. The greater preparation was Wombinda's alone, for only she could gather the strength and resolve necessary to expel the recalcitrant spirit. It was a strange, often taxing, relationship, for though *ondundu* had blessed Wombinda with curative powers, these powers were not easily directed. *Ondundu* was puissant, stubborn, and often mischievous, but Wombinda had treated such cases before. Some required night after night of dancing, and Wombinda had yet to meet an incurable patient. It was simply a matter of intensity, as with all diseases, and the course of treatment varied from one patient to another.

By midafternoon most of the original congregation had gathered near the work shelter, leaving behind their unfinished household chores. Though the air was hot and dry, many women stood in the circle with blankets tied about their waists. Among them were the two lionesses, one holding a baby at her side, apparently bewildered at reports of her previous night's struggle. A slight breeze stirred the air and rustled the drying leaves of a nearby tree. Movement and noise were everywhere in the homestead, and as the mistress stepped forward to initiate a round of clapping, she noted many eyes diverted by the infectious bustle. Turning to an older woman sitting beside a large mud hut, Wombinda nodded her head. Resting on the woman's lap was a drum. Straightway, she moistened the dowel and began producing a low, eerie tone that penetrated the myriad of sounds.

Soon the clapping began. At first it was slow and monotonous, but once the mistress felt every eye was upon her, the tempo increased. Sometimes the pace grew fervid, other times it mellowed, but always the clapping seemed to bear evidence of the congregation's confidence and expectation that something would happen. At the bottom of the circle, several women began swaying from side to side in gentle, uncomplicated movements, movements not provoked by a mystical agent. The clapping and dancing wore on, yet as the shadows lengthened, not a single movement or sound intimated the spirit's presence. Wombinda looked about her. The brilliant autumn sun, the bleating and lowing of livestock, the cries of children at play—it was an atmosphere *ondundu* found loathsome.

Hurriedly, she ushered the congregation into the aging mud house— a circular wattle and daub structure about the height of a man and perhaps five paces in width. Inside, the air was warm and dank, and the only source of light was a low, narrow doorway. Two stools were passed through the opening for Penguka and Wombinda and laid close together at the center of the house. The mistress and her patient entered and took their seats; the remaining company joined them, crowding around the stools. The drummer placed her chair near the ash-strewn threshold, and sitting with her back to the homestead, she stretched her legs and brought her feet to rest inside the somber hut. Reaching for her drum, she set the heavy instrument on her lap and directed its resonating chamber inward, toward the assembly. From within the hut, the drummer appeared as a shadow blocking the sun's light, but her music swelled and filled the interior with lush sound. A woman sitting to the left of Wombinda began to clap and soon the hut thundered, little by little closing itself to the outside world.

Wombinda and Penguka lifted slightly from their seats as their bodies followed the percussive waves. The mistress was summoning her powers—a sensation she felt identical to satisfying a deep hunger. It was a process that caught one unaware, for only after the chest had expanded, the mind had cleared, and the eyes began to see things differently did one recognize that change had occurred. The dark interior continued to resound, creating a mood of swirling, artificial motion—a perception of rapid movement amid relative physical stillness. Into this twisting atmosphere the mistress extended her arms and hands. Her eyes were closed and her countenance was peaceful. Several times she stirred, only to calm once again. Penguka turned from her mistress and pushed away her stool. Her eyes were also closed, and as she drew her ankles beneath her haunches, her head fell forward and her breathing waxed heavy. Moments later, her long, slender legs began to twitch and shake. Penguka rolled her head backward and strained her neck, softly moaning all the while. For a time, she held her awkward position without hint of bodily fatigue; then pearls of sweat began dripping from her long plaits. She rose to her feet and slowly lifted her arms in perfect accord, her fingers grazing the ceiling, lingering there for the briefest moment before tumbling to her thighs. Then, bending her knees, Penguka coiled downward to start the journey anew.

Her young limbs strained as she reached and stretched, climbing upward—only to fall back once more. Again and again she repeated the movement, though with each succeeding round her strivings grew less controlled. Now as her body rose, she struggled to find a sure footing. Her breathing was rapid and her eyes darted beneath their tightly closed lids. Her arms swung in lumbering circles and those closest to her shifted away lest they be struck. Her mouth opened ever wider and the rush of air from her lungs scattered the odor of her breath throughout the hut.

The clapping and drumming continued, and though her movements were faltering, Penguka strove to keep pace with the burgeoning tempo. Wombinda, who had seemed oblivious to her surroundings, came to life and looked through the darkness toward Penguka. Instantly, she rushed to her side and, recognizing the threat of collapse, slipped her own arms beneath Penguka's.

"Up!" she cried in whispers, "you must draw *ondundu* up! Don't let him fall, we mustn't lose him again!"

Penguka stood firm. The mistress ran her hands along Penguka's body, prompting her to follow the pattern that would drive the spirit from her. Moving, twisting, and lifting she pressed the *ondundu* upward—and it entered her chest. Wombinda grasped Penguka's arms and forced them into the high circular motions that would keep the spirit moving upward. Those who formed the inner circle recognized the signs of entry and hurried the pace, knowing that expulsion was imminent if Penguka could sustain her movement.

As her chest filled with the pain of habitation, Penguka's arms and legs grew suddenly fatigued, and only the mistress' sharp rebuke prevented her from dropping to the ground. Her eyes were fully open, staring into the darkness. Her mouth parted and she shrieked in anguish. Many in the congregation shuddered, and for a moment the percussion stumbled. Penguka now breathed in gasps and her throat bulged and swelled as the reluctant spirit was swept upward to her head. The *ondundu* was unhappy, for a spirit willingly acquiesces to no one, and when it must, causes distress at each point of its journey. Penguka's face was clouded with perspiration and she appeared distorted, her facial skin stretched and distended by the spirit's movement. Ever so gently, mistress reached over and tenderly stroked the sides of Penguka's face. The *ondundu* was rising through her head; Penguka could feel its motion. Her body trembled and then grew still. Suddenly, her head shook and twisted with ferocity as a final burst of movement propelled the spirit from her. Lunging forward, Penguka screamed and expelled a mouthful of yellow bile, her body tumbling to the ground. Everything stopped; for a moment the hut was drained of all sound and movement.

The mistress tucked a blanket around her patient while motioning to Dakata's mother. She left the hut and returned a moment later with a piece of steaming meat, for Penguka would have to eat. A weakened body would leave her vulnerable to the wiles of another spirit. But try as they would, Penguka would not be disturbed.

· 11 ·

Learning the Truth

... about troubling yet important conditions is part of Himba life. Wamesepa returns from the Opuwo hospital only to leave again. And what is to be made of the spirit exorcism? Is it genuine or a fraud, a self-imposed illness or a premeditated deception? Kavetonwa speaks about his father's decision not to be succeeded by one of his sons, and Masutwa must learn the cause of his wife's weeping eye.

Over a month had passed since I had left Otutati and the dry season had descended in full. As I drove along the dusty tracks, patches of green were rare and most of the deciduous trees had lost their leaves. A packet of photographs lay on the passenger seat. Margot had been safely born in Windhoek, and for a while longer, she, Elspeth, and Michelle would remain in the care of Michelle's parents.

Wamesepa had also returned, heavily medicated. As long as his supply of white tablets lasted, his spirits were good, but his lung condition was of a chronic nature and once the medicine was finished, his health rapidly deteriorated. Standing, walking, and simply rising to his feet became difficult, and he passed the greater part of his day in repose.

Several families without grown sons had closed their homes and trekked into the high mountain valleys with their livestock. Other households had sent portions of their herds and flocks into dry season pasture, entrusting their young men with the animals' care. It was a mutually agreeable circumstance, one that allowed fathers to remain several more weeks with their wives and younger children before dividing their time between responsibilities. For the young men—and the sisters who would accompany them—it was an eagerly anticipated break from the pressures of homestead life. Often, sons would press their fathers to send herds and flocks to new grazing before it was truly necessary, not realizing how obvious their intentions were. But as most fathers had done the same in their youth, obliging their own sons was not difficult. Besides, the livestock was truly in good hands, for the young men were building their own reputations as cattle herders, and gossip loved few things more than a slothful herdsman.

An unseasonably gentle breeze stirred the dormant branches of trees standing closely together along the footpath. Far ahead lay Katwerwa's homestead, its houses and shelters covered in winter dust. Voices rose faintly from a group of men gathered beneath a canopy and drifted toward the open plain. As the voices grew ever more distinct, a new structure on the homestead's westerly edge came into view. It was a curious framework made of four heavy posts set in the ground three or four paces apart, forming a square, connected at the top by narrow poles. Within the open framework stood a tiny slatted bench and table protectively draped in thorn branches. Lashed to the southeasterly post was a slender limb that rose above the framework; near its top dangled a banner no larger than a man's sandal. Dark stripes spiralled round all the posts and poles, and hanging from the timber nearest the table was a set of goat horns. The structure was a monument commemorating the place where Penguka had been freed from the *ondundu* spirit. On this bench and at this table she had eaten her celebratory meal. The horns belonged to the animal slaughtered for the occasion, the stripes had been painted from its blood, and the black flag, made from cloth dyed in its blood, marked the booth as specifically *ondundu*. The structure would now remain undisturbed till overtaken by natural decay.

"I'm not sure what to think," replied Kavetonwa's son-in-law, reclining on a cattle skin, his head supported by a carved pillow. At his side were the black cloth and leather strap that normally covered his hair, and the hairdresser knelt at his shoulders, sharpening a long knife against the palm of his hand. "I've heard the story from both Dakata and Katwerwa," he continued, glancing briefly at the framework. "But I'm suspicious of these foreign spirits."

The hairdresser moistened the man's neck and temples and began to shave them cleanly.

"When I was your age," said Masutwa's uncle, "these Angolan spirits were completely unknown—no one had ever been troubled by them. But now, all of a sudden, this woman and that woman are being struck down, and the talk is nothing but complaints of having to pay out money and livestock to rid our wives and daughters of these spirits." He looked downward, leaning heavily on his stick. "I say," he murmured, "I've given the matter a good deal of thought, yet I'm no closer to understanding this turn of events—why are we now afflicted by these spirits when they never bothered us before? Does simply being aware of their existence make us vulnerable to attack?"

"It could be so," replied an older man from Etanga. "Though perhaps not quite in the manner you think." His gravelly voice was serious and he hesitated slightly. "I say the spirits are real, but I don't believe our women are unwillingly attacked. I ask you this question: Does a woman ever become ill without knowing at least one other person struck by these spirits? My answer is no! And what does this mean? A woman sees a relative of hers afflicted by *ondundu*, she sees her eating meat, drinking liquor, and dancing with her friends. Perhaps she sees her with a new bangle or necklace and thinks, 'This kind of illness is a good thing—if I pretended to be ill, I could eat well and have my husband look after me!' So she begins to feign the symptoms, tempting the *ondundu*, and before long the spirit enters her body and she becomes genuinely ill."

Listening as he combed the long, dark strands, tinged with gray and white, the hairdresser lifted his eyes to follow the sound of laughter rising from a nearby work shelter. Settling back, he remarked, "Your words are likely true. Yet, here I sit dressing my friend's hair while these foreigners get rich from the spirits that follow them!"

The men laughed, and the dresser placidly laid aside his wooden comb to begin fingering the polished waves of hair. Carefully, he searched for any lingering debris, and when finished, leaned toward a pouch of dried herbs, withdrew a handful, and sprinkled them across the crown of the head.

Masutwa followed the conversation intently, though at times his eyes wandered across the dusty plain. Abruptly, he drew inward and pulled his stick nearer his legs, then bent forward slightly and looked cautiously at the other men. "I also dislike these spirits," he whispered. "Yet I don't understand why Mukuru and our ancestors can't drive them from us. Are the Hakavona healers more powerful than our fathers?"

Several murmured their agreement with the question, though none ventured a reply. Eyes fell to the ground and for a moment no one stirred, least of all the hairdresser. Walking from the direction of his homestead, Kavetonwa approached the silent gathering of men and found a seat. At his footfall, Masutwa turned and repeated the question within the old man's hearing. Kavetonwa raised his eyes as he listened to Masutwa's words, then lowered his head and brushed the creamy dust from his wrinkled shins.

"I think Mukuru could drive out the spirits if he wished to," he firmly responded. "But it seems he does not. And this, for me, is the true question: Why should Mukuru refuse to help us?"

"Ah," said the man from Etanga. "So you also believe these spirits are real?"

"Yes," answered Kavetonwa, "certainly they're real. If our own ancestors strike us with illness, shouldn't other spirits be able to do so?"

"Then why don't our ancestors heal us?" asked another.

Kavetonwa's posture slackened and his blue eyes drifted downward. "I must say," he began, "I have no true answer to this question, only a thought." Lifting his head slightly, he looked across the valley. "I've known Francisco for many years and I think he's a good man. Many of his kinsmen are also good people, but their spirits are evil, their intentions are evil, unlike the intentions of our fathers. I think we must be careful not to adopt Hakavona customs; let them live their lives and let us live our lives. It's when we turn from our ways to pursue the ways of the Hakavona or Vambo or Boer that we have trouble. And when we follow their ways, we cannot rely on our ways to release us from that trouble."

His words trailed off gradually into the warming breeze, yet the company waited as if expecting to hear something more, something different. But Kavetonwa was finished. He rested his back against a post and drew his legs to his chest. Soon, his eyes were closed.

The conversation weakened as the sun climbed higher in the sky. Most watched quietly as the dresser closed the freshened hair within the dark cloth turban, fastening and refastening the thin leather strap till its placement was exact. Kavetonwa roused at last and gazed at the men seated about him in the circle, straining to recall his present surroundings. Several of them stood, preparing to return home now that morning was finished. The older man from Etanga remained in place, delaying his journey, though he seemed unable to engage anyone's attention. Turning slightly, he noticed Kavetonwa's bewildered expression and rose to greet him formally, moving to the old man's side.

"Your father and my father were friends," he explained. "And I remember walking with him to your father's homestead when I was a lad—but you were already married by that time."

Kavetonwa's eyes searched the man's face. "You seem familiar to me," he remarked, "but I can't say that I know you. Who is your father?"

"My father is dead," replied the man.

Masutwa's uncle leaned toward Kavetonwa's ear and spoke the father's name.

"Ah, yes," said Kavetonwa, "I know that name. I remember your father. He wasn't a tall man, but his body was very strong and he was famous for killing a lion that had eluded the men of this valley. Isn't that right?"

"Yes," answered the man, smiling, "your words are true. And it pleases me that you remember my father, it makes my heart glad." His lips tightened and his breathing deepened, and several others joined the circle. "But I have a question," he continued, "something I've always wondered— perhaps you can explain it. I know Wamesepa is a great *muhona*, truly, the greatest of all. Still, I've always wondered why your father chose him, rather than one of his own sons, to succeed him."

Kavetonwa shifted his weight and sighed as he reached for his stick. "Yes," he said softly, "this is a question I can answer. It's a question I asked my father long ago, but only after my heart had cooled. One evening, I greeted him, entered his house, and sat beside him on the floor. For a while we talked of the local comings and goings, laughing at the mischief of certain people, but I think he sensed I had another purpose in visiting him. 'Father,' I finally said, 'I have an important question for you.' He knew precisely what it was, but allowed me to speak my heart. 'Father,' I asked, 'why did you choose Wamesepa to take your place?' He was quiet for a moment, then replied, 'My child, one day I will tell you, but that day hasn't yet come.' These were bitter words, but there was nothing to be done. 'Yes, my father,' I said, and left the house.

"The seasons changed, and on a warm evening, just after the cattle had been penned for the night, my father asked me to walk with him to the foot of the hill. I thought an animal was missing and he needed my eyes to find it. 'Why do you think the beast has wandered over here?' I asked him. 'A beast?' he replied. 'We're not searching for a lost animal. I believe the time has come for me to answer your question.' We walked to where we would not be disturbed, my mind moving rapidly from thought to thought. Father leaned against a boulder and began talking. I lowered my eyes and looked away.

" 'I understand why you ask this question,' he said. 'Your brothers haven't asked me. Perhaps it doesn't matter to them; perhaps they're afraid to ask. But I'm pleased you have—because I want you to understand my decision. There are several reasons why I've chosen Wamesepa to take my place. Firstly, he is my mother's sister's son, we belong to the same *eanda* [matrilineage], and as you know, my *eanda* has governed the affairs of people in this area for many generations. I would like this to continue. Wamesepa will also inherit most of my cattle—and this will make him a wealthy man. In some ways these things are important, but far more important is that I choose someone capable of properly looking after the needs of these people.'

"My father stopped talking, and I remember thinking how strange his voice was—he was speaking to me as if I were a boy, not a man. Only later did I realize he was speaking to me as a father, not a peer. 'My son,' he continued, 'tell me what a *muhona* is.' I looked at the sky and thought for a while. 'A *muhona*,' I said, 'is a great man with many cattle that other people may use.' This seemed essentially correct, but my father thought otherwise. 'So,' he replied, 'a *muhona* is simply a rich man—is this what you think?' It wasn't, of course. And I answered, 'No. I've met several rich men who would never be called *muhona*.' 'And why wouldn't they be called *muhona*?' 'Because,' I answered, 'they aren't generous with their wealth.'

"My father turned aside and cleared his nose. 'You're correct,' he said. 'A rich man with a bad heart can never become a *muhona* because he loves his wealth more than he loves people. A good heart is a gift from Mukuru, but it isn't a simple thing to maintain a good heart. Why Mukuru bestows wealth on some men and not on others, or why bad-hearted men are sometimes blessed with riches, I don't know. But a true *muhona* knows his wealth is a gift to be shared by many.'

"My father stepped away from the boulder, and I thought to myself, 'Why are you telling me such things? What does this have to do with me?' Then he asked another question, a difficult one. 'My son, how does Mukuru differ from our ancestors?' At first I thought it was a riddle, or a question without an answer, but he waited patiently for my reply. At last, I said, 'We learn that Mukuru is good, that he only blesses us and never curses us as our ancestors sometimes do. We also say that Mukuru answers "yes" to our petitions, though the ancestors may say "no."' Father nodded his head. But still I was perplexed—I had no sense of what he was trying to explain. And then he asked, 'Is Mukuru a *muhona?*' I looked at the ground—I couldn't grasp his intentions, I couldn't see the end of his words. Gradually, though, as I thought about his question, it became clear that *ovahona* and Mukuru were expected to behave in much the same way. So, I answered, 'Yes. I think Mukuru must be a *muhona.*' 'You are correct,' said my father, 'you are correct. And this is what I wish you to understand: a *muhona* does what Mukuru would do. This is precisely why I've chosen Wamesepa to take my position. I've watched him grow and develop and mature over these many years. I know his heart and his heart is good; yes, it is good.'

"I followed him back to the homestead without exchanging a word, confused, mulling over the things he'd said. It was a long time, though, before I understood his intentions. When this happened I was young and inexperienced, but now I'm an old man and somewhat wise to the ways of human beings, and I tend to see things as my father saw them."

The man from Etanga straightened his back. "Thank you, *Tate*," he said respectfully. "I thank you."

As the midmorning sun warmed the still air, Masutwa's younger son tethered a large goat to one of the work shelter's posts. Its thick, curling horns were dusty, as was its golden, tawny coat. A handful of people sat beneath the work shelter visiting amiably, some in the shade, others preferring sunlight, waiting for the diviner to arrive. Masutwa was nowhere to be seen and his wife remained sheltered in their house.

Several weeks past, Masutwa's wife awakened with an irritation in her left eye. She rubbed it, doused it with water, had a friend blow on it, but nothing gave her relief. By evening, her condition had worsened. The skin around her weeping eye was puffy and swollen and red, her head throbbed, and she had difficulty maintaining her balance. Masutwa asked me to come and examine her eye. A day or two later, he set his wife upon a donkey and walked her to the clinic in Opuwo. There she remained for a number of days until the infection had subsided, leaving the hospital partially healed. She had been given a small envelope containing tablets, and when the course of medicine was finished, Masutwa wished to know why she had become ill in the first place, lest the malady return. He set about making discreet inquiries, finally arranging for a diviner to attend his wife. The man was from Angola, born a Thwa, a people distinguished for its beautiful ironwork. As a diviner, he had acquired a reputation for consistency and accuracy in his diagnoses, and fairness in his compensation; indeed, Masutwa was relieved to have found such a forthright person to consult the oracle.

The diviner entered the homestead from the east with Masutwa at his side. He was short, his skin golden in color, and he wore simple cloth aprons about his waist. His head was covered by a fraying woolen cap, beneath which dusty, gray hairs glimmered in the sunlight. The diviner spoke in his native tongue, as did Masutwa, and gestured toward the goat, nodding his approval. It was large, it was male, its horns curved evenly, its coloring was proper, and it belonged to Masutwa's wife—all the characteristics necessary for the animal's veins, arteries, and intestines to reveal the ailment's origin. Masutwa led the man to a worn, metal-framed chair near the goat and settled him. A moment later, his wife emerged from their house, walked across the dung-scattered ground, and stooped to enter the work shelter.

The diviner pulled the blade of his knife along the sole of a rubber sandal, then gathered a handful of dust, sprinkled it over a smooth log, and began drawing the blade across the roughened surface, sharpening its edge. Once, a burst of wind scattered the dust, sweeping some of its particles into the diviner's eyes. But he cleared his vision and began the process anew. When at last he stood, Masutwa came forward, recognizing the man was ready to slay the goat; the chatter lessened as the onlookers turned their heads toward the beast. Masutwa quickly straddled the animal to hold it in place. His left hand grasped a horn while his right tightened round the goat's muzzle, its thin, golden beard caught between his fingers. The animal was confused, perhaps sensing danger, and began to struggle. Holding the knife firmly, the diviner pressed its blade just below the goat's right ear, and cut deeply and swiftly across the throat to the other ear. The animal kicked its legs and respired loudly through its nose. Its tawny form softened and, with Masutwa's help, fell gently to the ground. The diviner gathered the tethering cord and carefully wound it around the animal's forelegs, slipped it over a heavy beam, and pulled slightly to incline the goat's upper body. Masutwa tied the cord in place, then retreated to the shade.

Leaning inward, the diviner stood before the hanging goat, steadying the animal's chin with his left hand. With care, he laid the tip of his knife at the base of the chin and made a smooth, continuous cut to the belly, augmenting this incision with a small crosscut at the breast bone. His hands and forearms stiffened as he attempted to peel the skin away from the animal's throat. Probingly, his fingers touched the trachea and glided among the physical elements that would clarify the matter. The audience looked on in quiet fascination as the diviner's inquisitive hands pulled, rubbed, squeezed, and patted the arteries of the throat.

"Yes," spoke the diviner. "I'm beginning to recognize things—definite clues are appearing." His voice was soft, almost wispy, and could only be heard with effort.

"I see there's been trouble in this valley," he said playfully, "trouble where no trouble should be." The audience tittered a bit. "I see there has been unusual sickness among you. I also see that one man's wife is being very naughty while he's away at cattle post—far, far naughtier than he suspects!"

"Who is she?" called Masutwa's uncle teasingly. "Whose wife is being naughty?"

The diviner worked to suppress a smile, feigning concentration as he probed further with his eyes and fingers. "The identity is not clear. But this I can say: She'll never be satisfied with her husband again!" The onlookers burst into laughter, delighting in the man's humor. Then turning, the diviner grieved, "I see that someone's maize harvest is infested with insects because the storage bins were not repaired—despite what he told his wife." To the amusement of those present, other revelations followed that subtly and cleverly implicated the behavior of everyone in company.

Several more incisions were made across the throat and belly and the skin pulled aside before the diviner's knife more deeply penetrated the flesh to expose major arteries and lesser veins. In the same jovial manner, he continued revealing the secrets of Otutati life, making light of the pompous and ambitious, and keenly displaying his knowledge of local gossip; yet as he neared the animal's bowels, his buoyant tone increasingly softened. A thick, fatty membrane held them in place. And as the diviner readied his knife, the talkative onlookers fell silent, each one knowing the curvature and coloring of the bowels were key to divining the origin of the problem. In a single, rapid movement the diviner severed the membrane. Springing forward, Masutwa opened his hands to help contain the twisted mass of purplish gray intestines and lower it to waiting branches, maintaining, as best he could, its original configuration. The release of the bowels provoked a rush of foul air, causing even Masutwa's uncle to turn away.

Kneeling beside the branches, the diviner skillfully moved his hands amid the contorted circle, furling his brow as he did so. His thumb and index finger glided back and forth over a section of bowel. As he considered the changing thickness, its manner of entanglement, and the positions of several black spots, Masutwa stood behind him to glimpse the process of divination, though for him it was unintelligible. People chatted, yet Masutwa's wife remained mute, watching intently, aware that her well-being was at stake. An easy gust of wind blew through the shelter and the diviner paused to hold his skirts in place. As his investigation deepened, he nodded and hummed, indicating that readable signs were present and that he was engaged in their interpretation. A few moments later, he straightened his back and turned around.

"I think I've found the answer you seek," he reported calmly, "though it's not a very pleasant one." Returning to the bowels, he pointed at several peculiarities. "This twisting here, with those spots above it," he said, speaking to Masutwa, "these tell me that a group of men living beyond Opuwo are responsible. Unfortunately, the signs aren't strong enough to reveal their identities, but at least one of them has conducted business with you, and I believe you know him well." He broke for a moment, tracking a clue invisible to everyone else. "Ah," he breathed, "Do you see this? I searched this small piece hoping to find whether it was livestock or something else, but the signs are simply too weak." A moment later, he pointed to a thin, dark line, running along a stretch of intestine. "This mark is very clear and very strong; it shows the man's envy and hatred. He is malicious and cowardly; and to deliberately cause you misery, he and the others are working to injure your wife and children. Look here, see this sharp turn of direction followed by this thickness, this tells me their *omiti* is very strong, strong enough to ruin your wife's health."

The diviner glanced over the audience, then turned and lifted his cap. Feeling something on his right hand, he wiped it meticulously on a soiled kerchief. "Now," he said, speaking more loudly than before, "do you see that the intestines change color at this point? And do you also see how this section thickens and lays over the other piece? This is very important because it tells me your ancestors are countering the *omiti* working against you. Your fathers have healed your wife and prevented the sickness from attacking your children. But this thinness here, together with these tiny stripes, is a request, a request that you sacrifice a sheep to them. And these markings next to the stripes are a promise: If you make a sacrifice to your fathers they will be strengthened enough to thwart any further evil from these men." He lowered his head a bit to examine the liver. But finding nothing of specific value, he straightened his shoulders, looked at Masutwa, and retreated a few steps, marking an end to his reading.

Masutwa acknowledged the diviner's words by intoning his agreement. He also stepped back and for a moment looked away from the gathering. "I say," he murmured, turning to the diviner, "why should these men want to do me harm?"

"Beyond jealousy," answered the man quietly, "I don't know. The intestines revealed nothing more. But I could see *omiti* emanating from that group of men."

Relieved to know of the affliction's source and the helping role of his ancestors, Masutwa thanked the diviner and paid him, inviting him to stay for the feast. He called an elder son from across the homestead and asked him to fetch a sheep as quickly as possible. Two large kettles were moved to a hearth and several women began the task of drawing water to fill them. With his uncle at his side, Masutwa raised the goat from the ground in preparation for dressing. The two worked skillfully, and well before the large, dark sheep entered the homestead, a fresh goatskin lay atop the work shelter drying in the sun while its flesh simmered in the ashen kettle. The ancestors' sheep was handsome, but its steps toward the ancestral fire were reluctant. Masutwa stood tall, speaking a long, sober prayer before taking the sheep's life. Its hind legs were lashed together and the body hung from a tree. There it was readied for cooking and by midafternoon the feast was well underway. Eventually, the shadows lengthened and children began returning with the livestock. Adults rose, knowing the tasks of evening were fast approaching.

Wandisa came to me to borrow five liters of petrol to drive his father to Opuwo. For several nights, Wamesepa lay awake coughing and asking for tablets, strong tablets. I visited him and encouraged Wandisa to seek help for him in Opuwo. But Wamesepa was afraid. "Just this kind of illness killed my fathers. In my family we die because our lungs cannot take air. My father's brother died from coughing—he coughed and coughed until his breath was gone. My father also died in this manner. And now it's my turn." Wandisa finally insisted his father see a doctor and gathered skins and blankets to make him a bed in the back of the truck. A number of others wished to accompany Wamesepa and care for him during his stay in Opuwo. As the truck was loading, Wandisa handed me his father's medical record—twelve pages of folded notes detailing his visits to the clinic during the past six years. Curiously, in the box reserved for his date of birth, someone had neatly written the word "ancient." Amid the shouting, calling, and well-wishing, the engine turned over and Wandisa slowly drove along the bank of the dry river to where it dipped, struggled across the sandy bottom, and edged forward to the tracks. Masutwa and his two eldest sons were waiting there. Wandisa stopped and Masutwa strode forward to speak with him. A moment later, he motioned with his stick and the two young men slung their bundles into the truck and climbed aboard.

Masutwa stood at the tracks, watching until the dust settled. "My sons are leaving," he said. "It's a very sad day for me." Their departure was not unexpected. For some time the two had planned to seek their fortunes in the wider world, hoping to find jobs in South Africa and never return to the life of Otutati except for brief visits. From Opuwo they would find a ride to Windhoek, and from there to a mining center in South Africa. This, at least, was their ambition.

"It's now for Mukuru to decide," said Masutwa. "And may he go with them."

· 12 ·

Found and Lost

...are the cattle that mysteriously appear in Vita's enclosure and just as
mysteriously disappear. But so too is Wakamburwa's cosmetic beauty found
and lost—a loss Katere finds humorous. Winding his way to Otutati, a
preacher leaves before delivering a sermon. And Repuree finds a dream
troubling, yet loses his fears as Ngipore interprets the dream for him.

The night had been cold and long. Even as sunlight trickled over the
easterly hills, animals refused to leave the warmth of their huddles. A few
weak clouds floated listlessly above the motionless valley, their rolling tufts
changing hue as the sun edged ever higher.

Keeping a blanket closed tightly about her, Wakamburwa stooped
through the doorway into the chill morning air and walked to her cooking
hearth, blowing on a smouldering branch to keep it alive. Her free hand
picked through the ash to find a bit of kindling to feed the glowing ember,
and with charred twigs and a bit of dry grass she nurtured a tiny flame.
When the fire was set, she lifted a pail hanging from an ironwood tree,
but the water was slushy, too cold to drink. She returned to the hearth
and warmed her hands, her breath rising above her head in faint streaks
of white. The sun climbed slowly, and when at last its light fell across the
cold, dusty ground, other women emerged from their houses to begin the
day.

Wakamburwa pulled a goatskin pouch from beneath her blanket and
laid its contents near the fire. Shifting as her eldest daughter ventured
from the house, she awaited the girl's return, knowing she would wish to

bathe with *otjize* before starting her morning chores. The girl was beautiful and favored her mother with her long, playful eyebrows, large, full lips, and strong, white teeth. She was soon to be a maiden and Wakamburwa took pleasure in the child's growing interest in womanhood.

"Is your father still sleeping?" Wakamburwa asked after greeting her daughter.

"Yes, I think so," she replied. "He was rolled in his blankets and very still when I left the house."

"And your sisters?"

"They were stretching, but they're too cold to leave their beds."

The girl leaned forward and took the *otjize* in her hand, twisted its lid, and passed the container to her mother. Wakamburwa warmed the cream on her palms for a moment and then divided it. Together, they worked to refresh their arms and faces, shoulders and breasts, thighs and shins, feet and backs, pausing now and again to check for lapses in their work. Within the homestead, the rustle of activity grew and both mother and daughter found its sounds irresistible, lifting their eyes again and again to investigate. But nothing weighed heavily upon them and they finished bathing in peace.

Wakamburwa rose and motioned to her daughter. "Come," she said, "we must milk the cows." The fire was low, mostly ash, and as they passed the house, Wakamburwa turned, looking for signs that her husband was dressing.

They opened the entrance to the calves' enclosure with some difficulty and set the heavy posts to one side. "I'll stand here," Wakamburwa said, "to keep the calves from bolting while you fetch a cow." After a while the girl returned, reluctantly driving a contentious beast toward the pen. Immediately, a calf sensed its dam's presence and ran to begin suckling. As the calf drank, Wakamburwa stepped closer and slipped a cord round the cow's hind legs, hobbling the animal. By now, the milk flow was well established and she nudged the calf aside with a walking stick. The dam turned its head and snorted as Wakamburwa squatted down with a milking pail and roughly fingered its engorged udder. Closing a teat in her hand, she expressed a trickle of milk. The cow sharply rebuffed her action with a kick and was immediately disciplined, suffering a light blow to the hind quarters. Calling her daughter, Wakamburwa took a short leather strap and tied it round the cow's left hind leg, inserted a twig, and turned it several times to raise pressure on the upper limb. Dusting her hands, she returned to milking while her daughter struggled to hold the calf. The distressed creature bellowed and its mother looked around, finally lifting its tail and releasing a load of waste. The steaming dung cascaded forcefully to the ground and splattered Wakamburwa's freshly bathed ankles and shins. Angered, she stood, and the surly cow stepped forward, scraping the hoof of its tingling leg against the ground, raising a wave of powdery dust that covered Wakamburwa to the waist. "You stupid animal!" she cried, lifting her stick. But the calf burst from the girl's arms and ran to its mother, and Wakamburwa lowered the rod.

From beyond the enclosure, muffled laughter caught her attention and she turned. Katere stood there, leaning over the fence wearing a tattered, sleeveless cardigan, his skirts neatly gathered. Decisively, Wakamburwa lifted the pail and walked to him. "It's a man's duty to milk his cows," she shouted with acidity, thrusting the pail at him. "Woman!" he stammered, as she left the enclosure, "it's the husband's duty to tell his wife what to do—not the other way round!" But she paid him no heed.

By late morning the air was warm. Katere's daughters had long since finished milking and full pails hung from the enclosure fence so that the sun might hasten its curdling. Vita's younger son, a lad whose lower incisors were newly removed, walked along the edge of the homestead toward Wandisa's. Relieved to find the man at home, he delivered his father's request. "My father asks that you come to him if possible," he said.

Vita had journeyed to the south to attend the naming ceremony of a relative. He returned home several days earlier than expected, arriving well after nightfall, hungry and fatigued from the long trek. Vita's wife had spent a difficult evening comforting a feverish granddaughter to allow the mother some rest. Early the next morning, Vita arose and took the child to relieve his wife, and cradling the baby in his arms, he walked to the central enclosure to see his cattle.

"When I looked over the fence," he told Wandisa, "there were three cows and a large ox I'd never seen before. I thought, 'What's this? How can this be? Have my fathers given me so great a blessing?' Then I went to Daniel's house. 'Daniel,' I called, 'you must come and see this strange thing in the cattle pen.' I waited and waited, and finally entered the pen by myself. The animals were very tame and I checked their ear cuts. They weren't mine, and I didn't think they were Daniel's. When at last he came, I pointed to the animals and asked what he knew about them. Daniel walked around each one and examined the ears. 'Well, they're not my animals,' he said, 'and I haven't the slightest idea of why they're standing here with our cattle.' He looked at them again, shielding his eyes and clicking his tongue, and then returned to his hut.

"I walked beyond my homestead wondering if someone on his way to Opuwo had left his cattle here for the night, but there was no one about. I returned to the animals and had another look at their ear cuts. This time I noticed a difference in pattern between the cows and the ox—the cows shared the same marking, but the ox's was altogether different. And there was another curious thing: Two of the cows had full udders, yet there were no calves to drink their milk. By now the baby had fallen asleep and I brought her to my daughter, and asked her if she knew anything. When my son awoke, I asked him about the animals, but it was the first he'd heard of it."

Wandisa was puzzled. "I say, I've never known anything like this before. And no one around here remembers seeing or hearing anything out of the ordinary?"

Vita shook his head. "No," he replied, "and this makes their appearance all the more strange. Daniel watched my cattle yesterday and said when he penned them last night there were my eight and his three. And we all know cattle aren't like lizards—they're noisy. I got home late in the evening and my wife was up much of the night, yet neither of us heard anything—nor did anyone else. I came out here this morning and there they stood."

Wandisa walked around the enclosure, staring at the animals. Katere, who had come with him, also edged closer to the fence, but said nothing. After several long moments, Vita broke the silence.

"Didi," he said, "I wanted you to see this for yourself—in case I should ever be accused. But I'd also like your counsel: what should I do with them?"

Wandisa walked to his side, his eyes never leaving the ground. "I doubt they are a gift from Mukuru or the fathers," he replied. "But I think you must look after them as if they were your own. Strange cattle simply don't wander into another man's homestead. We'll pass the word around and

I'm sure the owners will eventually come. If a beast of mine were missing, I'd search until it was found." Wandisa looked again at the enclosure. "Yes," he added, "I think you must care for them and not let them wander away."

Vita and his son gently separated the two milk cows from the other cow and ox, and brought in a calf of their own. The calf trotted to one of the cows and maneuvered its way to the teats. The cow pulled away. But the calf tried again, this time drawing some milk. The cow pressed forward, but allowed the calf to drink, relieving the stress of its udder. Vita pushed the calf toward the other cow and began milking. The other beast was far more reluctant, but eventually relented. After milking, the four animals were led to graze with the other cattle, under his son's watchful eye. In the evening they were milked again, and once they were secured for the night, Vita and his son carried the morning and evening milk and poured it onto a sandy depression. It was a regrettable loss, but Vita had concluded the cows might well be sacred, possessions of another man's ancestors, and he was unwilling to weather the risk.

A faint clatter rose from the tracks. In the distance appeared a man on a bicycle, riding over the gravel, stones, and dust. Well before he reached the first of the huge trees marking Otutati, he dismounted and ran his hand over the rear tire. Moments later, he resumed his course, but his pace was slower than before and the noise produced as his bicycle clacked and rattled along the tracks drew many to the strange sight. Most looked on in wonder, never having seen a bicycle before. The rider was a young man with deep lines across his forehead. His face was shiny and his head glistened from the myriad beads of perspiration that clung to his neatly cropped hair. The instant he ceased pedaling, his bicycle came to a halt and he raised himself from the saddle in haste, knocking his sunglasses askew. He was dressed in dark blue: heavily soiled trousers and a clean, well-ironed, sleeveless, collarless shirt. On his feet were black, vinyl dress shoes, worn without socks. He was Herero and introduced himself as Thomas, from Otjirunda in eastern Kaokoland.

"I have come to heal you," he declared above the chatter of the people surrounding him. "I've come to heal your bodies, but I also want to speak to you of the Black Book." He paused to gauge the effect of his words, then pushed his bicycle forward, adding, "But first I must repair my tire."

The young man leaned his bicycle against an ironwood tree in the thicket where Katere and Makuva were playing mancala. From a wooden crate strapped to the rear of his saddle, he pulled tools, glue, and a long strip of dull, black rubber, and set them on a stone. Children gathered round to study the curiosities, commenting on the brightly colored tube of adhesive. Without a word, Thomas removed the crate, inverted the bicycle, adjusted his wrench, and began loosening the rear wheel. Most of those who had gathered beside the tracks now positioned themselves to watch the repair. Interest grew as the wheel was pulled from the chain and dropped to the ground—even the players abandoned their game for a moment. Searching the tread, Thomas found three large, gray thorns and began forcing the tire from the rim. The onlookers chatted, sometimes asking questions, but Thomas ignored them. After stripping away the inner tube, he ran his thumb along its surface till he found the punctures, and working fastidiously, removed the thorn fragments, cut pieces from the spare rubber, glued them in place, and laid the tube in the sun to dry. Children pressed forward to examine the circle of black rubber. Thomas crouched beside the crate and fumbled through his supplies, finally rising with a hand pump and gesturing toward Kuwiya's elder son. The boy came near and Thomas set the inner tube in his hands and began to pump. The tube stiffened and he laid his ear against the patches to listen. Satisfied, he finished mending the tire, righted the bicycle, and strapped the crate in place. He stepped from the shade and wavered a moment, then leaned forward and cleaned his hands on the knees of his trousers.

"I say," he began, noticing the crowd around him had grown, "how far it is from here to Otjitanda?" Though his eyes ranged over the gathering, his voice seemed directed toward the elder men. Katere and Masutwa spoke together quietly.

"Yes," replied Katere, emerging from the private discussion. "We both know Otjitanda—we've both visited people staying there. But our recollections of the journey's length are different. I say, if you had left early this morning and walked steadily all day, you would arrive in Otjitanda not tomorrow, or the day after tomorrow, but in five days." Katere held up his right hand and pulled down its fingers with his left to calculate the number of days. "However," he continued, facing Masutwa, "this man thinks if you left tomorrow morning and walked the whole day through, you should come to Otjitanda not the day after tomorrow, but near evening on the day after the day after tomorrow."

The young man looked at the ground. "I see, I see." He shook his head and clicked. "Now, which of these opinions is correct? Does it take three days or five days to walk to Otjitanda?"

"I've done it in two days," stated Kuwiya.

"Two days?" questioned Katere. "I don't see how that's possible unless you walked day and night."

"A youth walking very quickly," intervened Mukuva, "not even stopping to visit, could possibly make it in two days. But old men like us need at least three days."

A sudden burst of wind struck the top of the windmill, sending the creaking blades round and round and round.

"Ah yes, I see," said Thomas, "and I thank you. Now I have an idea of how far I must travel." Turning toward his cycle, he lifted a large tin from the crate. "Before I leave, is there anyone with a wound—a cut, a scrape, or a burn—that needs attention? I've brought medicines that can help."

He opened the tin and removed scissors, gauze, tape, ointments, pastes, bandages, and lotions. "Have you any tablets?" shouted someone. "A few," he answered, arranging things on the ground, "but not many." Scarcely had he made ready when the assemblage closed in upon him. New wounds, old wounds, chronic maladies, imagined maladies, and every manner of health complaint was brought before him. Patiently, he listened to each person but exhausted his supplies before too long. He apologized for the shortage as he gathered his things and repacked the crate. Wheeling his bicycle to the tracks, he was beset with grievances and bitter reminders of promised treatment and cries of favoritism. Thomas simply mounted the bicycle and pedaled away.

"I hope he comes again," sighed Wakamburwa as she gazed down the tracks, her hand closing tightly over several tablets.

The wind had blown for days, raining dirt, sand, and dust upon the valley. Few ventured beyond their houses except to attend the necessities of life. Those who watched the herds and flocks hid themselves behind boulders or in abandoned huts to escape the wind's fury. Strangely every evening after the sun dropped below the hills, the winds calmed for a time. Yet before the moon finished rising through the night sky, they returned, imposing an unbearable curfew. But the heavy winds were an element of the season and everyone knew they would soon come to an end.

The morning dawned tranquilly, with a few low clouds hovering above the southerly hills. After a long absence, Ngipore and his son returned from taking their cattle to dry season pasture near Oruwanje. Their homeward trek was wearying as they drove a score of milk goats over mountain ridges during the windiest days, arriving in Otutati late one afternoon. The wind had damaged the fence around Ngipore's house (built to keep the livestock from waking him too early) and his enclosures were also seriously weakened. These were haphazardly patched, yet every morning the goats were able to breach the pen and storm the walls of his house.

Few people were up and about in the early morning as Repuree passed homestead after homestead on his way to see Ngipore. Crossing the river-bed, he pulled a blanket over his shoulders to cover his bare chest and stepped quickly up the embankment. His movement was swift, swifter than usual, but as he approached Ngipore's house and saw the tightly closed door, his walk slowed. Several goats strode across the cool, dusty ground, but most had gathered near the kids' enclosure, trying to answer the cries of their hungry offspring. For a moment Repuree stood at the fence, staring at the door, then guardedly crept forward and listened. Hearing nothing, he retraced his steps and sat beside a fence post, drawing his legs under the blanket. From a distance, several goats began approaching him, advancing in stages as a thin, silvery haired beast led the way. Repuree watched each movement, allowing them to come near; his muscles tensed as he artfully reached for his stick. "Sik!" he cried suddenly, waving his arms. Spooked, the goats scattered in all directions.

The brief commotion had no effect upon the household. Repuree settled down again and slumped forward, gazing fixedly at the house, then around the homestead, at the rising sun, the dusty ground, the riverbed, the empty gardens, and back to his own feet. He repeated the course once more and then stood. "I say," he called, "is anyone inside this house?"

Without waiting for a reply, he walked to the door and knocked. "Is any-one in this house?" he called again. Crouching down, he listened and then withdrew beyond the fence to wait.

Presently, the door opened and Ngipore, stooping low, passed from the dark chamber, arranging his turban as he straightened his back. "What's all this noise?" he asked. "Can't a weary man sleep in his own house without being disturbed?" He lifted his right hand and shaded his eyes, straining on the image before him. The bleating of his animals momentarily caught his attention, but he quickly returned Repuree's stare. "Is that you, Repuree? Have you come to visit so early in the morning?"

"Yes," replied the young man, looking downward, "it is Repuree. I didn't mean to disturb you, but you're the only person who can help me. I had a dream last night, a frightening dream, and when I woke this morn-ing it was still clear in my mind. I think the dream is a warning, but I can't be sure. I'm hoping you might be able to interpret it for me."

"Ah, so you've had a dream," said Ngipore, nodding his head, "a fright-ening dream. Yes, well. Let's go sit over there in the warmth and you can tell me about your dream."

Ngipore slipped back into his house to fetch a chair. With long steps he walked to the hearth and placed it facing the sun. "Who's that over there?" he asked quietly, his chin pointing beyond the northerly edge of his homestead. "I don't know her name," replied Repuree, squinting, "but she's the old woman who lives in the house next to Wamesepa's day shelter." Ngipore shaded his eyes and fumbled his blanket. The woman was Kakara's grandmother, a sister to his estranged wife's mother. He waited till she came near, motioned to her, and greeted her kindly. "This child," he explained, "has had a dream and is going to recount it for me. Why don't you stay and listen?" The woman readily accepted the invitation and sat with her back to the sun. No sooner had Repuree begun his tale, when Ngipore silenced him and repaired to his house for an ember. Re-turning, he lit his bone pipe and handed it to the woman.

"In my dream," said Repuree, "I was no longer in this valley but in some other, and the land was hilly and uneven. I was running—running very quickly after a warthog. In my hand was a spear, and as I ran I looked down and thought to myself, 'Hey you, you must be hunting!' The warthog was very clever, always evading my spear. Then I remember stopping and leaning against a tree trunk. I looked one direction and then another, and to my surprise the warthog was walking in the high grasses and grubbing for food.

"Quietly, I sank to my knees and crawled toward it. The warthog didn't hear or smell me, and I raised my stick and crashed it on the animal's head. Blow after blow I gave it—and hard ones—yet it still wouldn't die. A friend of mine appeared from nowhere and started beating the animal. For some reason I stood up and walked backwards. I hadn't gone far when I tripped and fell over a stump. The warthog turned and looked at me. 'You're falling!' it said, as though it hadn't been beaten at all. Its voice was human and terrified me. I got up from the ground and continued walking backwards as seven dogs came running toward me and my friend. Suddenly, the warthog changed into a man—a man my friend knew well. My friend dropped his stick, but I took mine and began striking the man with all my strength, despite his screams and protests. The dogs gathered around me and watched. Then I awoke."

Ngipore breathed deeply. And Repuree watched him, giving him time to think.

"Well," he said at last, "can you interpret the dream?"

Ngipore pulled the blanket more tightly around his shoulders. "This, Repuree, is a strange dream, a very strange dream." He filled his pipe again and gave it to the woman. "One thing is clear to me," he said. "Your dream is a dream of comfort, a way for your fathers to assure you of their presence. As for the events of the dream, I don't know whether they correspond to something real or if they're merely suggestive. But it's obvious that someone was trying to bewitch you with intent to kill. I say your friend was really no friend at all but an enemy, jealous of you, only pretending to be a friend. The warthog is not a clever animal and only *omiti* could have allowed it to evade you. When you and your friend beat the warthog, all your blows came to nothing; but your friend knew it wasn't truly a warthog, only a vessel of his jealousy, his wrath, his *omiti*. This is why he stopped when the warthog turned into a man. You didn't recognize the man, but you sensed he wanted to harm you. And what did your friend do? He simply stood aside. The dogs, I think, were your fathers. They ran to you, they surrounded you, and they gave you strength. Your fathers came between you and the *omiti* that might have killed you." Ngipore turned slightly and ran his hands over his face. "Yes," he concluded, "I think your fathers are concerned that you remember them so little; they want you to know how often they protect you."

His explanation was finished and the old woman stood and pushed out her lower lip, smoking one last time before returning the pipe. Nodding her head, she murmured, "I must be going."

Repuree also rose to his feet. "I thank you," he said, closing his eyes. And lifting his hands to the level of his chin, he noiselessly clapped them. "I thank you very, very much."

Daniel had been in Opuwo for several days consulting a doctor about his eyes. Before leaving, he asked Vita to watch his cattle. Vita obliged him and herded the animals together with his own livestock and the mysterious cattle. The pasturage around Otutati was fully exhausted, making the daily round of driving the animals to and from grazing areas increasingly difficult. Farther and farther they had to be led, and with the number of burdens upon his own shoulders, Vita charged his younger son with the animals' care. Daniel had been gone for three days when Vita's son arrived home in the evening and told his father the mysterious cattle were missing. Immediately, the two returned to pasture and searched until nightfall. Early the next morning they retraced their steps, scouring the hillsides and riverbeds, looking behind large clumps of trees, and walking through every patch of scrubland until Vita felt the search was lost. Day after day, his son continued looking while the livestock grazed, but it seemed the mysterious cattle had vanished without a trace.

"My husband is with the goats," answered Vita's wife. "He said to expect him back at midday." She turned from the strange men and glanced at Watumba. "If you wish," she said hesitantly, "you may rest yourselves here and wait for him to return." Pointing with her eyes, she added, "My daughters are roasting maize. When it's ready they'll bring you some—and a gourd of soured milk."

"Many, many thanks," said the elder one. "Your hospitality is indeed welcome."

The three men settled some distance from the work shelter where Vita's wife and Watumba sat with their young children grinding maize into meal. The sight of the men on donkeys standing at the edge of the homestead had frightened the two. But when Kupika announced they were searching for missing livestock and had been riding south for two days after hearing of the mysterious appearance of cattle in Otutati, the nature of their business was clear. Vita was a stranger to them, but as his name was mentioned in the story, when they arrived in Otutati, Katere and Mukuva easily directed them to his homestead. Vita's wife felt she must invite them to wait, knowing her husband should properly inform them of the cattle's disappearance.

Kupika and his companions were silent as refreshments were brought to them. Standing back several paces, Vita's wife cautiously looked at the men's faces while the girls served them, their eyes politely averted. "Is it as I thought?" asked Watumba, as soon as they returned to the shelter. "Yes," answered Vita's wife, "his eyes are very red." The two spoke quietly, discussing whether the redness of Kupika's eyes was due to fatigue or if it might be a sign of malice, of hatred, of *omiti.* The men ate and talked among themselves, taking care that their words fell only where intended. A few clouds drifted overhead and a slight breeze blew from the east. The breeze was friendly and cooling, and too weak to lift the dust from the ground.

Vita approached his homestead from the north. At first the strangers remained invisible, but as he took notice of the three men his eyes strained toward their faces. He hurried his step to greet them, entering the homestead as the sun passed behind a cloud. Deep shadows fell across the strangers' faces.

"Does the day go well for you?" called Vita in an amicable voice.

"Yes," returned Kupika, "the day goes well and your wife has been very hospitable."

"Thank you," said Vita, looking for a place to sit. He dusted a flat stone with his foot and lowered himself, holding his front skirt in place. "You seem familiar to me," he continued, looking at Kupika, "but I don't know exactly why—perhaps we've met on another occasion. But tell me now, what's your news? Why have you come to visit me?"

"Our news," answered Kupika, "comes from news of you. We hear of cattle appearing in your homestead that don't belong here. And since cattle belonging to us have disappeared, we thought we'd better come and look over these beasts of yours."

"Ah, I see," said Vita. "I am truly sorry, but you've come too late. The cattle are no longer here."

Kupika dashed his stick against the ground. "What do you mean we've come too late? Where are the cattle?"

"I don't know where they are, but they are gone," replied Vita. "All I can tell you is what I know." Patiently and unhurriedly, he recounted the cattle's discovery, his efforts to learn of the circumstances of their arrival, and the counsel of Wandisa. "I followed his advice, but one man can't do everything so my son began herding the cattle. One evening, he returned home saying they were lost. We looked for them until dark, and in the morning we continued our search, but found nothing. It was all very curious because the cattle had been grazing together the whole time—the strange ones never separated from my herd. Truly, my son and I searched and searched without finding even one of them. And this is all I know." The strangers shook their heads and one of them clicked his tongue. "Do you think they just wandered off?" he asked.

"I say, I don't know what to think," answered Vita. "Put yourselves in my place—after several days' away from home I return and find strange cattle standing in my enclosure. No one has any idea of how they came to be there. And barely has the moon finished growing when the cattle disappear, and as before, nobody knows how or why. Now, I ask you, have you ever heard of such a thing happening before? I haven't, and I don't know why it's happened to me."

Vita's words were fervent and he lowered his eyes after speaking them. The youngest of the three responded, breaking an awkward silence. "If there's nothing more you can tell us about the cattle's disappearance, perhaps you remember their colors and ear markings. If you do, we'll be able to know if the beasts belong to us." His companions nodded their approval.

"Yes," said Vita, "I think I can help you with this."

The four spent considerable time discussing the subtlety of colors, spots, stripes, horns, and ear cuttings, restating the combinations again and again until at last Kupika was satisfied.

"Vita, my man," he said, "I believe your words, and your words tell me the mysterious cattle are ours."

They rose to their feet, Kupika saying he would speak with Wandisa before they continued on to Opuwo. Vita watched until they had mounted and passed beyond the woodland. His wife strode toward him and joined him at the homestead's edge. "The men believe the cattle are theirs," he whispered. "They also said the beasts were stolen."

13

When Words Are Spoken

. . . they resonate with virtue or vice, and their messages ring true or false. Wamesepa returns to Otutati, but not before consulting with the diviner, Mbuwene. Watuwamo has also been to Opuwo, but her words bring both sadness and hope. Kuwiya drives his flocks to drink and finds the words of a man speaking with Francisco shameful and unworthy.

Many, many years ago, three maidens went berry collecting in the mountains. Before leaving, their parents admonished them to use their words cautiously, warning them not to swear even if they should they stumble against a tree or a stone. As the day progressed, the first two slipped several times. But remembering their parents' advice, they held their tongues in silence. By and by Nihova, the youngest maiden, tripped over a large, jagged stone and swore an oath against it. The other two rebuked her, reminding Nihova of what their parents had said. But she countered them, asking, "What should I do if a stone hurts me?" A great many berries had already been collected, yet the maidens decided to walk across the slope to another wooded area. Blocking their way, however, was a huge boulder wedged between the steep cliffs. The first two maidens stood before the boulder and sang, "Oh rock belonging to Nauyamba, please open for me. With the bead on my head, I also belong to Nauyamba—and the one who swore at you is not yet here!" The boulder opened and the first maiden walked through the cliff. The second maiden repeated the song and the boulder obeyed. When Nihova approached the cliffs, she also began to sing; yet the boulder refused to open. Her companions urged her to sing more forcefully, but it was to no avail; the boulder would not open and she was left behind.

※

At the behest of his daughter, Katere stood gazing to the east, his left hand cupped against the small of his back. The girl's young eyes were keen and perceptive, for in the distance was a man. His pace was moderate and his course seemed directed toward Wamesepa's homestead. Upon his shoulder rested a walking stick bearing a large, cumbersome bundle—a bundle made from the same brightly colored cloth as the man's turban. Katere's daughter ran back to her playmates, upsetting birds in a nearby tree as they busily gathered nesting material. Her father slowly made his way to the work shelter where her mother sat with friends. All eyes were on the traveler, though no one fully recognized the man. When at last he came near, Katere greeted him politely.

"Yes," replied the stranger, "the day goes well for me." He was a younger man, dusty from his walking, but cleanly shaven. He lifted the stick from his shoulder and eased the bundle to the ground. "I'm looking for a man named Katere, the nephew of Wamesepa Ngombe," he calmly announced. "Do you know where I can find him?"

"And why do you seek this man?" asked Katere.

"I have a message from Wamesepa and Wamesepa's son."

Katere leaned heavily against a post. "I'm Katere," he confessed, "the son of Wamesepa's sister."

The stranger looked around as if he would sit, but Katere remained standing against the post.

"So you are Katere," said the man, "then let me give you the message. Wandisa says this: Your uncle has been released from hospital and wishes to return home. Wandisa's truck won't move, and he asks you to arrange transport for his father. His father is staying in Katwerwa's hut in Opuwo, not far from the hospital. Wandisa asks that this be done as soon as possible." The stranger paused and furled his brow. "Yes," he said, a moment later. "I believe that's everything."

Katere spoke to his wife, and the stranger was given a gourd of soured milk to drink. He turned slightly and motioned for me to follow him. "You've heard what this man has said?" he asked. "Your father and my father has great need of us." Katere's intentions were clear.

We arrived in Opuwo midafternoon, and as Katere had frequented Katwerwa's townhouse many times, he guided us to the small, plastered hut without a single wrong turn. It stood between two other houses made of corrugated tin and sticks. A chest-high fence separated Katwerwa's town-house from the others, and as we stood peering over the briary pickets, the hut appeared empty and the door securely bolted. Not a moment had passed when a wandering neighbor told us that Wamesepa had gone to see Mbuwene that morning and was now traveling home by donkey cart.

The man called Mbuwene lived in a secretive compound near the foot of a flat-topped mountain, northwest of Opuwo. He was a seer, a diviner, a revelator; and conspicuously little was known of his origin. Rumors that he was a Xhosa from South Africa were widely spread, though others thought him Angolan; but whatever his birthright, Mbuwene spoke all of the local languages with perfect fluency. His dark, matted hair fell below his shoulders, and he was of average height. Mbuwene was renowned for his disguises and often accused of masquerading as other personas. His underground popularity was enormous, and this, it seemed, was rooted in the flow of gossip. Of the many and varied stories that circulated about him, it was nearly impossible to sift truth from error. Two things, however, were of common agreement: that he was an exceptionally gifted diviner, and that he often dressed in the Victorian costume of Herero women and walked the feculent lanes of Opuwo handing sweets to children who called him beautiful. Many had encountered such a man (with a scarf pulled round his cheeks and chin) and warned their sons away from him. But since he was renowned for his talent as a diviner, his sweeping prome-nades were tolerated.

Wamesepa's lungs were healthy when Dr. Forster signed his discharge from the hospital. Katwerwa helped him to the townhouse where he would convalesce before returning home. The old man was pleased with his treat-ment but feared another relapse and several times called Wandisa and Katwerwa to his side to discuss a final cure. Both agreed his present good health could only be temporary, but after so many attempts to secure a lasting solution, neither of their attitudes were anything more than realistic. It was known that Mbuwene was in town, and though Katwerwa and Wandisa had low opinions of diviners in general, for Wamesepa's sake, and in the unlikely event that Mbuwene could offer a genuine remedy, they agreed to arrange a consultation. The problem of conveying Wamesepa to Mbu-wene's home was solved when Katwerwa borrowed a large, rickety cart and two thin donkeys from a shopkeeper. The man, a Portuguese mulatto, ordered a servant to hitch the donkeys and bring the cart to Katwerwa's townhouse. And after the briefest instruction Katwerwa was on his own, never before having driven a team of animals. A hastily fashioned bed was lowered into the cart, and when Katanga pronounced it good, Wandisa helped lift his father onto the bed and then covered him with a blanket.

Abruptly, the cart pulled away from the house and headed for the tarred road, raising a cloud of dust in its wake. Wamesepa chatted a bit, but mostly rested as the morning bustle of Opuwo became ever more distant. The path narrowed through a glade of ironwood trees before running parallel to the banks of a dry watercourse. Pulling the cart through a dip in the embankment, the donkeys struggled across the sandy bed and up the other side. Far ahead, Katwerwa sighted a tall fence made of upright timbers that conformed to the various descriptions given him of Mbuwene's compound. As they neared the homestead, the gate opened, but the passage was far too narrow for the cart and Katwerwa urged the donkeys into the shade of a tree. "We are here, *Tate*," he said, forcefully pulling the reins. Easing himself from the driver's bench, Katwerwa walked to the rear and helped Wamesepa from the cart. Together, they entered the compound and hesitantly looked about, not knowing how they should properly announce themselves.

They were alone but a moment when Mbuwene walked from the large doorway of his rectangular house. "Great one!" he called, "I'm pleased you honor me with this visit. Has the morning gone well for you?"

Wamesepa cleared his throat. "Yes," he replied.

Mbuwene's salutations were extensive, but finally his words ceased and he ushered Wamesepa toward his house. Katwerwa wavered a bit, uncertain whether he should follow his uncle. The old man turned and looked over his shoulder, and Katwerwa quickly stepped to his side. Passing through the doorway, they entered the dark and smokey house. Carefully, Mbuwene led the two inside and seated them on wooden stools near the center of the room. His figure was shadowy as he moved about, lowering his head to avoid the many bundles dangling from the rafters. His preparations appeared methodical and precise, and when they finally ended, he sat on a goatskin at Wamesepa's feet.

"Great One," he began in a low, groveling voice. "Your nephew has solicited my powers on your behalf and the oracle is ready. But first you must help me understand the problem you wish to set before it."

Wamesepa took a deep breath and turned his head toward the doorway. "I've been with many of your kind," he lamented. "My problem isn't new and I doubt you can resolve it—still, I must try." He drew his knees together and laid his stick upon the floor. "It's my health, my breathing. It's the thing that kills the men of my family—always the lungs. I'm an old man and I've learned that much of life is beyond our control, but I'd like to know whether my sickness can be cured, and if it can, what it is my fathers expect of me."

Mbuwene lowered his eyes and crouched beside the hearth. The smouldering wood was blown into a weak flame and strengthened until its heat could be felt. Returning to the skin, Mbuwene said, "So it's a lung illness that troubles you, and you wish to be healed of it." Wamesepa nodded affirmatively. Mbuwene sat quietly for a time, then leaned forward on his knees and stood. "I'll prepare to set this problem before my oracle, and I assure you, Great One, my oracle is powerful. It knows all things and reveals the feelings of one's heart and mind. It speaks to all the powers and medicines in the world—nothing can hide from it."

Mbuwene bent slightly at the waist and stared at the burning wood. Some of the light generated by the growing flames rested upon a long, cloth drapery hanging at the edge of the room. Within this veil of privacy Mubwene kept his oracle. It was an object whose viewing was forbidden to all but its servant. The oracle was said to be hot, approachable only by Mbuwene, and only when his own body was sufficiently heated to allow his intellectual powers to fuse with the oracle's revelations. He removed his sandals and unbuttoned his shirt, then stepped to the fire's edge and warmed himself, slowly bathing his skin in the rising heat. Wamesepa watched for a while, but the events seemed not to engage his attention. Lowering his head, he opened his snuff tube and reached behind his ear for the spoon. His aged lungs inhaled with effort, but then he relaxed— as oblivious to the silent incantations of the oracle's servant as Mbuwene was of his patient's casual indifference.

The diviner left the fire and retreated behind the drapery. Kneeling down, Mbuwene was mostly hidden from view, speaking in a tongue neither Wamesepa nor Katwerwa recognized. The conversation was lengthy and spirited, and at its conclusion Mbuwene exhaled mightily before lapsing into silence. Moments later, the curtain parted and he walked from the presence of the oracle, utterly spent. Katwerwa laid his hand on Wamesepa's arm to awaken him. The old man opened his eyes and looked about; Mbuwene strode forward and took his place on the skin.

"Great One," he said, "I have an answer for you." Wamesepa blinked and cocked his head to one side. "The medicine tells me your grandfather is displeased with you, that you haven't sufficiently remembered him. The sickness in your lungs is to remind you of him because he too suffered from that sickness." Mbuwene paused and surreptitiously glanced at the two men. "The medicine warns you that so long as your grandfather is aggrieved your lungs will not heal. He asks that you honor him by sacrificing a bullock. He wishes to bless you, to withdraw the sickness from you, but cannot unless he is shown proper respect." The oracle's servant inhaled deeply and raised his voice. "So speaks the medicine!" he concluded.

Katwerwa had turned, peering through the doorway, listening as a group of children passed along the riverbed. Mbuwene's head deliberately sank as he waited for Wamesepa to speak. The old man stared at the fire. "I don't understand," he quietly replied, "why my grandfather should think I've neglected him. Perhaps it is so—I might have done something to offend him. But I don't think so." He sighed heavily, for it was the same old diagnosis—one so difficult to fathom. He reached for his stick and was ready to leave.

Walking across the open courtyard to the cart, Katwerwa helped Wamesepa to his bed. Mbuwene stood by himself, leaning against the trunk of a tree waiting for Katwerwa. "Is your uncle pleased?" he asked when the man came near. Without answering, Katwerwa handed him a hundred rand note and stepped away.

Feeling the shake of a rubber whip, the donkeys started across the riverbed.

Wandisa was still sitting in council when they returned to the townhouse. A number of people waited there, hoping to find a ride to Otutati. Spread over the ground were rolls of bedding and parcels of cookware, sugar, maize meal, salt, and other goods to be delivered to homesteads and cattle posts. Katanga had neatly gathered Wamesepa's things and set them near her own bundles. The arrival of braying donkeys temporarily broke the ongoing conversations and lounging men rose to their feet in greeting. Katwerwa climbed from the seat but Wamesepa remained in his bed, tired and longing for home. It was past midday and the activity of the neighborhood was beginning to settle into its afternoon quiet. When at last the council head called a recess, Wandisa hurried along the narrow footpath leading to the townhouse and stooped to climb through a break in the fence. Amid the jovial commotion, he sought Katwerwa's eye, and quietly, the man slipped away to confer with Wandisa.

"Mbuwene claims his grandfather has something against him," Katwerwa answered. "This is why the sickness always returns. His grandfather has requested that a bullock be sacrificed if the illness is to be cured." And deflecting slightly, he whispered, "I don't honestly think your father was satisfied with the explanation—though he's said nothing about that to me."

Wandisa wiped his lips and chin. "Yes," he said. "I see." His eyes moved downward. "In any case, my father will have to decide what to do. If he wants to make a sacrifice, we will do so. And even though I have doubts about Mbuwene, I'm still the son, not the father."

Their words soon ended and they rejoined the crowd. Wandisa visited with a few people before speaking at length with his father, and taking notice of the descending sun, he returned to council without mention of the message he had sent Katere. Baggage and people were carefully loaded around the contours of Wamesepa's resting form, and the two donkeys, straining with a heavily overburdened cart, pulled away from the townhouse and walked toward the main road.

After hearing of their departure, Katere and I decided to return to Otutati. The narrow lane adjoining Katwerwa's townhouse led to the main road, and as we drove away from the small shanty town we passed a large sow grubbing through a collection of household rubbish. Katere looked at the animal with disgust. "How could anyone eat the flesh of such a revolting creature?" he asked. Children played near the road, kicking tins from one to another and clapping hands. As the petrol station came into full view, Katere knocked rapidly against his window and pointed with his chin. Standing in the shade of a pepper tree in the municipal building's forecourt was Watuwamo. A large goatskin bag hung from her left shoulder and tied on her back was a baby, an infant not her own. We crossed the road, slowed to a halt, and offered her a ride home.

Watuwamo had been in Opuwo for several days visiting her daughter, a girl born to her while she was yet unmarried. The baby had become a toddler when Watuwamo was taken to wife, and she accompanied her mother in marriage. The girl was soft-spoken and a good companion, and Watuwamo's husband treated her affectionately. During a cool, dry season, the girl, now a maiden, traveled north to visit her grandparents and met with a group of soldiers fighting in the Border War. This temporary association gave her a taste for alcohol. "She was no longer my daughter," said Watuwamo, "but another person. She thought of nothing but drink. We tried to help her, tried to keep her away from alcohol, but she resented us and refused to see what was happening to her. My daughter became a thief, stealing things from us and then returning home sick. One day I told her she couldn't stay in our homestead, that her heart no longer worked. I so hoped she would change, but she didn't." The young woman moved to Opuwo and made her way begging and granting easy favors. She and her mother remained in good contact, and in her sober moments she was warm and receptive. Her sickness, though, worsened, and when she told her mother of a coming baby, Watuwamo was afraid. The baby was born in Opuwo, away from its maternal home, but Watuwamo was a frequent visitor. "This time I feared the baby might not live, so I asked my daughter if I should take her home with me. She finally agreed it would be best."

Now the tiny girl slept at her grandmother's bosom.

The tarred road soon ended and we drove the tracks leading westward, looping behind the Opuwo hill. In places the dust was thick and deep and would have been impassable had the tracks not been partially solid. Ahead lay a narrow span of concrete resting atop a large culvert. As we drew closer, a group of people clustered on one side of the culvert waved at us, warning us to stop. Katere and Watuwamo leaned their heads through the open windows, peering toward the shade of a tree growing over the dry streambed where Wamesepa lay on his skins and blankets. The cart had been driven too close to the edge and the left wheel had stumbled. One side of the cart rested on its axle—but the donkeys managed to keep their footing while people and possessions were hastily offloaded. No sooner had the cart been emptied when Katwerwa admonished the donkeys to pull, and their traction, combined with the lifting power of four or five men, eventually set the cart aright.

As we stepped from Old Rover to greet the travelers, we noticed a short, fragile looking woman descending the hillside along a well-worn footpath.

She was dressed in a heavily soiled blouse and skirt, both yellow, and chatted vociferously with herself. Katwerwa came forward to greet us, explaining the mishap in some detail and asking whether Wamesepa might ride home with us. After a time, we climbed down to the streambed to talk with Wamesepa and collect his belongings. The strange woman's chatter was ever present and at someone's insistence we turned to see her dip a metal pail into the sandy bed as though she were drawing water. Everyone stared, but it was Katanga's gaze, as she paused from her bundle gathering, that seemed to vex the woman. Rising truculently from the dry stream, she placed the pail on her head and walked toward Katanga, cursing her very existence, accusing her of having stolen her husband's affections. The poor woman stood no more than an arm's length from Katanga, screaming the same ugly words again and again. Wamesepa leaned forward on his elbows and stared at the woman, baffled by her demeanor. Finally, Katanga took a step in the stranger's direction and raised her chin. "You, Mama," she calmly said, "are speaking as a fool. And your words are as filthy as your breath." Immediately, the woman fell silent, turned, and placing her left hand on the pail to steady it, began walking up the hill.

Wamesepa and Katanga, along with their possessions, were loaded into Old Rover. Having decided to return the cart to its owner, Katwerwa patiently led the donkeys beyond the concrete and turned them around. Still apprehensive about driving over the culvert, he walked the cart across the span of concrete and stopped beside those wishing to return to Opuwo. A handful of others elected to wait beside the tracks, hoping to find their way with another traveler.

Along the northeast horizon, far above the mountaintops, heavy, gray clouds had begun to gather. The clouds would surely not bring rain, but were a hopeful sign that the coming rainy season might be long and wet. The valley was slowly awakening from its cold, dry slumber, and everywhere modest, new buds of fresh, ebullient green rose from the soil, from tired, dusty branches, and from long dormant vines. Yet it was only a hint of the changing seasons, the merest suggestion that the time of want was nearing its close.

Wamesepa's return home had lifted his spirits though his health remained fragile. Wandisa said his father thought often of Mbuwene's words, but was still uncertain whether or not he believed them. Many rainy seasons had passed since he had visited his fathers' graves, but this, he felt, was not due to willful neglect but to his own physical decline. The graves lay a fair journey from Otutati, and in his enfeebled condition such an undertaking would be difficult. Still, Wamesepa had not dismissed the idea entirely, choosing instead to be certain of its usefulness before asking Wandisa to make preparations.

The new morning proved cool and breezy, and the blades of the windmill hummed as they spun round and round, the only pieces of the water-drawing pump not to have lain idle since the end of the previous rainy season. On several occasions Wandisa requested that the pump and mill be mended, but was reminded that many such pumps needed repair. Water reserves around Otutati were low. The perennial fountains still ran at a trickle and provided fresh water for people, but the water available for livestock was dwindling. The once full reservoir was shrunken and muddy, yet the area's herdsmen were dependent on it. Under his father's direction, Wandisa called a meeting of all the men currently residing in and around Otutati to discuss the problem. It was agreed that water was critically short, and following Wamesepa's advice, it was decided that the animals be allowed to drink only once every three days. A rough schedule was devised to stagger watering days, as well as the time of day each man should bring his livestock to drink, and the plan was put into effect.

Kuwiya had asked me to help him with his large flock of goats as he led them to water. Narrow paths crisscrossed the creamy soil through dense ironwood groves and along the often deep channels cut by flood waters as they rushed from the mountains and hills toward the reservoir. Everywhere we walked the spoors of goats, sheep, and cattle had been pressed into the ground, forming serpentine patterns of movement in the finely textured dust. The animals had also worn pathways through tightly clustered bushes and shrubs growing along the channels, their bodies pressing against lower branches and limbs until the woody barriers were forced aside. Kuwiya's goats had spent the morning in their enclosure to avoid the far lengthier trek from pasture to reservoir, and the creatures, now anxious to end their fast, were distracted by any edible pod or shoot and had to be urged at every turn. Kuwiya clicked his tongue and raised his stick to keep the flock moving. His two young sons followed the same methods in driving the animals forward, but the goats were no longer fat and had difficulty sustaining their usual pace. We had only passed beyond the two small hills when the scent of water reached the animals' nostrils. Immediately, Kuwiya ran ahead to divert the goats lest the flock run headlong to the reservoir and cause a panic. Shouting directions, the two boys and I loosely flanked their father, and with stones, sticks, and threatening moves, slowly brought the charge under control.

Kuwiya sent his elder son to see whether it was time for the goats to approach; the boy returned with an unwelcome report that other flocks were drinking. Progress had to be slowed, but the animals' thirst was far stronger than the staff, and again and again the goats broke rank forcing us to scramble. Kuwiya decided to advance in stages and maintain order as best we could. Stopping a hundred paces from the reservoir on a slight rise from which we could view the coming and going of livestock, the usual scene of visiting, gossiping, and laying plans had given way to discussion. Francisco and several other Hakavona stood opposite a tall Himba man. A small gallery of onlookers had gathered on the fringes, and as none of them was talking, Kuwiya surmised the discussion was not friendly.

The tall man was called Tjiuma and lived in a modest homestead near Oritjitombo. His broad shoulders, firm musculature, and deep, resonant voice set him apart from the others. He was also rumored to be a distant kinsman of Katere, though the two never visited and never publicly acknowledged the relationship. Francisco and his son-in-law, also a tall man, were answering questions, but the three youth who accompanied them had left the conversation at Francisco's request to gather their animals.

"It is our turn to water the animals. This was decided when all of us met with Wandisa," Francisco said to Tjiuma. "And I don't recollect seeing you at the meeting."

"I didn't attend the meeting," roared Tjiuma, "but I'm Himba and you're not! You have no claim to water your animals here when I need to. This isn't your land, this is Himba land!"

His body strained and trembling, Francisco lowered his head. "The privilege to water my animals at this reservoir was given me by Wamesepa Ngombe. You don't even live around Otutati. I've never seen you at the homestead of Wamesepa. So I ask you, who are you to be claiming such privileges for yourself?"

A ripple of wind filled Tjiuma's rear skirt and he stepped backward, lowering an arm to keep it in place. Francisco raised his head and looked directly at Tjiuma. Glancing about, the tall man saw the growing audience on the shore, and from their silence and downturned faces he realized his words had found little support. It was perfectly still, except for animals' voices; even the children had stopped their play. Tjiuma kept his head high, never casting his eyes downward, yet entirely avoiding Francisco's gaze. The audience's silence was the silence that follows a breach of civility.

Standing with his shoulders peaked, Tjiuma turned to face Francisco, his eyes fixed on some distant object. "We call you servants, we call you slaves!" he thundered. "You aren't Himba!" He lifted his stick and walked down the slope to where his wife and elder daughter stood. "Bring the animals home after they have drunk," he ordered. "I won't stay here any longer."

Tjiuma left, heading westward toward Oritjitombo. Most of the bystanders watched his tall, handsome figure till it disappeared from view. His sheep and goats had long since finished drinking and simply loitered in the mud, but his wife made no effort to gather them. At last, a goat broke through Kuwiya's guard and then the entire flock surged toward the reservoir. His sons clicked and threatened, but Kuwiya stood motionless, allowing the animals to have their moment. Then he walked to the water's edge and invited Francisco to bring his livestock.

14

The Living and the Dead

. . . derive comfort from one another. A missing woman is sought and eventually found and her soul brought to peace. Wamesepa calls for Ngipore to hear his dream and wishes to visit the grave of his father once more before he dies—a journey requiring the help of many. And Mukuva bids farewell to the woman he called his second mother.

Rain had fallen two successive evenings, clearing the dust and nurturing a delicate aroma of soil and plants that filled the air until overshadowed by the midday sun. It had rained more heavily in the pasturelands north of Otutati, prompting several women to return and begin the work of clearing their gardens. Once settled though, they saw their intentions were premature. Wamesepa's health remained steady and any thought of following Mbuwene's advice had fallen from discussion. Yet the idea of cleaning his father's grave and dedicating another heifer to him was ever-present.

On a calm, windless evening, as Katere sat dining with his wife, several men on foot approached his work shelter asking whether anyone had seen their mother in the past few days. She was an elder woman of noted maturity and sapience who lived in a cluster of homesteads on the eastern side of the valley. Her husband had died in his middle years; and though her natal home of Otjinungwa was far away, she chose to remain with her husband's people. Her sons and daughters-in-law had long since driven the cattle to dry season pasture, leaving behind a favorite granddaughter to tend her and keep her company. But not many days ago, the maiden arrived at the cattle post conveying her grandmother's greetings as well as a message that she had decided to visit her sister and was sending the girl to post to enjoy the remainder of the season with her friends. The brothers felt uneasy about the turn of events and two of them journeyed homeward to call on their mother.

The search had greatly expanded as her only living sister had seen nothing of her. The few people around her homestead reported greeting the woman on the morning she had left; a child mentioned the old grandmother had asked him to lock the door when she was gone because her fingers were too sore to do so. Nothing more was known. With the help of other men, the brothers scoured various footpaths leading in the direction the woman had likely traveled without uncovering a single clue. Their mother had vanished. The brothers decided to visit each homestead in the valley, hoping someone might have seen her or spoken with her on the day of her disappearance. Katere and Wakamburwa listened with great interest to the unusual story before asking the men to join them at supper. Food was all they could offer.

At the request of his father, Wandisa had been away seeing that Wamesepa's herds and flocks were in good condition. It was a task rarely undertaken for the reason that only trusted kinsmen husbanded the livestock—herdsmen who approached their responsibilities with competence and skill. Wandisa was at first reluctant to undertake the journey, but did so because his father seemed earnest in his request. When he returned, he reported that three beasts had died from lung sickness and an old ewe had been lost to a predator. Otherwise, the livestock was doing well.

The morning after Wandisa's return, once the air had turned warm, Wamesepa repaired to his day shelter and waited for his son. Restlessly, he sat in his chair, shifting his weight from one leg to the other, finally settling a bit when he noticed the outline of a man approaching the shelter. "Good morning, *Tate*," said a voice, "do things go well for you?" Bending forward, Ngipore entered through the low doorway and stood before the old man wearing a pale yellow coat with rhinestone buttons. The collar and cuffs were heavily tinged with *otjize* and the coat's hem struck just above his knee. "Ah, it is you," replied Wamesepa, looking at his face,

"I'm glad you've come to greet me." Ngipore moved forward a step or two, probing a bit of fallen thatch with his stick. "You needn't stand," said Wamesepa. "Come, sit here beside me and tell me your news."

Holding his front skirt in place, Ngipore crouched downward and sat on a withered ironwood limb. Despite the fact that Ngipore was a relative newcomer to Otutati, Wamesepa knew him well. During his own youth and throughout most of his adult life, Wamesepa had been on close terms with Ngipore's father and grandfather, and commented from time to time on the characteristics the three of them shared: wit, genial companionship, and unusual wisdom and prudence in assessing matters of import. For a long while, the two chatted amiably, but as Ngipore rose to take his leave, Wamesepa asked that he stay until Wandisa arrived, adding he had something to share with them both. Ngipore respectfully obliged.

"Do you remember what that foreigner told me about my sickness," Wamesepa asked, "—that my grandfather struck me because I've forgotten him?"

"Yes," answered Wandisa. "I remember."

The old man lifted his chin. "I would like you both to listen, for I see things clearly now. I understand what this sickness means, so please hear me and tell me if you think I'm right."

Ngipore and Wandisa stretched their legs and turned their heads aside, each in a different direction.

"Didi," the old man said, "my father died when you were a boy. He died from a lung sickness and I remember so well the sound of his breathing, the smell of his breath. Mukuru had blessed my father with good fortune and nearly everything he attempted went well. I know that beyond his ears some called him a jackal, but I never thought he was a jackal—he wasn't clever in that sense. The truth is our fathers loved him and blessed him.

"During this very season, but long, long ago, I sat with him near the ancestral fire. He had summoned me from dry season post, and as a son who loved his father and respected him as a man, I did whatever he asked of me. When I arrived, he was sitting beside my mother, but not a word passed between them. I remember thinking, 'This is a strange thing—my father and mother sitting there like two stones.' They were both loquacious people, yet there they sat like a couple of trees. I greeted them and my father motioned me to his side. Mother left us to fetch a pail of sour milk and when she returned we drank. We were all alone in the open part of the homestead, just the two of us drinking. At last my father said, 'Wamesepa, my child, I've learned something I feel you should know. I've learned that my death will come soon.' His words seemed abrupt—as if something were missing—yet he said nothing more. I was puzzled that he should speak so openly of such things and I asked him, 'How can a man know of his own death? Who could possibly have told you this?' His eyes and lips held steady, but finally he made a reply. 'This knowledge came to me in a dream,' he said.

" 'Several nights ago I woke from a dream, a very simple dream. I was at the foot of the Ojtihapa mountains, where I spent much of my youth. I saw all kinds of animals, wild ones as well as cattle and sheep. The sun was about ready to set and from its direction came a large blackbird, flying toward my home. For a time it soared among the clouds, then lighted forcefully upon a springbok. Immediately, the springbok fell dead. The bird flew back to the clouds but dove again, this time landing on the head of a white sheep. It too died. Stretching its wings, the bird returned to the clouds, dipping low, then soaring high. The blackbird did this again and again, searching, searching, searching for something on the ground below. At last, the bird spied its target and swooped down, resting easily on the back of a jackal. I cried out and then awoke. I was sitting in my bed, yet already the dream's meaning was clear. I've always been called the jackal, even as a boy. The jackal is my animal and the blackbird has come for me.' "

Wamesepa drew himself forward in his chair. "My father died during the season of cold, not long after the cattle were taken to post again." Easing back, the old man's face was resolutely still, his eyes calm, and his breathing steady. "Last night," he said, "I had a dream like my father's. It was exactly as he described it, except the mountains were these over here, where I played as a child. A blackbird came from the west and circled in the sky, gliding, gliding—never flapping its wings. Suddenly, it swooped and landed on a huge kudu—the name of my father's people. It was an old buck with large, tall horns, and the bird lighted so gently the kudu seemed unaware, but it opened its mouth and fell to the ground. The bird flew into the bluest part of the sky, searching and searching for its next victim. It saw a cow, and I recognized the beast as one of those belonging to our ancestral herd. The bird circled around the cow's head, confusing the animal, and then perched on its horns. The beast collapsed and blood ran from its mouth. The blackbird stretched its wings and flew higher and higher till it was lost among the clouds. I looked across the sky, but I couldn't find it. Then I lowered my head and saw the bird. It had flown right here, in this very homestead, hovering above the ancestral fire. On the hearth lay an old lion with a tattered mane. The bird came to stand on the lion's shoulders, but unlike the other two animals, the lion felt the bird's talons, and it trembled and squirmed and died an agonizing death."

Wamesepa turned and looked at Wandisa. "I am that lion," he said, "I know that clearly. And like my father, I know my death is near." He put his head back and closed his eyes. A period of absolute quiet followed his words.

"*Tate*," said Ngipore, hesitantly breaking the peace. "I have heard you now, I have listened very carefully. What is it you wish me to say?"

Opening his eyes, Wamesepa replied, "You are good with dreams, my child. I wish you to tell me whether or not I understand my dream."

Ngipore paused and lowered his head.

"I think," he said after a time, "that your interpretation is good. But I do question the timing of your death, *Tate*. The lion struggled and did not die immediately, as did the kudu and the beast. It may be that though the bird has come, your death is not as near as you think."

"Are you speaking the truth," asked Wamesepa, "or simply placating an old man?"

"*Tate*, I speak what is in my heart."

Wandisa leaned forward. "Father, what do you think? What do you have in mind?"

Wamesepa coughed. "I'm not anxious to die," he whispered. "And when I was your age I wasn't anxious either. We're forbidden to speak of it, but I think every old man and old woman is afraid to die—and why shouldn't we be?"

He turned abruptly, the sound of children at play upsetting his train of thought.

"Didi," he continued, "this is what I have in mind. When my father died and I watched his grave being filled, I wished I had taken him to *yambera* his father's grave. Now I have a great desire to clean my own father's grave and dedicate a heifer to him. But I'm too old and feeble to arrange this myself, so I ask you, Wandisa, my elder son, to do this for me. I'd like everyone to attend the feast, not just my paternal kin. This is what I'd have you do."

Wandisa straightened his shoulders as his father relaxed against the back of his chair. To organize a *yambera* would require considerable time and effort. Word of the event would have to be circulated and a proximate day fixed; the length of travel from northern and southern Kaokoland would need proper calculation, and the *yambera* animals would have to be brought from their sundry grazing areas to Otutati. But in due course, Wandisa assured his father, all the arrangements would be made.

With the warm afternoon breeze came the news that the missing woman had been found. The details were spoken quietly and only among adults. After the brothers had finished their search of the valley, they returned to their homestead, never having opened their mother's house. One of the two examined the door and found that though it appeared to be securely locked, the door was not actually bolted and could be opened and shut at will. Pulling the door toward him, the man looked inside and saw his mother's body hanging in midair. The woman had tied one end of a long strip of ironwood bark around her neck and the other to a point in the ceiling where a rafter met the tall, central pole. The discovery was shocking, and not one person could understand why the woman should have taken her own life. The body, already beginning to smell, was released from the cord and laid on the floor. Several messengers were dispatched to inform those who needed to know in order that burial arrangements could be made.

It is impossible to know all the sorrows and problems that lurk in people's hearts. The outside of a human being may be far from the inside, and the person who commits suicide can only be pitied that his burdens were so great he saw no other resolution. Mukuru understands such people—he and he alone. Only Mukuru can see into a person's heart and comprehend the motivations behind such an act. This woman had lived with a heart so heavily laden her closest kin were blind to it; no one but Mukuru will ever be able to penetrate the mystery of her death.

The walk to the homestead was long but pleasant in the midmorning cool and many from Otutati had decided to attend the funeral. The circle of homes where the woman had lived was large and its work shelters teemed with friends and relatives preparing the burial feast. The deceased's body lay ready for interment in the house where she had taken her life, wrapped in a leather cape; only her face was visible. On the western edge of the homestead, just beyond the fence, stood a temporary hut constructed of saplings, blankets, and skins. Before its entrance stood an ever expanding throng of people awaiting their turns. At intervals long and short, one group would leave the house as another entered on its heels.

Mukuva and his wife, together with her mother and sister, stooped low and walked into the dusky hut. It was warm inside, and seated along the eastern wall were the deceased's four sons, her sister, and three other close kinsmen Mukuva had never met. The women wept openly, occasionally striking their breasts and wailing at the top of their voices to express the depth of their grief. The displays were momentary, and as Mukuva positioned himself, the cries began to soften.

Standing erect with his eyes cast downward, his hands joined at the small of his back, Mukuva began to speak. "Your mother was a good woman," he said in a strong, clear voice. "She was kind and generous, especially to children. As you all know, I spent time in your homestead as a boy and a youth—I played with you and I worked with you. Always, your mother was my mother. She fed me, she talked to me, she pulled thorns from my feet, and she provided me with a bed. She came to my wedding, she came to the namings of my sons and daughters; she was with me at the death of my father and my mother. She was a good woman, she cared for people."

As Mukuva ended his prepared words the mourners lifted their cries. The family acknowledged him, and then it was time for his wife to remember the deceased. When the last member of his party had had her turn, the women cried again and Mukuva left the hut. Company after company visited with the family, conveying their associations and remembrances of the dead woman. Their numbers, though, had swollen beyond all expectation, and when at last the family emerged from the hut, the sun was low in the western sky. The brothers hastily gathered and conferred, deciding to conduct the burial and sacrifice on the following morning, inviting all those visiting the homestead to join them in an evening meal.

We returned the next morning with many others. The fire-keeper approached the ancestral hearth and spoke to the fathers of the woman's

deceased husband. Her sons carried the body on a litter to the graveyard,
quite a distance from the homestead. There, beside several rows of her
husband's kinsmen, a deep grave had been dug. The sons lowered the
corpse to the ground and prepared her stiffening body by lifting her torso,
drawing her knees to her chest so that the soles of her feet faced forward,
and raising her chin that her closed eyes would look the same direction
as the soles of her feet. With particular care, the body was set in the grave
facing east, the vantage point of the immortals, and all in company pushed
a bit of earth into the grave. The women present wept and howled until
all of the mourners had had their turn. Two men with spades completed
the task as the congregation of mourners returned to the homestead and
gathered at the ancestral fire. Drawing water from a wooden bowl, the
fire-keeper sprayed the consecrated fluid over the mourners to cleanse
them from their association with a decaying body, purifying them so they
could rejoin the world of the living.

Cattle and sheep were slaughtered for the feast and the preparations
were well underway. There was but one remaining difficulty—the disposal
of the woman's house. An entire homestead may be abandoned at the
death of one of its prominent members and the deceased's hut will be
left to decay naturally, though other houses and enclosures may be dis-
mantled and reassembled elsewhere. But this woman's death was highly
unusual, for it came not from the workings of *omiti*, but at her own hand.
There would be no inquiry, no reason to secretly establish the party responsible for the use of *omiti*. Yet her house could not be allowed to stand,
and after a lengthy discussion it was decided the hut should be burned to
the ground and the charred remains left to disperse according to the
winds.

The day had been busy with friends and kinsmen arriving for the com-
memoration ceremony. And as evening finally settled over Otutati, the
light of cooking fires dotted the plane south of the dry rivercourse. Three
ancient men had gathered in the sandy riverbed near a curve where a
pathway had been worn by children. They sat round a small fire in the
middle of the bed, leaning against their sleeping bundles. Wandisa's wife
had sent a daughter with a gourd of sour milk and a basket of warm
porridge to offer the men; the girl approached them warily, leaving the

food without answering their questions. One of them rubbed long shreds of brittle tobacco between his palms, his empty pipe lying at his knees. The milling was easy and he filled the pipe, lit it with a burning twig, and shared its pleasure with his two friends. The men had come to be with Wamesepa—the four of them were all that remained of the scores of youths circumcised in the year of the great bush fires. Wamesepa had guessed they would wish to sleep in the riverbed and had even considered joining the solitary encampment, but his weary bones longed for his own house, his own bed.

The short, thick man sitting with his back to the empty gardens inhaled slowly. The glow of the pipe reflected in the only lens of a pair of black spectacles he had inherited from a distant uncle. Turning his head, the firelight caught the tiny fragments of glass pressed into its bows, causing his companions to blink. Their conversation never waned but moved seamlessly from the beauty of the night sky to the condition of Wamesepa, from tomorrow's *yambera* ceremony to recollections of the past—their boyhood dreams, their youthful fancies, their failed romantic conquests, the changes they had witnessed, the things they had shared, and the people they now missed. The fire burned low, its coals grown black and gray, and the men unrolled their bedding and lay still against the easy sand.

Tempered by long, white clouds, the morning sun began rising above the easterly hills, casting streaks of darkness across the valley floor. The air was still and slightly warm and carried the angle of light that most fully revealed the delicate, new growth emerging from limbs, branches, tuffets, and vines. Children walked gingerly among the huts looking for playmates, but those who would later journey to the graves and witness the touching of the heifer were slow to leave their chambers, taking special care with their grooming. Well before the first guests had arrived, Katwerwa and Dakata had walked to a northern pasture to gather a number of suitable heifers to lead to the graves. These beasts would join a much smaller herd from Otutati—already en route—and from their combined numbers, Wamesepa's father would choose the animal he wished to possess. Wandisa believed the two herds of cattle would be in place before his father arrived at the graves and hoped the ceremony could begin by early afternoon.

Visiting our fathers' graves is a time of happiness and remembrance. It is also a time of hope, hope that the heifer will be well received by the deceased father, hope that the ancestors will no longer consider themselves forgotten, that their hearts will turn favorably to their living kin and the problems that beset them. Our ancestors are never fooled by mere display, by a simple following of long-standing traditions; they read our hearts, and if we yambera *a father out of duty or fear, rather than genuine affection, the ceremony is a fraud. We may have our meat and porridge and drink, but we do not have our father's approval. And the heifer that was to represent him, represents only a folly, a bit of trickery, an attempt to deceive those who already know the intentions of our hearts.*

An assemblage of people, mostly men, departed the homestead while the morning shadows were still long, heading for a small tract of sacred ground beyond the southeastern mountains. Among them were local men and youths, but the greater part was composed of visitors—trusted friends and relatives who had come to honor Wamesepa and his father. In all, sixty to seventy people began the pilgrimage, walking to a place few of them had ever seen, most carrying nothing more than a herding stick. Wandisa stood watching their piecemeal departure, while Katere stood beside him. The sight of so many people moving in a single direction was rare—a scene difficult to describe. Children were largely oblivious to it, but many of the remaining adults paused for a moment to observe the unceremonious procession.

"When shall we leave?" asked Katere.

"We'll let them get to the hills before we start," replied Wandisa. "But first I have to round up my own animals."

Wandisa had delayed the *yambera* until his truck was repaired, knowing his father would otherwise be unable to clean his father's grave and witness the cattle charge. He had also invited his father's circumcision friends to ride along with them. Katere had anticipated such an arrangement and on the previous evening approached Wandisa about his sore back and an aching hip. "This is a glad occasion," Wandisa had told him. "And I wouldn't want you to miss it. You may sit with the men in back. My father will ride up front with me."

Wandisa and one of his daughters led the animals to pasture. They crossed the riverbed and tracks, and followed a well-worn path that wound through ironwood groves and across a stony flat on its way to the northerly foothills. The homestead at their backs slowly began to fill with activity as women gathered to grind maize, some of them carrying heavy containers of a fermented drink made from sugar and grain. Nearly every household in the surrounding area contributed pots, kettles, and other large cooking tins, as well as baskets, gourds, and pails—all the kitchen furnishings needed to prepare a feast of this scale. Firewood, water, and freshly cut boughs for the banquet table were carried to the homestead in waves. The cattle to be slaughtered when the company returned were pastured nearby, and the boys who tended them were charged to keep the animals within sight. Wandisa's wife, along with Katwerwa's wives and Katanga, oversaw the preparations, taking pains not to appear meddlesome lest the throng of helping hands take offense.

The wind against his skin felt cool and Wamesepa wrapped himself in a blanket before climbing onto the black, dusty seat. Katere had changed his clothes, preferring brightly colored skirts to the drab, soiled ones he had worn earlier. The four men arranged themselves comfortably in the back, one of them leaning against a large jerrycan partially filled with petrol. The journey to the graves by motorcar was shorter in time, but far longer in distance. Wandisa would have to drive to the outskirts of Opuwo and find the tracks leading southward to Kaoko Otavi, then head overland to the foothills of the lower Ojtihapa mountains. His battered, yellow truck soon disappeared down the gravely tracks, though its clattering engine could still be heard.

As the sun reached the top of the sky, Katwerwa recognized features in the landscape and knew the graves were nearby. Calling his younger son, he pointed to a small formation overlooking the hilly terrain. The boy skipped ahead of the plodding cattle and quickly disappeared. The stone outcropping stood atop the tallest of three connected hillocks, and as the boy looked over the countryside he set his hands above his brow and gazed as far as he could in all directions. Twice, his young eyes scoured the landscape, finding nothing that resembled a graveyard. But looking southward again, something caught his attention: beneath the only large tree in the area he spotted a tall stake. Attached to the stake were a number of cattle skulls neatly stacked one on top of the other. The boy lifted his stick in the air and mentally sketched a course leading from the graves to where his father and brother stood waiting. As he turned from the outcropping to begin the descent, he noticed a long cloud of dust hanging in the near distance and quickly retraced his steps.

Dakata walked slowly along the narrow trail, bringing the cattle to a halt before the ravine widened. His father had gone ahead to wait for Wandisa at the graves. It was a lonely and forlorn place, and had become such when a prolonged drought forced Wamesepa's father to remove his family and herds and flocks from the valley lying beyond the graveyard. Still, this small patch of ground held four generations of fire-keepers, and when he died, Wamesepa would be placed beside his father. Cooled by the growing shade, a score of graves lay in the glittering soil, each facing the morning sun, many outlined with stones. The mounded earth had washed from three or four graves on the lower end, but the wooden stakes bearing the skulls of cattle slaughtered to honor the more recently dead stood true. The skulls themselves were creamy white, but the once lustrous horns had turned dark, brittle, and fibrous. Katwerwa walked easily to a stunted tree south of the graveyard and inspected a notch where three stones had been placed to warn away strangers.

Wamesepa sat in the truck while Wandisa and Katwerwa finished preparations. The two small herds of cattle were now one and the old man was anxious to visit his father's grave. Knocking against the door with a single finger, he caught a young man's attention and was able to open the door and step from the seat. Leaning heavily against his stick, he lifted his long, spindly legs and walked toward the graves. It was a journey of forty or fifty paces and his chest rose and fell with each one. All alone, Wamesepa entered the graveyard and moved steadily toward the only grave with a headstone. In earlier days, the long cement brick must have borne an inscription, but its message had long since worn away. Many watched him from afar, for it was Wamesepa's privilege to peacefully enter and greet his father away from the company of others. The old man drew his legs together and dropped a leaf upon the grave. He stooped as low as he could, stretching his right hand toward the marker and lowering his eyes. "My father," he whispered, "I have come to remember you." His fragile outline wavered little and his lips were still. Wandisa walked to the edge of the graveyard, his eyes following his father's every move. The old man began to turn, shifting his weight from the right to the left foot. Raising his stick, Wamesepa lodged it between stones; but one of them gave way and he slipped and tumbled to the ground. His gentle fall provoked a rustle in the branches above him, followed by a stilted cry as a bird stretched its wings and abandoned the tree. Wandisa lifted his father from the ground and led him to a chair from which he could safely view the cattle's advance.

Everyone stood back from the graveyard. On the lower side, people crouched among the ironwood trees; others gathered on the rocky slopes north of the graves, leaving just a few stripling herdsmen to keep the animals in place. Wandisa laid a handful of grass cuttings on his grandfather's grave—not as an enticement, but as a token of appreciation for the heifer his grandfather would choose. Katwerwa gave the signal and the beasts were allowed their freedom. At first there was a rush of movement, but it quickly lapsed into a simple plod as the cattle lowered their heads and searched for bits of vegetation. Filling the open ground, they trudged closer and closer to the graves. Wamesepa's eyes widened and he leaned forward slightly, looking from heifer to heifer. A hornless, tawny-skinned animal with a long, straight back entered the graveyard. Several others followed it, walking clumsily between the burial mounds while turning their heads from side to side. None of them lingered for more than a moment, but passed from the shadows and moved toward the groves with the greater part of the herd. And as more and more cattle reached the ironwood trees, the people waiting there rose from their cover and whistled and clicked at the beasts, hoping to drive them back.

A golden-brown heifer with creamy spots across its body and a creamy nose walked in front of Wamesepa. The animal was young and cautious, yet ventured nearer and nearer the graves in company with a solid black heifer. Several paces from the old man's chair they spooked each other and the golden-brown animal clipped away toward the groves. The other one hesitated, then walked between a row of graves searching for grass. Edging ever closer to the headstone, the smoky beast turned its head downward, raised its left hind leg, and scratched at its belly. Suddenly, a blackbird flew from the tree—its flapping wings the only sound it produced. The heifer lifted its head and bounded away, yet hardly a moment had passed when the golden-brown guardedly returned. Walking tentatively into the graveyard, the animal found a silvery green tuft and wrapped its tongue around the blades and pulled. As it tore the shoots from the crusty ground, its soft, brown eyes caught Wamesepa's, and for an instant the creature froze. But chewing steadily, the heifer moved forward, turning firstly to the left and then to the right. Uncannily, the beast stopped beside the faded headstone. Wamesepa rose to his feet, staring at his father's choice. The heifer's body quieted and it laid its nose upon the grave.

Using his stick, Wamesepa stepped cautiously into the shade, allowing the heifer to see him lest the animal move away. Standing at the foot of his father's grave, he touched the heifer's flank, then let his hand fall. Hunched over, he raised his chin and spoke. "This is your heifer, the one you have chosen, my father. She and all of her offspring are yours. Their milk and their meat will only be used by your sons, and we shall never forget they are gifts from you." He took a backwards step and reassured the beast.

Mukuva and Dakata crept forward and gently restrained the animal, slipping ropes around both hind legs. But the heifer grew nervous, visibly shaking as Wandisa stood at its side holding a knife. The three ancient friends surrounded their ancient companion and supported Wamesepa as best they could. Placing his arms around the animal's head, Katwerwa wedged his body against its neck, and when he felt secure, Kuwiya approached the chosen heifer from the other side. Grasping the horns and the tail as Wandisa raised the knife, all four men strained to prevent the creature from bolting. The left ear was pulled taut and Wandisa cut deeply into the ear to mark the heifer as a beast belonging to his father's father. Holding the excised skin in his left hand, Wandisa swiftly cut the right ear. The men in front relaxed their grip and stepped aside. The bewildered animal bellowed and the hind legs were released. Wandisa passed the cuttings to his father, watching as the heifer ran to join the herd. Wamesepa maintained a steady hand; already his palm was streaked with red.

A few young herdsmen took charge of the cattle, allowing them movement while keeping them loosely sequestered. Hurriedly, people gathered at the borders of the graveyard and waited for Wamesepa to finish his work. The old man stood facing his father's burial mound and stretched his left hand above its center. "Father," he said, "I give you these ear cuttings, for the heifer is now yours." And, inverting his palm, the two limp pieces fell to the grave. The ceremony was over.

A score of Wamesepa's paternal kinsmen pressed forward to clean the graves—removing debris, realigning stones, and bickering from time to time over who lay in which grave. Wamesepa sat in his chair watching the men at work. In a year's time, after his father's new heifer had calved and its udder was full, he would return with a pail of its milk and pour it over the grave for his father to taste.

* * *

Wandisa was beset with ardent requests to return to Otutati by truck. He accommodated as many as possible, choosing those who would be of most help in slaughtering, dressing, butchering, and cooking the two oxen and several goats for the evening's feast. The sun was still high as the truck drove to the south, meandering along the plain until Wandisa found the tracks leading to Opuwo. The others trekked northward, over the hills and mountains, and soon formed two parties: those responsible for the cattle's return, and those responsible only for themselves. Both parties arrived before dusk to find a homestead filled with people and chatter and simmering foods. The married men congregated around Wamesepa in the *otjoto* canopy, the younger children stayed with their mothers beside the cooking hearths, and the youths and maidens gathered wherever they found a bit of seclusion. It was an evening of eating, drinking, and good cheer. Stories were told and favorite pieces of gossip rehearsed. The middle of the night sky was awash with brilliant starlight. But as a waning crescent moon passed beyond its apex, falling slowly toward the western hills, sleeping children were carried home and the elderly retired to their beds. Leftover meat was carefully stored for use on the morrow and the once burgeoning fires fell to ash.

Morning came early and the livestock's bleating and lowing was ignored for a time. Only the children stirred at their usual hour. To the rear of Wamesepa's house lay a large ironwood limb. When the old man rose, he would take the ancestral fire from his house to the hearth and summon Katwerwa and Wandisa to carry the limb and place it behind the fire among the many other limbs set there to mark *yambera* ceremonies. In time, perhaps, Wamesepa would place a carved bowl belonging to his father, or a bead from one of his necklaces, on the limb. For the limb was his father's and stood behind the fire to represent his presence to his children, grandchildren, and great grandchildren.

The ancient man's youngest son left a small hut on the southern edge of the homestead and walked to the cattle pen. Chatting and laughing at each step, he leaned his right side against the fence and raised his front skirt. Soon, a puddle formed near his feet. The playing children hid themselves to watch the unusual display. The man lowered his skirt when he was finished and moved to the ancestral hearth. Standing there for a moment, he fell silent and lifted his right arm. An instant later he turned, passed beyond the large circle of homes and headed east.

· 15 ·

Offering the Pipe

. . . is a sign of friendship and comradery. The news from Katwerwa is disconcerting: The cattle thieves have been apprehended and will stand trial in Otutati—but all four men are local folk. The accused are heard, a judgment is reached, and punishment delivered. Now, the life of the community must go forward.

More rain had fallen and the verdure of the new season was everywhere present—in the delicate feel of infant leaves, in the spreading blanket of grasses, and in the rising scent of bark washed clean by droplets of rain. Here and there, roofs were being repaired or entirely rethatched with thick-stemmed grasses ripened and cut the previous year. Some laid fresh plaster on long neglected walls and silos while others mended livestock enclosures. Many worked steadily in the maize gardens, removing old stalks and turning the idle soil. And though a sweeping, tumultuous downpour had yet to soak the ground, all the signs of a hopeful season were in place.

Kuwiya toiled in his second wife's garden, burning the stubble and hoeing the weeds. She had begun to clear the field, but the arrival of her third baby was imminent and the heavy labor was more than she could bear. The newborn would be Kuwiya's fourth child and Katanga believed it to be a boy.

People were gathering at the thicket of trees where mancala was often played. The vibrant new leaves growing on the slender upper limbs shielded the widening circle of chairs, logs, and stones from the late morning sun. Men from around the valley, as well as from neighboring valleys, chatted and mingled easily as they waited for others to arrive. Most were arrayed in their finest clothing, wearing neatly folded skirts and turbans with the discarded woolen jackets of another world. Skin glistened with *otjize* and necklaces had been polished with an ebony cream. Rapidly, the thicket was coming to life, yet the occasion bringing them together was a somber one. Only five days had passed since Katwerwa returned from Opuwo with news that those responsible for the local cattle thefts had been caught and would stand trial in Otutati. Most of the cattle would not be recovered as an agent thief had already taken them to Vamboland for resale. The permanent loss of the animals was indeed bitter, but bitterer still were the thieves' identities. For each of them was a local man, three from Otutati and one from Oritjitambo.

The circle beneath the trees grew to an extended oval and the most prominent seats—those at the middle of the two lumbering crescents—were eventually filled by men of the senior generation. The morning sun was still climbing as a man sitting on the northern end of the oval stood and called for order. He was tall and his thick, graying eyebrows easily rose and fell above his narrow, deep-set eyes. His family was known and respected in Oritjitambo. As he would be absent from the gathering, Wandisa had asked Takame to steward the proceedings, knowing his conduct would be orderly and wise. Four younger men had been recruited to act as bailiffs, to keep the defendants separated from one another as well as from the court's discussion. Dakata had agreed to work as Takame's chief officer. He would summon the men when needed for questioning, guard the company's walking sticks and knives (safely lodged at the foot of a tree outside the oval), and should the court so decide, administer corporal punishments.

The four thieves had been caught in circumstances so incriminating that any pretense of innocence was futile. Their guilt was duly confessed, and what lay before the court were issues of resolution and punishment, of whether or not the thieves could be reclaimed, of how to ensure they would pose no further threat to the community, and who should take responsibility for their parole. Cattle theft was a serious crime and the four thieves had roused deep feelings among the people of Otutati.

Takame clicked his tongue, signaling the end of lazy conversations; and as quiet slowly fell across the oval of men, old Solomon rose from his chair. Moisture beaded in the folds of his mouth and trickled onto his gray beard, and his watery eyes shone as he lifted his right hand.

"I say," he uttered sharply, "nothing's worse than the kind of people we'll question today. It's bad enough to steal cattle from a stranger, but to steal from one's own family and friends is unthinkable. When I was a young man, if a lion stole one of our cattle we pursued it and brought it to death. These criminals are thieving lions and ought to be treated as such!" Solomon's tone was deliberately exaggerated and his polished statement brought a ripple of laughter. Yet, the underlying sentiment was shared by many who felt such grievous stock theft could not be tolerated. A few of the older men still remembered tales from their fathers and grandfathers of cattle-raiding Damaras who so decimated their forefather's herds that many of them fled across the Kunene to save their lives, becoming a generation of paupers.

"Yes, *Tate*," came the reply, "we understand your words." And taking several steps toward the center of the oval, Takame continued, "Before we question these people we should be familiar with their individual crimes. They may have done far more than we know, but all I've heard is their confessions about specific cattle thefts and only these thefts will be discussed today."

Many of the gallery shifted about in their seats and Takame paused for a moment.

"The first man we'll question is Daniel. He lives here in the homestead belonging to Vita and has stolen cattle from Etengwa and other places, and sold them in Opuwo. Many of you recognize the man sitting beside Mbitjitwa. Four of the six cattle Daniel's confessed to stealing belonged to him. He claims these are the only animals he's stolen—though we can't know for certain if this is true."

The man drew a long breath and turned his head slightly.

"In a different series of thefts, we'll question three lads who worked together to steal at least ten head of cattle. Zondoka, whose father sits with us here, will be the first to answer. Many of us have known him since his birth and have watched him grow into his youth. The lad's admitted taking cattle from other valleys, but he was caught with animals belonging to Katwerwa. He's also confessed to stealing a beast from his own father. All the cattle were led to Opuwo and sold. Katwerwa was fortunate to have recovered one of his, but Vita's ox is gone. This is the second time Zondoka's appeared in court for stock theft."

Discreetly, a few men looked in Vita's direction, though most restrained themselves out of respect for the man.

"His friend, Nondo," continued Takame, "has also confessed to the thefts. For those who don't know him, he's an Ngambwe lad who lived for a time at Okangwati, but came here to be with an uncle who stayed by the deep river. His uncle has since moved north again and Nondo is alone in the homestead. So far as we know, Nondo owns no livestock and has no garden. Aside from theft, it's unclear to us how the lad makes his living. He's been to court twice for fighting and once for stock theft, and I believe his case requires very serious reflection.

"The final person is a young man from Oritjitambo, the lad we call Tall One. He lives in his father's homestead and has been to court at least four times for cattle theft; still, he remains a thief. We think he's the one who planned these thefts and persuaded the other two to join him. We also think Tall One has a long-standing contact with the Vambo who bought the stolen animals and drove them to Oshakati. It seems likely that he's been involved in other thefts, perhaps other crimes. But Tall One comes from a good family—though as yet, no one's been able to help him."

Takame looked down for a moment, then took a sideward step.

"I say, there's nothing new in this—we've all been discussing it for several days. And learning the details of the thefts is only part of what we must do. As the thieves will pay full compensation for the animals they stole, the primary matter for us to settle is their future: what we should do to help turn them from cattle theft. The two cases are different. Daniel lives here as a stranger; his people, his ancestral fire, his uncles are elsewhere and there is no one to watch over him. The other three are young, but they're also convicted thieves. And if we do nothing to help them, their paths in life won't change. I know anger comes easily when we discuss stock theft, but two of the young men's fathers are here with us and their sorrows could just as easily be our sorrows."

Takame took his seat. Men whispered back and forth, some praising his well-spoken words, others feeling his lack of harshness might work against the proceedings.

Dakata walked to a shady embankment where a bailiff stood watching Daniel. "You have been called," he said, gesturing for the defendant to rise. Leading the way, Dakata brought Daniel to the thicket and then stood aside, allowing him to pass through the line of men and enter the oval.

His legs were dusty and his skirts deeply soiled and uneven, and draped over his head was a square of dark cloth that hung to his shoulders. With his head covered and slightly bowed, it was difficult for him to find the center point of the oval, but at last he rested his feet upon the warm, sandy ground.

"I say," declared Solomon, "what's that absurd-looking thing on your head?"

"It's a cloth," Daniel replied softly. "My eyes have been bothering me of late. The sunlight is painful and the cloth keeps it from my eyes."

"It's dark and shady under these trees," Takame said. "And it would be much better for us to see you directly."

"Please," he asked, "let me keep my eyes covered."

As Takame knelt to confer with the most senior men in the oval, a younger man leaned his way and whispered, "I saw Daniel earlier this morning with his goats. His head was uncovered, and if his eyes were troubling him then, there was no sign of it."

"We know what you mean," replied one of the seniors. "Daniel's intentions are more than obvious, but I think his unwillingness to face us directly brings him even greater shame. I say so long as he isn't flippant in answering us we should allow him this foolishness."

Takame returned to his seat. "Daniel," he called, "tell us why you are here."

The shrouded head moved to find the speaker's voice. "I am here," he replied, "because I stole cattle and because I was caught doing it."

"Is it wrong to steal cattle—or anything else?" asked Katwerwa.

"Yes, it is wrong."

"Then why did you do it?"

Standing quietly before a silent gallery, Daniel prepared his answer. His head cloth edged downward, touching below his chest.

"I say," he responded, "you have asked me something I've asked myself many times. The reason is simple: I stole those few cattle because I needed money to bring my wife and baby to see a doctor in Opuwo. I'm a poor man and could think of no other way of raising the means."

"Daniel," said Solomon, rising to his feet. "Do you think the doctor charges several head of cattle to be seen? Don't stand here and speak feebleminded words. You know you're well liked and that had you need of three or four rand to go to the clinic, you could have borrowed it from one of us—or exchanged a young goat. We all do that from time to time. I say, my child, answer us rightly!"

Daniel moved to his left, but made no reply.

"We ask you again," a senior man entreated. "Why did you steal those cattle?"

"Because I wanted money," he answered.

"Did you need money—were you in trouble?"

"No, I wasn't in trouble. I just wanted money."

Takame straightened his back. "Daniel," he said, "this answer tells us very little. We want to know *why* you stole those cattle, how a man of your age—someone who knows what's right and what's wrong—could threaten another man's livelihood. This is the question we'd like you to answer."

Daniel's long, dark veil swept slowly from side to side. "It's not a question I can answer," he began. "I'm just an average man—not wealthy, not too poor—and I don't know why I stole those cattle. It wasn't something I'd planned to do. I didn't rise from my bed one morning and say, 'Today I'm going to steal cattle.' It was nothing like that. This whole business started when I was grazing my own herd, way over there near those foothills. Other cattle were in the area—untended cattle—and all day long I watched them, wondering why no one came to see after them. It occurred to me how easy it would be to steal them, and once my mind settled on that thought it wouldn't leave me alone. Again and again, I devised ways of taking them. But they were only thoughts, nothing I'd really do—much like considering different ways of building a fence or where to take animals during a drought. They weren't desires and they weren't intentions.

"But day after day, my thoughts gave me no rest; my mind rehearsed them again and again and again. And when I'd heard from others how much cattle fetch at the market in Opuwo, I could think of little else. There were things I wanted to buy: tobacco, sugar, maize meal, salt, Mint Punch, coffee, small stock, even cattle. I walked way to the north to steal an animal, and when I came down those hills over there, I led the beast to Vita's enclosure for the night. A day or two later, I took the ox to Opuwo and sold it. The theft had gone so well I decided to do it again, and then again."

Daniel paused and looked for Takame.

"Honored Sir," he said, after settling his feet, "you've asked me why I stole those cattle. The only honest answer is this: I did it for want of money. And I can truthfully say I had no intention of ruining anyone's livelihood."

An elder man from Oritjitambo leaned forward. "Daniel," he asked, "are you a man?"

"Yes," replied Daniel. "I am a man."

"What you've said seems truthful to me," continued the elder, "and I'm pleased with your candor. But don't you realize all men have such thoughts, that everyone's mind tells him to do such things? It might be expected that a boy would follow an evil thought and fall into trouble, but a man is stronger than that. A man knows that stealing is wrong, and by your own admission you stole for things you really didn't need. Answer me now, are my words correct?"

Daniel lowered his head. "Yes, what you've said is true. A man should say no to things he knows to be wrong, and I've gained nothing from my thefts."

Francisco rose to his feet. "I say, Daniel, I have a question for you. I'd like you to tell us what you've done with the money from your thefts. I think we're all interested in learning what a thief does with his spoils."

Daniel shifted from leg to leg, but made no reply.

Again Francisco rose. "Must I repeat my question?" he asked.

"No," answered Daniel. "I heard the question. Only its answer shames me further, for I have no money remaining from my thefts—I've spent it all."

The gallery murmured heavily at his disclosure.

Daniel turned, sensing the growing discontent. "I've confessed my crimes," he said, "and I'm ready to bear my punishment and my shame."

"Your shame?" cried Kavetonwa, amid the glowering voices. "You speak only of your shame? You've disgraced yourself and you deserve to be shamed. But are you so absorbed in your own matters that you can't think of the shame you've brought to others?"

"Do you mean to my family," asked Daniel, "to my wife, to my daughter and son? Yes, I think about their shame."

"No!" answered the man from Etengwa. "Are you so blind to what you've done? You've brought shame on another man's house. You have no real life, no homestead of your own; you live with Vita. And where I stay, word has spread around of stolen cattle being harbored not in your homestead—because you have none—but in Vita's. His good name is associated with your theft and your shame. It's easy enough for you to take your beating and pay me compensation, but how are you going to restore Vita's good name?"

The man's words were strong and piercing, and Daniel made no attempt to respond. Standing among his peers, he was wearied by their questions, their accusations, and their challenges. When at last he was dismissed, the bailiff led him to a place on the riverbank to wait until his fate had been decided.

The range and quantity of spectators had increased by the time court reconvened. Older boys and youths leaned against tree trunks beyond the oval, while shadows on the thicket's fringe gave cover to a handful of women and maidens. Takame stood and called the gathering to order and asked that Zondoka be led to the thicket. As he walked along, the lad looked about him uneasily, recognizing many of the people seated on the ground. His breathing was rapid as he stood before the court and his face was shiny and moist. Like his father, he was short, but unlike him, his eyes were tinged with red and his lips quavered each time he parted them to draw a breath. The youth's dusty, blue trousers, cut at mid-thigh, and his faded, yellow shirt were all that he wore; his circumcision plait had been cropped and his once shaven head was covered with hair. Glancing furtively around the oval, his eyes never resting for long, Zondoka noticed his father huddled in his chair, staring at the ground.

"My child, why are you here?" asked Takame, examining the lad's appearance.

Zondoka lowered his eyes and answered. "I'm here because my friends and I were caught stealing cattle."

"Were you involved with Nondo and Tall One?"

"Yes," he replied, "I was."

"Is this the first time you've engaged in cattle theft?"

"No. Last year I was also caught stealing and was brought before this court."

"That's correct," said Takame. "And as you remember, last year we decided you were still a boy; now, however, you'll be treated as a man."

For a moment Zondoka stood idle, waiting for the next question.

"Tell us," began Mukuva, his copper whistle resting on his tongue. "How, precisely, did you steal these cattle?"

Zondoka turned in Mukuva's direction, keeping his eyes on the ground.

"It was Tall One's idea," he answered. "He is very clever with such things. He told Nondo he knew someone in Opuwo who wanted to buy cattle. It was a man from Oshakati or Ondongwa who bought cattle from Himba and sold them to Vombos. Tall One said if the three of us worked together, it would be an easy way to make some money. At first, Tall One and Nondo did the stealing. They took cattle while they were grazing in the field and led them deep into the woodland. Then at night, when the moon was straight overhead and everything was quiet, we drove the beasts toward Opuwo. We always walked at night and always along a course where no one lived.

"Three times we took cattle to Opuwo. The second time, we walked near the foothills till we reached the outskirts of town. The cattle were so tired we had to prod them to keep them moving. We found a thicket of trees—like this one—away from any path, and we stopped there while Tall One went to fetch the Vambo. They returned after sunrise and the man inspected the beasts. He said he'd take them, but quibbled about their condition, telling us they weren't in good shape and that he'd have to pay us less. Tall One wouldn't hear of it, and the two of them talked and talked and finally agreed on a price. When the man left the thicket, we sat down and decided how to bring the cattle to his house without raising any suspicions. I walked two of the beasts to his hut; the distance was short and I felt relieved that it was nearly over. When the three of us arrived, the man inspected the cattle once more; he looked satisfied, then told us there was a problem. He couldn't afford to transport the beasts to Vomboland and said we'd have to pay those costs ourselves. When Tall One reminded him that transport was included in the price, they started to argue. The man threatened to go to the police, so we took his offer and each of us got a hundred rand."

Zondoka suddenly looked upward as a high gust of wind stirred the canopy of leaves. And before he could continue, Katwerwa had raised himself in his chair.

"My child," he said, "are you telling us you gave the Vombo four head of cattle and all he paid you was three hundred rand?"

"He offered us three hundred rand for each beast," replied the lad. "But since he had to charge us for transport he could only give us three hundred rand for all four of them."

"Don't you realize what you've done?" pressed Katwerwa. "You sold healthy, mature cattle for the price of a large goat!"

"We knew it was too little money," said Zondoka, his voice steady and unchanging. "But the man assured us if we brought him cattle again, he wouldn't have to charge us for transport. That's why we stole three more animals."

Zondoka's revelation caused a stir.

Mbitjitwa leaned toward Kavetonwa. "This lad can't be Vita's son," he whispered. "It's simply not possible—his wife must have been with another man while Vita was at post." Kavetonwa nodded, then closed his eyes.

"So tell us now," said Masutwa, as voices settled, "did you steal more animals for this man to buy?"

"Yes," Zondoka replied, "we did."

"How many?"

The youth held up three fingers.

"And how much were you paid this time?" asked Solomon.

"The same as before—the man gave each of us a hundred rand."

"I say," groaned Katwcrwa. "Did you learn nothing from your first encounter with this Vambo?"

The lad made no reply, only gazed stonily at the ground.

"My child," said a man from Oritjitambo, "I'd like you to tell us how you were caught and why only one of these animals was recovered."

Speaking softly without raising his eyes, Zondoka answered the man. "The Vambo loaded the cattle into a small truck and drove through Opuwo to the petrol station. Two policemen came from their building and talked to him while the girl filled the tank. They said they were checking for stolen animals and asked to see his papers. One of them thought he recognized the earcuts on the ox and ordered the man to bring the animal from the truck. He looked more closely and was sure the beast was stolen. The Vambo said he had just bought the cattle and gave the police a description of us—told them we were waiting for the shops to open. So one policeman stood holding the ox, the other came to find us. And by the time we reached the petrol station the Vambo had driven off with the other two beasts. The police took us to their building. We denied everything, but another man sitting at a table inside the building remembered Tall One and Nondo from other thefts and we were put in a small room."

Zondoka's voice had grown so soft that everyone strained to hear.

"My child," Solomon gently asked, "tell us why you do such things. You come from a good family, your life is good—how can you be involved in cattle theft? Every family here lives from its cattle. When you steal them you're endangering the well-being of your neighbors."

Zondoka straightened himself and looked beyond the men seated round him. Three of his friends leaned against tree trunks, boys who were circumcised with him, their thick plaits dressed in cloth. His eyes fell again.

"Did you hear the man's question?" asked Takame.

"Yes," replied Zondoka, holding his hands behind his back. "I know that we're people of the cattle, and I know stealing is wrong. But when I steal, I don't think of the owners, I think only of what I want."

"And what is it you want?" Masutwa asked, looking at the youth.

"Things," he answered. "I want things. I want clothes. I want shoes. I want music. I want food and drink from tins and bottles. I want all the things we don't have."

"Many of us sitting here also like these things," said the man from Etengwa. "All of us would like to increase our herds and flocks and our personal comforts, but it isn't right that we should steal another man's cattle to do so.

"You tell us that stealing is wrong, yet this is your second time in court for cattle theft and we can only wonder whether your mind works properly."

Other men quickly voiced their assent and then settled back.

"I know it was wrong of us to steal. And truly, I'm sorry for what I've done."

Francisco leaned forward in his seat. "I'd like to know whether your sorrow comes from your theft or simply from being caught—and I'd like your answer to be honest."

Hesitating a moment, Zondoka breathed deeply. "If I'm to be honest," he began, "I must say that I'm sorry I stole the cattle, but I wish we hadn't been caught."

Francisco nodded his head.

Looking about the oval, Takame stood. "Answer us this, my child. Are you going to steal again?"

"I will say no," spoke Zondoka. "But I don't know for sure."

"Is there anything else you wish to say before we send you down?"

"No, honored sir. I've nothing more to say."

* * *

Moments after Zondoka was led away, another bailiff entered the thicket with Nondo at his side. As the young man stepped unaccompanied into the oval he tightened a length of black cord that drew the heavily worn fabric of his golden coveralls toward his waist. Nondo was taller than Zondoka but lanky, and his face—with its fine lips, small nose, high cheek bones, and whispery brow—was very handsome. Curly hair grew in mounded tufts across his scalp, and his demeanor was quiet and peaceful.

"Tell us your name, child," said Takame.

"I am called Nondo."

"And who are your people that we may know you?"

"I am Ngambwe, from the Omukwendata clan. My home lies beyond the Kunene at a place called Ohungiarundu. My father was taken into war, my mother still lives at Ohungiarundu. I have one brother and three sisters, but I don't know whether they still live in my mother's village or if they've moved elsewhere."

"How is it then," asked Mukuva, "that you've come to reside in Otutati?"

Nondo's eyes swept over the gallery of men.

"I came here because of the war," he answered. "I wanted to live in peace, so I crossed the river into Himbaland. I had known Himba in Ohungiarundu and worked well with them. I hadn't any idea where I should settle, and came to Otutati by chance. Not long after I arrived, I met *Tate* Wandisa who gave me work cutting wood for a cattle enclosure. Then he hired me to help him build a house and then to build a shelter for his wife. I worked hard for him and I think we had a good understanding. One day he asked me if I'd like to be sponsored by a man who had no sons, to help him with the cattle and sheep, and to live in his homestead. I told him that I would and *Tate* Wandisa brought us together. And this, honored sir, is how I came to live in Otutati."

"Was this man good to you?" asked Mbitjitwa. "Did he treat you well?"

"Yes," the young man replied. "I wasn't received as a foreign laborer but as a nephew, and I called the man 'uncle.' I stayed with him and worked for him for nearly four years. He treated me well and I was happy living in his homestead. But when the drought came and he decided to move everything north, I told him I was afraid to go with him and wished to remain in our homestead. He left me a small flock of goats and asked me to care for them."

"I know of you," declared Solomon, edging forward in his seat. "And I know the man you called 'uncle.' I remember he spoke favorably of you. But I also recall seeing you in court before. This isn't your first time, is it?"

"No," replied the young man, lowering his eyes.

"Why have I seen you here before?"

"I've been here twice for fighting and once for cattle theft," Nondo answered.

"So, this is your fourth time—and still you haven't learned how to behave?"

"No," he replied softly. "I haven't yet learned."

Takame lifted his hand and called for Nondo to explain the recent thefts. Though the young man recounted the events in much greater detail than Vita's son, the two reports were in broad agreement, differing only in the breadth of Nondo's involvement with Tall One. As Nondo described things, his role was as minor as Zondoka's.

"Did you or didn't you help him carry out all the plans?" asked Masutwa.

"Some of them, yes, but not all of them," Nondo replied. "I didn't go with him to fetch the buyer."

"And because of that," said Masutwa, "you're asking us to believe that your own actions are less culpable than Tall One's?"

"Honored sir, I'm only telling the truth when I say the idea was Tall One's from the beginning. I did nothing to plan the thefts, I only helped carry them out. If I had conceived the idea then I would bear that responsibility too."

Takame called Dakata to remove Nondo from the oval that the senior men might confer without his presence. Their discussion was brief and the defendant was soon returned.

"You have spoken cleverly," said Takame. "To conceive an idea is one thing, to act upon it quite another. All of us here have likely conceived bitter ideas but have had the wisdom not to carry through with them. Thus, we feel the greater wrong lies in action, not conception, and that your words, though clever, are unfounded."

The young man changed his stance, but his expression remained sedate, his lips and eyes even.

"Now, my child, we want you to explain to us why you do such things. Wandisa was good to you. Your 'uncle' was good to you. The people of this valley have been hospitable to you. So why do you repeatedly steal our cattle?"

Nondo looked downward and the company drew still.

"Honored sir," he answered, "I didn't steal cattle out of anger or spite or a desire to ruin someone. I only did it because I wanted money."

"Are you offering an excuse?" asked Katwerwa. "Didn't it ever occur to you that you had no right to take another man's property?"

"I sometimes thought of such things when we stole cattle," Nondo replied, "especially in the beginning. But I didn't mind. In my heart I cared more for money than I cared for people. And more than anything else, I thought about what the money would bring me."

The man from Etengwa lifted his head and closed his eyes. "Tell me, my child," he said, "are these still your thoughts? Do you regret the loss of money to spend more than the hardship you've caused the owners of your stolen cattle?"

Taking his time, the young man made his reply in a low, unwavering tone. "What I did was wrong," he confessed, offering a statement rather than an answer.

Again, Nondo was removed to the riverbed that his words could be discussed. Men of the gallery quickly rose and stretched the discomfort from their limbs. "I see no signs of remorse," said Takame. "And unless the lad is earnest in his regrets there isn't much we can do to help him." But many in the oval disagreed with Takame and spoke well of the young man's sincerity. It was finally decided that the matter be placed before Nondo himself, that he be given opportunity to answer the court's reservations. And once the men were seated, the lad was summoned from his isolation.

Takame looked directly at the young man and asked him to approach. "My child," he began, "you've properly confessed your crimes and you've answered our questions. But this is a difficult matter to resolve. We've taken in a lad—a stranger, a foreigner—and given him place, given him food and work. He's become one of us, part of our community. And then he steals our cattle, not just once but twice—perhaps even more than we know. We have regard for the young man and have tried to help him find his way, yet now we don't know what more we can do. We don't know if we can trust him. We could banish him, force his removal, and this might serve our interests well, but it does nothing to help him. And this, you see, is our problem."

Leaning back in his chair, Takame asked, "Nondo, how do you answer us?"

The young man stood quietly, his lips pursed. "I understand your words," he replied. "And if you're asking me to answer them I can only say this: I think I'm trustworthy, but I don't know it absolutely."

Satisfied, Takame called for the bailiff.

Before Tall One entered the oval, his aging father left his seat and retreated to the lowering shadows. The young man stood erect, his large shoulders and heavily muscled arms stiff and unmoving. His neck was thick and strong, as were his hands and feet. A long, deep scar divided his face, rising from his nostrils to the tops of his ears, and then cutting sharply along the back of his head. The young man's brightly colored skirts were held in place by a wide leather belt, and a drab, faded shirt covered his back. His face was downcast and its look defiant. As he had been reluctant and combative in previous court appearances, a strapping bailiff stood beside him to help temper his behavior. Takame asked him to recount the three thefts and his subsequent arrest, and Tall One followed the sequence of events outlined by Zondoka and Nondo.

"How much money were you promised for each beast?" asked Katwerwa.

"Three hundred rand."

"And how much money were you actually paid?"

"We each got a hundred rand."

"Did it occur to you that the animals were worth many times that?"

"Of course it did."

"Then why did you sell them for so little?"

"Because they were stolen," answered Tall One in a flat, discourteous tone. "The Vambo knew they were stolen and the buyer always has an advantage over the thief. There was nothing else we could do if we wanted to avoid being caught."

Katwerwa eased back, his lips curving downward.

"I say," remarked Solomon, sitting forward in his chair, "your voice and your remarks are very disturbing. I've seen you too many times before in this court. Have all of our words and good intentions been wasted on you? Are you still beyond seeing the damage your thefts cause yourself and others?"

Tall One stared blankly at the ground. "My cattle thefts don't hurt any-one," he replied. "I never take more from one man than he can afford to lose—I'm careful about that. As for all of your words and intentions, they are simply your words and your intentions. I haven't asked for them and I don't feel bound by them."

An immediate murmuring rose from the court. Yet it was difficult to know whether Tall One spoke honestly or if his words were deliberately insulting—for many considered him an enigma, a thoroughly inscrutable young man. For generations, his people had lived in an area south of Oritjitambo and his father was respected for his veracity and kindliness, well known among his fellows for his patience. But he was deeply worried about his son and at a complete loss as to what more he could do. On many occasions he had supplicated his ancestors on his son's behalf. He had also sought counsel from the men of his patriclan and followed it as best he could. Yet no true change had overtaken Tall One, and now, it was rumored, the man was afraid of his own child.

Settling the court, Takame raised his chin and spoke. "We have a final question for you, Tall One—a simple one. Will you steal again?" Takame paused, then added, "Think about this carefully and give us a truthful answer."

The young man turned and looked toward the distant folds of a rocky mountainside. Beads of perspiration gathered at his temples and fell to his cheeks. His jaw stiffened. "In my mind I know stealing is wrong," he said. "But I also love to steal; it gives me great pleasure." He stepped back a pace or two and let his eyes drift downward. "I say, this is an honest answer."

The shadows of late afternoon had fallen across the ground as the court's final discussion began. Under Takame's guidance, the merits of alternative judgments were weighed, all reasonable concerns were addressed, every-one's opinion was heard, and finally, a general consensus was reached.

On Takame's instruction, Dakata absented himself from the court's de-liberations that he might gather and prepare the things necessary to com-plete the work of the proceedings. Only once did he interrupt the discussion when he called aside several men to help roll a large, rusting petrol drum into the center of the oval. Then, leaving the thicket, Dakata followed the river course and searched among the clumps of willowy bushes looking for a bough of proper thickness and pliancy. He ran his hands along several different branches, and finding two of them suitable, he patiently bent their tips and watched the branches spring. He cut the larger of the two and smoothed the shaft by removing the leafy growth. It was nearly as long as his leg though its base was slightly rounder than his thumb. He switched the cane in the air and watched its quivering movement before turning his ear to its subtle trill. Again, he struck through the air, and finding the cane in order, he retraced his steps to the thicket. Quietly, he pulled a small bundle from the crook of a tree. A long piece of black cord fell to his lap as he opened the bundle, and setting his knife aside, he held one end of the cord against his upper lip and twice wrapped it around his head. Deftly, he severed the piece and cut three more of identical length, tying together the ends of each and carefully setting them aside. Once more he raised his knife to cut a wispy branch. And after dividing it into four pieces, each the length of his forefinger, he gathered the four circles of cord and the four dowels and slipped them into a pouch.

Daniel walked into the oval, his head still shrouded in cloth, and stood at its center. Both of his legs were firm as he awaited the court's decision.

Takame rose from his seat. "Daniel," he said, "we've counseled together and agreed on a course of action, and soon a messenger will be sent to your mother's brother in Ondova to inform him of the court's decision. Firstly, you are required to compensate the owners of the cattle you've stolen with seven head for each of the beasts they lost. This, as you know, is the law. We've also decided you're to be banished from this valley for several years and put under the protection and care of your uncle who will look after you as a child—because you are a child. A man of your age and responsibilities doesn't engage in stock theft.

"And furthermore, to ensure that Vita's name is not associated with your crimes, Wandisa will notify all the headmen in Kaokoland that it was you, and not Vita, who harbored stolen cattle at Otutati. Because of your age—though some felt otherwise—we've decided not to have you caned. We hope that you will have learned from this and that your disgrace won't be associated with your children."

Takame took his seat.

"Now, Daniel," said Katwerwa, "tell the court whether you will ever steal again."

"No," he answered quickly, "my heart tells me that I'm finished being a thief."

"Do you have anything further to say to us?"

"No, honored gentlemen, I have nothing left to say."

Daniel was dismissed from the oval but was free to remain in the thicket.

The court had decided that Zondoka and Nondo should stand together to hear their sentences. As the bailiffs brought them forward, they averted their eyes and entered the oval of men, Nondo assuming the lead. His calmness had fled and his companion's face shimmered with perspiration. The thicket was now filled with people and Takame waited for them to quiet before speaking to the young men.

"Our children," he began, "your thefts are grievous. Not only have you been caught stealing for a second time, but you've taken cattle from men who've been like fathers to you. We've discussed whether or not you're capable of being helped and we simply don't know. However, we hope never to see you in court again. As you are young, and to lift some of the burden from your families and guardians, we've decided that you, along with Tall One, will pay compensation together. Both of you are to pay two head of cattle for each stolen beast. We've also decided that you'll wear the nose string and receive a caning—perhaps a bit of pain will teach you something. Before you leave this gathering, each of you will be placed under a guardianship. Zondoka, your father will act as your guardian; and you, Nondo, will be my responsibility. Vita and I have agreed to help you regain your direction and clear your minds. Everyone here will assist you. All of your movements will be watched and you must remain submissive. If there's any serious infraction you'll be turned over to the police in Opuwo and dealt with by their laws. Do you understand the court's decision?"

Each responded briefly.

Immediately, Takame called on the bailiffs to help Dakata apply the nose strings. And scarcely had he finished his command when Nondo stepped toward his chair.

"Please," he whispered, "I must talk with you privately. My body's in no condition to take a beating."

"Ah," replied Takame. "And why is this?"

"I'm sick," answered Nondo. And gesturing cautiously with his hands, he continued, "I'm sick down here. It's very bad, I need to get to Opuwo."

"Well, my child, if what you say is true, you won't be beaten, but you must submit to the nose string."

Asking Masutwa and Kuwiya to join him, he led Nondo from the thicket of trees into the sunlight and beyond to a nearby garden. There, the young man unfastened his belt and opened his coveralls. The three men looked carefully at his groin, but there could be no disputing the blisters, sores, and fleshy growths. Nondo could not endure a beating, for the thrusts of the cane would split his bowels.

They returned to the gathering and the bailiffs directed Nondo to a patch of ground on the side of the oval opposite Zondoka's. Already Dakata had laid a circle of cord and a dowel beside the lad, and as soon as Nondo had taken his seat he placed a nose string within his view. Kneeling behind the young man, Dakata lifted the circle of cord with his middle fingers and pulled it taut. Evenly, his hands rose above Nondo's head and slowly brought the rigid cord to rest just below his nose. Pulling back on the string, Dakata drew the tails across Nondo's cheeks and above his ears until they met at the base of his skull. The movement was practiced and smooth, and with one finger Dakata held the two loops while his other hand quickly worked the dowel into place. Round and round he twisted the dowel, tightening the nose string while lightly rubbing a finger against the cord to check its tension. It seemed too loose, and he twisted the dowel several more times. Nondo whimpered and moaned, and Dakata left him to engage Vita's son.

The effect of the nose strings was rapid and the two could no longer sit upright—their limbs had weakened and their upper bodies fell over their wobbling knees. The muscles of the neck became flaccid and their heads drooped to one side, their glassy eyes rolling upward. By now the initial quiet had lifted and many of the gallery commented openly on the young men's crimes. But there was no frivolity, no disrespect.

In time, Zondoka began to pant, the heavy, rapid breathing a sign of his growing pain. Takame took notice of his state. After several moments' hesitation, he called to the lad, "My child, will you ever steal again?" Zondoka heard the question and worked to shift his eyes as his head could not be moved. And looking toward Takame, he moaned a quiet no.

Nondo had rolled on his side and lay on the ground hardly able to move. His crying and his paralysis seemed unusually harsh and Takame motioned for Dakata to feel the tension of the nose string, fearing it might be overly tight. There were, however, no tears on Nondo's face, not even in his eyes; and when Dakata touched the string, he found that it had somehow come loose. Resetting the dowel, he twisted it again and again it until it bore deeply into the young man's skin, and those along the oval watched as Nondo's distress became real.

Takame left him to suffer and watched the shadows lengthen before turning to question the young man. At first, Nondo chose not to respond and the question was repeated. Finally, he mumbled an answer and both Nondo and Zondoka slipped from consciousness. Dakata released the nose strings and the two friends lay on the ground as sensation gradually returned to their bodies.

Dakata handed the cane to Takame and watched as the man lifted the rod and felt its weight and tested its spring. When he finished, he passed it on to the senior men for their inspection. A bailiff standing beside Zondoka helped the lad to his feet as another set branches and stones along the drum to prevent it from rolling. The seniors approved the cane and returned it to Dakata. Nondo was positioned on the ground to witness his friend's beating as another bailiff led Zondoka to the drum and asked him to remove his clothing. The lad handed the man his shirt and then stepped forward. Quickly, he loosened his shorts, kicked them to the ground, and hurled himself to the rusting surface, hoping his genitals would not be widely seen—for they were private, so private their names could only be whispered, and when spoken in normal voice, were the foulest of all oaths.

Dakata stood at Zondoka's right and firmly planted his feet on the ground. Concentrating his eyes on the fleshy mark, he incisively raised his hand overhead. The crackling sound of the cane falling heavily across Zondoka's buttocks jarred some of the onlookers. The lad's throat tensed and then lengthened; his head rose, his face trembled, and a deeply held breath rushed from his mouth. Yet before his stiffened body could ease another blow was struck, and then another, and another, and another. The strokes were clean, drawing no blood, and after the crack of the fifth lash Dakata laid aside the cane to allow Zondoka a brief respite. Four more strokes would follow.

Nondo had not watched the beating, only listened as his friend gasped at each stroke. But now he turned to hear Masutwa's question. "Tell us, lad, will you ever steal again?"

There was no response, just the sound of his body shaking against the hollow drum. Takame rose and looked for breaks in the skin, and finding only inflammation he repeated Masutwa's question. Zondoka turned his eyes and then looked downward. And lifting the cane, Dakata swiftly delivered the final blows.

Vita watched stoically as his son was disciplined, and when Dakata stepped away from the drum, he approached Takame, requesting that his son receive additional strokes. "I've not been able to reach my boy's heart," he said. "Perhaps another caning will help him remember this day." But his request was declined and two bailiffs came forward and gently lifted Zondoka from the drum, one of them helping the lad replace his shorts. Nondo stood by and observed his friend's retreat before finding a place in the deeper shadows.

Chattering voices died away as Tall One entered the oval and stood before the seniors, flanked by two bailiffs. Takame remained in his chair for a moment, gazing at the young man, and then leaned forward.

"Tall One," he said, his voice rising in tone. "Too many times you've stood before this court because of cattle theft, knowing perfectly well how serious a crime it is. We've listened to all your words and considered them carefully. Your explanation of why you continue to steal—the pleasure it gives you—is particularly disturbing. Furthermore, we are troubled by your demeanor, your lack of respect for others. But we credit you for your honest answers, even if they offended our ears. As we told Nondo and Zondoka, the three of you will pay compensation together, and we've decided that you will pay three head of cattle for each beast you stole. Your father will take you into his care and you will obey him. If there's any violation of this arrangement you'll be handed over to the police in Opuwo. We've also decided that you should wear the nose string and be caned for your thefts."

Takame eased back. "There's one more thing, Tall One. I must say how unfortunate it is that your young and handsome face carries the scars of the nose string. It's shameful that you haven't yet learned to behave as a man."

Dakata stepped into the oval and walked toward Tall One. The bailiffs moved back slightly to allow him a place on the ground, but Tall One refused to kneel. Dakata held steady and looked at Takame. The bailiffs laid hands on the young man's arms, but firming his legs, he resisted their pressure. The gallery murmured. And shaking his head, Solomon cried, "Isn't it enough that you're a thief? Must you also be a coward?" Tall One glared at the old man as the bailiffs forced him to his knees. Dakata secured the cord and tightened the dowel, and the young man's reserves began to dwindle. His knees weakened, his arms fell. Finally, as his breathing increased and the blood vessels crossing his temples strained ever larger, his body slipped downward. His eyes closed for a moment but opened as Takame spoke. "Do you promise never to steal again?" he asked. Tall One's eyes widened, and with a sudden, rapid movement he grasped the dowel and pulled it from the string. The bailiffs dashed forward and held Tall One to the ground while Dakata replaced the dowel and tightened the cord. One of the bailiffs left the oval, returning with enough rope to bind the young man's hands. Soon his body lost its composure and tears coursed from his eyes. He began moaning in waves as he gently rocked his head back and forth. Then, slumping over his knees, Tall One heard Takame repeat his question. He refused to answer and the oval grew quiet as the onlookers watched the young man's anguish.

Moments passed and Takame rose from his seat. "Will you ever steal again?" he cried. Tall One rolled onto his side and pressed his fingers together to prevent their quaking. His eyes were closed and their lids drained of color. Calmly, Takame stepped to the young man's side. "Do you promise," he quietly asked, "to stop your thievery?" But the words seemed not to have reached the young man's ears. Remaining at his side, Takame watched his head throb and his breathing lessen, and believed him to have fallen unconscious. But the young man moaned, "Yes."

Dakata released the nose string and untied Tall One's hands. A gourd of water was set within his grasp and slowly, he awakened.

Tall One was stripped of his shirt and asked to remove his back skirt. Reluctantly, he lay across the drum and eyed the four bailiffs standing within the oval, ready to hold him in place should he refuse to accept his punishment. The cane rested motionlessly on Dakata's shoulder as he waited for the sign. It was long in coming, and though Tall One rested his head against the warm metal, his eyes wandered around the thicket. Without a warning, Dakata raised his arm and slashed the tapered shaft over the young man's buttocks, the drum beneath resonating from the force of the stroke. Again, the cane thundered upon the flesh and Tall One cried out in pain. As a third blow fell sharply, the young man's muscles tensed and he jumped to his feet. Struggling against the bailiffs, he was maneuvered back to the drum and thrust down, his arms and legs tightly held that he should not escape again.

"Lie still," shouted Katwerwa, "and take your punishment like a man!"

But Tall One would not submit. He straightened his powerful arms and legs and held them stiffly as the cane bore down on him again and again. Then, exerting the strength of his torso and thighs, he drew upward and forced his body to collapse stiffly, his chest bounding off the metal drum. The bailiffs scrambled to maintain a grip, but finally subdued the young man. Takame stood and walked to him and carefully examined his skin, and ordering Dakata to begin anew, warned that any further defiance would increase the number of strokes. The young man softened his limbs but clung tightly to the drum; Dakata stepped forward and laid the first blow. No longer did Tall One resist, only wept and cursed the pain. The succession of strokes was quickened and when Dakata was finished, two of the bailiffs helped Tall One from the drum and brought him to rest on the sand, away from the crowd.

Court was now over and the men of the oval stood. Joined by others, they mingled in conversation, though nothing was said of the proceedings and the punishments. Daniel leaned against a tree on the gathering's edge, and having removed his veil as the evening shadows were deep, he took a hesitant step toward his friends. The sound of livestock returning for the night drew little notice. Zondoka and Nondo stood awkwardly amid the crowd, occasionally passing a word or two. Vita chatted with Tall One's father and Makuva as he took a pouch from his belt and searched for his pipe. Filling it, he lit the grayish-green tobacco and inhaled deeply. His eyes sifted through the crowd and he moved slowly, following a looping but deliberate path. Finding himself on the other side of the thicket, he held the pipe to his lips again. And as his lungs released the smoke, he handed the pipe to the man at his left. "Here, Daniel," he said. "Share my pipe with me." And when the tobacco was finished, Vita walked another direction and stood beside his son.

The Road Is Filled with Dust

. . . and nothing more can be seen. The time has come to leave the Himba and many farewells are spoken. With the help of Dakata and his brother, Old Rover is packed and gifts are readied for distribution. Once the sun has lifted above the easterly hills, I will be gone.

Kuwiya's son had been born after a difficult labor and delivery. The baby was strong and there were many hands to help with his care. The mother was still weak but feeling better, and Kuwiya slaughtered goat after goat that she might have meat to strengthen her body. Daniel and Watumba were preparing for their move. Both Vita and Takame had visited relatives and gathered some of the animals Zondoka and Nondo needed to pay the compensation for their crimes. It was likely that another rainy season would pass before the compensation was fully paid, and Zondoka and Nondo would need many years to return all the cattle their relatives had loaned them to cover their debts.

The evening was warm and a thin layer of clouds covered the night sky. The ground was still a bit soft from the rain of the previous day, and having finished their evening meals, children played around the houses and work shelters. Wamesepa had asked me to visit him and I walked toward the fading glow of his cooking fire and unfolded my chair.

"Didi tells me the day after tomorrow you will leave us," he said.

"Yes, *Tate*, it is true. The day after tomorrow I'll return to my people."

"But your wife isn't here. And your daughter and baby must greet me before you go."

"Yes, *Tate*, I know. We had hoped it could be, but it hasn't been possible for them to return, much to our regret."

"Then why don't you bring them here and stay? There's land enough for your family and all your fathers and uncles will give you cattle to start a herd. Or don't you find our life a good one?"

"Your life is very good and so is your offer, but the matter is complicated and many people are involved. Sitting here with you, I can easily see your house and the house where Wandisa lives. Over there is your sister's hut, and on the other side is where your sister's child stays. If I walked around the homesteads I'd find many of your relatives. But my family and Mikila's family live far from Otutati and we wish to be near them in the same way you wish to be near yours."

"Ah, yes," replied Wamesepa, blinking, "this I can understand. What do you call the place where you stay?"

"When we leave here, we'll go to a place called England."

"And how long would it take me to walk there if I should want to visit you?"

"It's far, very far—almost to the other edge of the earth. If you started walking tomorrow and walked each day through, perhaps two more rainy seasons would pass before you reached us."

"It is far," he said, "too far for me to imagine. Do you think you'll come again to see us and bring your wife and children?"

"I hope so, *Tate*, I hope so. But I may be an old man before it is possible."

"Ah," he said, "I see. Then it is for Mukuru to decide, my son."

As the sun rose above the easterly hills, pushing a few lingering clouds toward the far horizon, I walked along the rivercourse looking over the surroundings that had become so familiar. The people, their sounds, their words, their expressions, their personalities, their houses, their work shelters, their fields, and the places where so many things had occurred were vivid in my mind. It was difficult to believe that on the morrow they would be nothing more than memories. Goats and sheep finally stirred, and then the few milk cows not at dry season pasture; at last, their masters left their skins and blankets and walked into the soft morning light. In time, pails and gourds were taken to the enclosures and the round of morning chores began. After watching the familiar pattern of work and people, I turned to my own encampment. The journey to Windhoek would take the whole day, and though my belongings were few, it seemed best to order and pack them well ahead of time. Already people had come to inquire about the things I would leave behind, believing that water jugs, plastic to lay beneath the thatch, cooking utensils, rope, string, blankets, tins of fruit, and anything else they had seen were part of a vast estate to be divided on the following morning.

The hide of a black ox had been drying for several days on the canopy of shade cloth above the tent. It was stiff and rigid as I pulled it down, but folded easily after being salted for the third time. The hide was a tangible memory of a recent feast sponsored by Wamesepa and Wandisa. Francisco offered his thumb as he saw me struggling to tie a knot; behind him stood Wombinda. They had brought a carved wooden pail and a pillow he had made for Michelle, as she had once admired Francisco's work. In his other hand was millet seed. "Take this and plant it in your land, then you'll remember me year after year," he said. They stayed for a while and watched me sort through my belongings, reminiscing on the past year's events. When they rose to leave, Francisco announced, "Tomorrow morning, I'll stand by the tracks, and when you come by I'll wave, and I'll stand there even when the road is filled with dust and watch till I can see no more and listen till I can hear no more." We said our farewells.

Clouds returned in the late afternoon and shielded the valley from direct sunlight. My work was finished and I laced my boots and set out for the southern hills along the path I had often walked to be alone. The groves were turning green, and here and there flies collected around patches of sunbaked dung. A light wind had begun to blow as the path led up the side of a tall hill. The angular stones were unforgiving and the path ended near the top. From the summit Otutati appeared small, but the maize gardens, the house where Watumba had given birth, the dry riverbed, Vita's homestead, and the *ondundu* shrine were all clear and precise. It was a beautiful sight.

As evening fell, the visitors left and I watched the cattle as they were driven home for the night, and beyond them, a brilliant red sun as it slowly fell behind the westerly hills. When darkness had come, I walked to Kavetonwa's house. He had asked me to visit him, to keep him company one last time. We talked until his eyes closed; then his wife guided him into their house and I left. It was quiet, no dancing, no singing, just the sounds of insects and livestock. The sky was clear and bright and draughts of cool air spread across the valley floor. By the time I reached the tent not a fire was burning in Wamesepa's homestead.

Morning came after a night of little sleep. I washed and dressed as the light of the rising sun fell upon the eastern side of the tent. By the time I had finished packing the last of my things Dakata and his brother had arrived. Katwerwa had also come to help me break camp and we greeted one another as I stepped from the tent.

"Does the morning go well for you?" asked Katwerwa.

"Yes, thank you," I replied, "and you?"

We chatted for a while before Dakata's brother took a broom and began sweeping the back of Old Rover, preparing it for loading. The contents of the tent were few, but I had bought many bags of maize meal and sugar to offer as parting gifts. These, along with the things I thought people would find useful, were carried and set beneath a tree. The other belongings were quickly loaded into Old Rover. We turned to the shade cloth, and as Dakata and I lifted it off the poles, Katwerwa and his other son guided it to the ground, folded it in quarters, and rolled it in a bundle. The poles were for Katwerwa to keep and he carefully laid them aside. We pulled the stakes and removed the supports and the tent collapsed to the ground. It was folded, rolled tightly, and set in its bag. By now a crowd had gathered and many hands helped load the last of the equipment into the canopy and assisted me in securing the tent and the shade cloth to a metal rack.

During the previous week I had quietly delivered particular goods— water containers, pots and pans, blankets, and leftover seasonings—to those who needed them most. And now that a crowd was pressing toward the tree, I was asked to distribute those goods as well.

"The sun is rising too quickly and I must be on my way," I replied, "so Wandisa will divide those things just now."

Some who had gone to the tree and stood next to a bag of meal or sugar were reluctant to lose their positions, but most drifted back toward

Old Rover to bid farewell. Katanga, Ngipore, Watumba, Daniel, Wandisa, Rikuta, Dakata, Wakamburwa, Watuwamo, Masutwa, Vita, Kavetonwa, Mukuva, and many, many others came to offer personal goodbyes—words of regret, words of remembrance, and words of greeting for Michelle and the children. When all these were said, I walked with Kuwiya and Katere to see Wamesepa. The old man stood and reached his hand toward mine.

"Remember," he said, "that you're a son of this fire and this house. And may Mukuru bless you and your wife and your children and your cattle. And may he bring you back to this place once more, the place of stunted ironwood trees."

The engine was running smoothly and I eased forward, moving slowly to avoid any of the children running beside Old Rover. I returned their waves for the last time as I headed down the embankment and across the riverbed. Climbing up the other side, I heard a shout and saw the reflection of Kuwiya's elder son running toward me in the mirror. I slowed to a halt, and as the boy drew beside me, he touched the open window. "My father says, 'Mukuru must go with you,'" he panted, then stepped back and waved.

A long way down the tracks I spied a donkey, and standing beside it was Francisco. He offered his hand. "Goodbye, my friend," he said, "goodbye," and walked to the side. I drove slowly along the tracks. But when I looked into the mirror for a last glimpse, there was only dust.

The End

Conclusion

Leaving Kaokoland and the Himba and eventually returning to our own world seemed an uncomplicated transition, though for Elspeth the journey back to a life she had never really known proved more difficult than expected. The seasons have turned a number of times since our departure, yet only the occasional day passes without my mind reflecting, for at least a moment, on the time we spent among the Himba. Some of this has to do with various reminders—wooden pillows, milking pails, small baskets, gourds, and photographs—situated in places prominent and obscure throughout our home. But far more striking are the times when a picture or a memory comes to mind of its own accord, an image of a person, a life somehow out of place given the circumstance in which it occurs, but an image that demands attention and temporarily returns me to Otutati.

When people ask us what it was like to live with the Himba, it is difficult to respond—not for lack of something to say but for the sheer inability to satisfactorily convey what we have lived. I can easily discuss Himba kinship and the morality that underlies it, or inheritance patterns and judicial procedure, but such discussion is inevitably abstract, once or twice removed from life as lived. To be sure, our sojourn in Otutati was no great feat or heroic deed; however, from a certain vantage point it was, perhaps, unusual, even adventurous and exotic. And I cannot deny that a trace of these elements occasionally hovered near the surface of our experience. But such raptures were short-lived, for the glittering layers of adventure and exoticism were quickly stripped away as a day to day, working and acting world, a world in so many respects like our own, asserted itself against such romantic notions. Still, it remains difficult to portray a world so near and yet so distant from our own personal journeyings.

Inevitably, such statements provoke the question of what, if anything, this strain of experience ought properly to mean? The corresponding expectation of an answer of singular profundity is, however, something I am not poised to meet and deliver. All I can offer is a brief personal reflection, the barest hint of an idiosyncratic direction.

Several things have distilled from our time among the Himba, and they vary but slightly in their significance. The first is nothing more and nothing less than a body of memories of the events of that time, of the many acquaintances we made, and the several friendships that grew from these. Despite the simplicity of these words they are things of great wonder. For it was a proper combination of mutually connective personalities, experience, perspectives, and interests—on the part of both the Himba and ourselves—that made these relationships possible. And that this could have happened between people so widely separated by geography and cultural purview strikes me as remarkable. It must then follow that something deep within us—a species of human soul, for want of a better term— is not only present but perhaps even more influential than culture. And it is this, coupled with the largely unalterable movement of human life, that allows human beings to step beyond their limited confines and experience commonalities with people who, at first blush, appear so utterly different. Admittedly, this deep-seated human ability is imperfect, for it does not allow a complete mutuality. This fact, however, is but a slight detraction from the experience of commonality. It merely underscores the difficulty and ambiguity of human associations generally—of knowing someone yet not fully knowing, of feeling close for so long a time, then discovering a hidden pocket that creates a stark distance. It is a closeness and a distance that exists as easily between brothers as between persons far separated by time and space. That such an assertion falls widely afoul of current intellectual fashion is not only clear to me, but also irrelevant, for intellectual fashions have yet to create long-term experiential truths of any consequence whatsoever.

Finally, there is the role of "belief" in human knowledge, and the power and confidence belief engenders in empirically unverifiable ideas— whether those ideas relate solely to the material world or to the material and immaterial worlds. This seems to me a fact that touches not only the Himba and myself, but certainly all people—that within the human mind belief creates the impression of knowledge where certain, verifiable knowledge cannot truly be known. And more curious still is this strange corollary: that we rather easily recognize the role of belief in the ideas others hold to be true, ideas at odds with our own, yet fail to make that connection between ourselves and our own deeply held conceptions about the nature of the world. In the end, I doubt that much of what we profess to know to be fundamentally true of the world, whether material or immaterial, can ever escape the loop of simple yet profound belief. Thus, we are left with a strangely annoying fact: We human beings do not exist without the perception that our fundamental understandings of the world and human life are anything other than timelessly true and universally valid; yet empirically, we can never know them to be what we think they are.

These have been the fundamental distillations born of this experience, and though of great value to me, I grant they may be of little consequence to others. It is possible that I might have happened upon these lessons without my stay in Otutati. Yet I cannot help but suppose the circumstances under which they were learned, and even more, the persons who unknowingly guided me to them, imparted a certain richness and flavor unique to themselves and their world, such that these lessons could not have been learned in quite this way in any other setting.

Epilogue

Three and a half years after leaving Kaokoland we were able to return to Otutati for a brief stay. Wamesepa had died the previous year and preparations for his *yambera* ceremony were underway. His onetime bustling homestead was empty but for a handful of families, and the many persons drawn to Otutati because of his patronage had settled elsewhere once Katere assumed management of the cattle herd. The men of the area had chosen Katwerwa to succeed Wamesepa as headman of the region. But he declined, saying his leg was weakening and that he felt unable to carry out the responsibilities of a headman. Wandisa then consented to do so, though he retained his position on the provincial council. Since his father's death, Wandisa has returned to the dress of a Himba man, and Katwerwa, now the keeper of the fire, was slowly training Dakata in the knowledge and practices of the fire as he will someday assume that responsibility.

Daniel and Watumba had moved long ago and no one knew much about them anymore. Dakata's first wife, Yapura, had given birth to a son—a source of great happiness for her. Kuwiya's second wife was buried not long after our departure; apparently, she never recovered from the strains of childbirth. Her son, though, was strong and healthy and followed his older brothers everywhere. Vita's son, Zondoka, had left with Nondo one day, and it had been years since Vita had heard anything from him. And while he was uncertain, Vita believed the lad had gone to Windhoek or crossed the border into South Africa. Kavetonwa's wife was recently deceased and he missed their companionship of many years. He had moved into a house beside his daughter where she could more easily see to his needs, but for a man of his years he was still vigorous and his mind was keen and alert.

Ngipore had moved farther north. After a lengthy separation, he and his wife had come together again and it was said they were happy. Katanga too had moved. And after so many years as a widow she found a man she truly loved and married him. News of our return had found its way to her husband's homestead and the two of them made the three-day journey to see us. Her husband was kindly and soft-spoken, and though it was strange to see him at her side, they seemed very content. Katanga was especially curious to see Margot, or Katanga katiti (Little Katanga) as she was called, recounting with her the details of her prenatal care.

Most of the others were well and commented on how we had aged, and reminisced with humor about the events of our previous stay. It was a good thing to be among them once again and to renew the ties that bound us together.

A Final Postscript

Shortly after finishing this book, we had opportunity to travel to Namibia and visit the people of Otutati. That visitation has caused me a good deal of reflection on the future of Kaokoland and the Himba, and though I have decided to retain my original epilogue—as it reflects the state of affairs current at that time—much has happened that might be of interest to the reader.

During the last months of 1996, Kavetonwa died and was buried at the foot of his father's grave. Wamesepa's wife, Ekuta, also died, but on a chilly winter's evening. She and Zorondu had settled down to sleep beside a handful of glowing coals in the center of her house. The thatched roof somehow caught fire, and while Zorondu was able to escape with only minor burns, Ekuta never found her way out and died as flames engulfed the hut. Vita's son, Zondoka, had returned to Kaokoland only to involve himself again with cattle theft and was now in prison at Omaruru, in west-central Namibia. Kuwiya had also participated in stock theft, and a day or two after our arrival he returned from Omaruru, having served a one year sentence.

It was clear in May of 1999 that a transformation of Otutati life was well underway. The images, subtle and otherwise, of a brand of African modernity—peculiarly enticing to youths and young men—were everywhere to be seen. Among them, traditional Himba dress was fast becoming an indicator of primitivity, a symbol of a dark, benighted past. Most young men desired shoes, shirts, sweaters, and socks, combining them with their brightly colored skirts to cultivate the image of a person with money enough to purchase desirable consumer goods. Much of their clothing was paid for with stolen livestock. A few enterprising street merchants operate in Opuwo selling filthy, betattered, and often grievously colored clothing—clothing that arrives in Namibia from charitable organizations, only to find its way into tertiary markets—to an ever growing clientele.

Clothing, however, is but a frivolous symptom for what elder Himba see as the real problem: the growth of individual liberties that work to erode the basis of their civil society, a society rooted more in collective good and obligation than in individual pursuits. Civil order was maintained by an unavoidable respect shown to the elders and the ancestors—regardless of how one felt inside—and a mild suppression of individual desires because of strong obligations to others. It is a social order that has worked very well, but it demands a degree of patience, acceptance, and self-restraint wholly inconsistent with modern human rights and the global capitalist market. Whether correct or not, the elder generation identifies the school classroom and the efforts of Christianizing missionaries as the sources of change. For the schools teach of a wider, national political order, one that supersedes the prerogatives and authority of the Himba, while teachers of the new religion instruct their pupils that the sacred fire and all of its attendant ceremonies, as well as the concept of powerful ancestors, are not only false but morally corrupting. Thus, the traditions, ideas, and morality by which the elder generations govern themselves are deemed old fashioned and seriously wrong.

Interestingly enough, the principal manifestations of this sudden awareness of rights and liberties among the younger generation are theft and a reluctance to work for their parents. The consumer market in Opuwo, pitiful though it is by European standards, offers an array of clothing, foods, toiletries, music, and other entertainments highly valued by young people. And because the idea and the practice of generating a bit of pocket money is utterly foreign to the traditional Himba economy, young people who wish to indulge in modern life have no means to do so. There is simply no such remunerative work available; hence, the continuing rise in stock theft as well as the all too common refusal to work without any immediate reward. According to Himba, this state of affairs is not peculiar to Otutati but to be found everywhere in Kaokoland. Parents and communities feel at a loss as to what can be done.

Complicating things is the emergence of a strong desire among many— a desire, I suspect, that has always existed though was rarely given overt expression—to acquire wealth as rapidly as possible and at nearly any cost. Since increasing a herd's size or waiting for an inheritance can be painfully long processes, the belief among many Himba is that younger men are seeking out a new brand of Angolan entrepreneur that offers the cultural equivalent of a "get rich quick" kit. These traffickers offer the sale or hire of personal *omiti* or *embari*, unseen powers that can attack, weaken, or kill others standing in the way of one's personal success, or be used to quicken the reproductive capacity of one's animals. The consequence of the belief in the availability of such individual powers is the assumption of their widespread usage; and grave suspicion is now sown among people as they consider their own illnesses and economic downturns to be caused by close relatives.

It is far from simple to explain this change, but placing the means of controlling one's own fortunes within one's own grasp, rather than through a chain of relatives and the ancestors' hands, must be very tempting. For now it is possible to obtain a rapid, though surreptitious, means of success, an ability to remove sundry obstacles, including human beings, for the sake of profit. It is even rumored that some forms of *omiti* and *embari* require the sacrifice of a loved one or relative: the power will do the killing, but only when the sincere human passion for the deed is present in the owner's mind. Wandisa lamented, "Our whole world is being turned upside down, and I doubt my grandchildren's children will know anything about our life."

The changes now sweeping through Himba life are part of an encroaching world, a vast globalization (the currently fashionable word) of which they have little understanding, and, as they see it, over which they have no control. I, of course, am no seer, no revealer of things to come. But what is clear is this: The great bustling life of Otutati that once was is no more. Gone are the personalities, the human skills, and the collective will that made it possible. The once great homestead of Wamesepa Ngombe is respectfully falling back to the earth, and many of its former inhabitants have settled elsewhere. Life there is still good, very good. And though change was to be seen everywhere, my mind's eye easily recalled the pleasant, vigorous, and familiar life that used to exist on that patch of ground. I suppose this book is now but a memory of that life, a life gradually ebbing toward an unknown future, and as the Himba once desired for me, I now wish for them: Mukuru must go with you.